D1520751

The Political Economy of
International Trade

The Political Economy of International Trade

U.S. Trade Law, Policy, and Social Cost

Jae Wan Chung

LEXINGTON BOOKS

A division of
ROWMAN & LITTLEFIELD PUBLISHERS, INC.
Lanham • Boulder • New York • Toronto • Oxford

LEXINGTON BOOKS

A division of Rowman & Littlefield Publishers, Inc.
A wholly owned subsidiary of The Rowman & Littlefield Publishing Group, Inc.
4501 Forbes Boulevard, Suite 200
Lanham, MD 20706

PO Box 317
Oxford
OX2 9RU, UK

British Library Cataloguing in Publication Information Available

Library of Congress Cataloging-in-Publication Data

Chung, Jae Wan.
  The political economy of international trade : U.S. trade law, policy, and social cost
/ Jae Wan Chung.
       p. cm.
  Includes bibliographical references and index.
  ISBN 0-7391-1291-0 (cloth : alk. paper) — ISBN 0-7391-1292-9 (pbk. : alk. paper)
  ISBN 978-0-7391-1291-5   ISBN 978-0-7391-1292-2
  1. Foreign trade regulation—United States. 2. International trade—United States.
3. United States—Commercial policy. I. Title.
KF1976.C458 2006
343.73'087—dc22   2005027294

Printed in the United States of America

⊗™ The paper used in this publication meets the minimum requirements of American
National Standard for Information Sciences—Permanence of Paper for Printed Library
Materials, ANSI/NISO Z39.48-1992.

To my parents

Contents

List of Figures

List of Tables

Abbreviations

AD	Antidumping duty
ACTP	Advisory Committee for Trade Policy
APEC	Asia-Pacific Economic Cooperation
ASEAN	Association of South East Asian Nations
ASEM	Asia-Europe Meeting
CAFTA	Central American Free Trade Agreement
CEA	Council of Economic Advisors
CFTA	Canada-U.S. Free Trade Agreement
CVD	Countervailing duty
DSB	Dispute Settlement Body
EC	European Community
EPC	Economic Policy Council
EU	European Union
FRB	Federal Reserve Board
FTAA	Free Trade Area of the Americas
GAO	General Accounting Office
GATS	General Agreement on Trade in Services
GATT	General Agreement on Tariffs and Trade
GATT_{1947}	pre-Uruguay General Agreement on Tariffs and Trade
GATT_{1994}	post-Uruguay General Agreement on Tariffs and Trade
GSP	Generalized System of Preferences
ILO	International Labor Organization
IMF	International Monetary Fund
ITA	International Trade Administration
ITC	International Trade Commission
ITO	International Trade Organization
LTFV	Less-than fair value

MAI	Multilateral Agreement on Investment
MFA	Multifiber Arrangement
MFN	Most Favored Nation
MRA	Mutual Recognition Agreement
MTN	Multinational trade negotiations
NAFTA	North American Free Trade Agreement
NSC	National Security Council
NTBs	Nontariff Barriers
OMA	Orderly marketing agreement
OMB	Office of Management and Budget
OTCA	Omnibus Trade and Competitiveness Act of 1988
RTAA	Reciprocal Trade Agreements Act
SDR	Special Drawing Rights
S-H	Smoot-Hawley Tariff Act of 1930
TEP	Transatlantic Economic Partnership
TMB	Textiles Monitoring Body
TPC	Trade Policy Committee
TPRB	Trade Policy Review Body
TPRG	Trade Policy Review Group
TPRM	Trade Policy Review Mechanism
TRIMs	Trade-related Investment Measures
TRIPs	Trade-related Aspects of Intellectual Property Rights
TPSC	Trade Policy Staff Committee
UNCTAD	United Nations Conference on Trade and Development
UR	Uruguay Round
USCS	U.S. Customs Service
USDOA	U.S. Department of Agriculture
USDOC	U.S. Department of Commerce
USDOL	U.S. Department of Labor
USDOT	U.S. Department of Treasury
USGPO	U.S. Government Printing Office
USTC	U.S. Tariff Commission
USTR	U.S. Trade Representative
VER	Voluntary export restraints
WTO	World Trade Organization

Preface

Free trade has been a long-standing U.S. policy position. For over half a century prior to the Uruguay Round, U.S. trade policy was largely based on the $GATT_{1947}$. The United States has played the leading role in this free trade framework and made a significant contribution to it through successive rounds for multilateral trade negotiations. As both trade deficits and fiscal deficits steadily increased during the early 1980s in the United States, however, free trade policy has not stood without its own share of backlash. Protectionist sentiment began to emerge in the United States and succeeded in persuading Congress to enact the Omnibus Trade and Competitiveness Act of 1988 (hereafter referred to as OTCA). The United States diverged from free trade ideology, primarily with the enactment of the OTCA. This act comprises the trade remedy provisions, the principal trade policy instruments at present. The 1988 law effectively determines U.S. trade policy today. The objective of this policy is to promote "free but fair trade," implying that the United States aims at open, fair, and equitable access to foreign markets on the one hand and protection of the domestic firms or industries from foreign competition on the other hand. This shift from conventional trade practice to a trade remedy regime tied to multilateral, regional, and bilateral agreements, often referred to as a managed or administered policy, marks a significant turning point in the history of U.S. trade policy.

The following statements made by top policy makers in the executive and legislative branches in the recent past reflect the current and likely future U.S. trade policy stance:

> "Our fair trade laws are the bedrock on which free trade stands." "The United States believes in free trade but not blind adherence to it." "You just have to work this day in and day out, every month, every year, and every issue to make

sure that we have not only free trade but fair trade." "We've got to be more aggressive."

The U.S. economy is massive. In the latest issue (2004) of *Economic Report of the President*, the Council of Economic Advisers reports that the real
gross domestic product of the United States in 2002 was $10,083 billion. Al-
though the proportion of its foreign sector was not as large as that in many
foreign countries, it has been steadily increasing over time and is now large
enough to affect significantly not only domestic economy but also foreign
economies. As the largest trading nation in the world, the United States accounts for roughly 20 percent of world goods trade and 16 percent of world
services trade. Trade policy is a key determinant of the size of the foreign sector. In addition to such a dominant force in world trade, the United States is a
main source of the intellectual and ideological inputs into the ongoing evolution of the world trade order. The impact of U.S managed trade policy of the
present era on the world economy is undoubtedly considerable. The OTCA
requires U.S. trade institutions to implement trade policy through complex
statutory processes. International trade agreements are incorporated into U.S.
trade laws and thus trade policies. The coordinated use of multilateral, regional, and bilateral agreements is the central part of today's American trade
policy. To this day, the United States believes that free but fair trade policy
has benefited the country; free trade agreements have reduced domestic
prices and provided consumers with more choices. The United States is likely
to make more new free trade agreements and continue to oppose economic
isolation in the future.

The $GATT_{1947}$/WTO has made a considerable contribution to freer trade for
over half a century. During this period, trade barriers decreased significantly,
and the volume of world trade grew substantially. The number of member
countries has dramatically increased; the scope of trade expanded from goods
($GATT_{1947}$) to goods-services (Uruguay Round) and continues to expand to
goods-services-agriculture (Doha-Round). Unlike cases under the $GATT_{1947,}$
settlements of trade disputes are largely successful under the WTO system.
Nevertheless, recurrent trade disputes among countries have become a serious issue. Trade disputes, especially between the United States and foreign
countries, are recursive and pervasive, as the United States intensifies the
managed trade policy. Despite a history of trade remedy policies in the United
States lasting for periods long enough to test their effectiveness, the routine
enforcement of trade remedy laws as mandated by the OTCA leaves the long-
term problem of trade disparity unresolved.

American trade policy is a crucial subject to not only the United States but
also foreign countries. It encompasses a broad spectrum of economics, trade

laws, and international agreements as integral components. A systematic understanding of this particular interdisciplinary area will enhance the prospect of fair trade practices and thus reduce trade disputes. Given the global nature and universal scope of issues and problems on international trade today, however, they do not flow exclusively in classical ways of economic behavior and hence laws and agreements may not adequately deal with trade conducts in the real world. The framework of international trade maintained by the United States for over half a century since 1947 is based on the rationale for free trade of the GATT$_{1947}$/WTO. Free trade presupposes perfect competition. However, most markets are not competitive. The frequent trade disputes stem from industrial sectors of imperfect competition. The social cost for settlement of disputes is enormous to the United States and the rest of the world.

The objective of this book is to explore American trade policy from the standpoint of U.S. trade laws and international agreements and to discuss the optimal trade law enforcement that minimizes the social cost and the ultimate need to reform the present U.S. trade policy and the GATT/WTO trade framework.

The book consists of two parts. Part I is concerned with *de jure* rules—U.S. trade laws and international trade agreements. As a main building block of this book, they constitute the legal foundations and framework for American trade policy. Part II is concerned with *de facto* policy—actual practices of U.S. trade policy. As another main building block, they include policy institutions, actual implementation of trade policy, trade disputes, and settlements, the decision-making behavior of the policy institutions, and commentary on the trade policy in the face of controversies. Classical trade differs from modern trade. The central argument here is concerned with free trade rules and framework for classical trade under the assumption of perfect competition applied to modern trade of imperfectly competitive firms/industries. Most trade disputes stem from this duality under the single set of rules. The social cost incurred from the processes of trade dispute settlement entails needs for optimization of trade intervention and ultimate reform of the U.S. trade policy institution and the world trade system in accordance with real world markets.

Part I includes the first five chapters and Part II includes the last five chapters. Chapter 1 outlines the constitutional mandate for U.S. trade policy. Although Congress has increasingly delegated this authority to the executive branch, the fundamental authority to set the overall direction of U.S. trade policy rests with Congress. Trade laws dictate trade policy. The legislative process for a trade law is usually long and intricate. Once established, trade policy tends to be inflexible. Without political consensus in the legislative branch for making a new law or amending existing law, no single government entity can easily alter the policy course. Trade policy is often tied with vested self-interests. This chapter explores a question on how a particular policy is upheld or compromised in practice. Chapter 2 makes a general survey of the primary U.S. trade laws enacted since 1930: the Smoot-Hawley Tariff Act of 1930, the Reciprocal Trade Agreements Act of 1934, the Trade Expansion Act of 1962, the Trade Act of 1974, and the Trade Act of 1979. It is important to keep in mind that a considerable portion of the trade law at present is a version evolved from them. The purpose of the survey is to trace the historical origins of trade laws and policy of the present era. It focuses on the legislative background and economic consequences of each law. Furthermore, the latter four (1934–1979) are the laws oriented toward free trade. Moreover, this chapter assesses intellectual underpinning of U.S. trade rules, i.e., long-held free trade ideals, by asking exactly what free trade ideals are and how they are reflected into U.S. trade laws. A great majority of trade economists, especially in the West, are consciously and unconsciously conditioned by these ideals, although their arguments and behaviors are coupled by short-run interests that may conflict with these ideals. Chapter 3 focuses on the dominant trade law of today: the Omnibus Trade and Competitiveness Act of 1988. It outlines the statutory composition of the law, its primary provisions, and the key features of each provision. Chapter 4 examines the chief trade remedy provisions included in the Trade Act of 1988: enforcement of U.S. rights and responses to foreign unfair trade practices, identification of trade liberalization priorities, identification of intellectual property rights priorities, countervailing duties, antidumping duty, and escape clause. These are the legal bases and instruments of managed trade policy of the United States. Their historical origins and quasi-judicial processes for implementation are also a focal point in this chapter. Chapter 5 presents international trade agreements: multilateral, regional, and bilateral. During the $GATT_{1947}$ era, all member countries were obliged to observe GATT rules. The Uruguay Round Agreement, Doha Declaration, NAFTA, and various bilateral agreements are the primary concerns of this chapter.

Chapter 6 discusses U.S. trade policy institutions at present. It focuses on collaborative policy processes between the legislative and executive branches. These processes frequently involve intra- and interbranch politics tied to special-interest groups. The three primary policy agencies are the Office of the U.S. Trade Representative (USTR), the International Trade Administration (ITA), and the International Trade Commission (ITC). Chapter 7 analyzes multifaceted trade policies in action by means of the coordinated use of multilateral agreements, regional arrangements, and bilateral initiatives, along with enforcement activities by trade remedy measures. It describes policies to identify the pattern of foreign unfair trade practices in the 1980s,

1990s, and the early 2000s. This chapter discusses selected specific issues regarding theory-practice nexus. It responds to questions on how real world outcomes do not coincide with the theoretical results and how specific political pressure is reflected in protectionist tendencies in U.S. policy-making. It is also concerned with to what extent U.S. pressure on developing countries to open their economies is justified and how their protests against U.S. policy and WTO agenda affect U.S. rules in law and practices in policy and multilateral trade negotiations under the WTO. Chapter 8 deals with questions on: given a specific trade dispute between the United States and any foreign country, what the primary cause of dissonance is, how they reconcile it, what the roles of the two governments and the WTO are, and what differences in perspectives of the United States and the developing countries on U.S. trade policy are. This chapter further examines the patterns of trade disputes and then highlights the disputes between the United States and the EU settled by U.S. trade policy institutions and the WTO. American trade policy encounters a number of problems. Trade disputes are not transitory. Mutual retaliations are increasingly prevalent. U.S.-initiated retaliations tend to boomerang. Many trade disputes remain unsettled for several years or occur again. Chapter 9 reviews empirical research done on the decision-making behavior of policy institutions, rules (principles), or discretion (politics), and the effectiveness of U.S. trade remedy policies. The overall results are: self-interested groups abuse the legal provisions; the ITC is based on rules, but discretion is not eliminated; U.S. trade policy is marginally effective; and trade disparities remain unresolved in the long run.

The framework of GATT/WTO presupposes free, interindustry trade under perfect competition. The United States has played the leading role within this framework. In the real world, however, most markets are not competitive. Given an imperfectly competitive industry structure, especially prevalent in developed countries, intra-industry trade is the dominant pattern. Trade disputes are heavily concentrated in the industrial sector of intra-industry trade. As long as imperfect competition is permitted to exist lawfully in the market, trade disputes will continue to arise. American trade policy institution *per se* is sound overall. However, strict enforcement of trade remedy laws as mandated by the statutes is a costly misjudgment. Chapter 10 discusses the social cost incurred from the settlement of disputes, requiring the U.S. trade policy agency and the WTO to undertake their leadership to optimize trade policy interventions for all countries. In the long run, it is necessary to reform the U.S. trade policy institution and the world trade framework in accordance with the real world market. This chapter makes specific recommendations for changing the U.S. trade policy and the world trade system.

Drawing from inferences made throughout this book, the epilogue addresses that U.S. trade policy/institutions and the world trade framework need to make a radical change by embracing the real world market.

At the end of the book, three appendices present components of the General Agreement of Tariffs and Trade, components of the Uruguay Round Agreement, and an outline of the North American Free Trade Agreement.

Acknowledgments

During many years required for me to complete this project, I owe a significant amount of intellectual debts to my colleagues of the Economics Department of George Mason University. Donald J. Boudreaux, Carlos D. Ramirez, Roger D. Congleton, Joseph Reid, and Willem Thorbecke facilitated me to form an overall idea on the manuscript or read parts thereof. I thank them for either their support or valuable comments and suggestions. I am also grateful to Philip R. Wiest for his support and suggestions on the policy-oriented program that motivated me to complete this project. All of my research assistants at George Mason University in the past helped me greatly with enthusiasm and devotion. They are Anthony de Carvalho, Mark L. Lynner, Michael Morrison, and Nicola Tynan. I would also like to acknowledge gratefully a significant contribution made by a large number of students in graduate and undergraduate classes I taught for many years. I have many fellow economists to thank for their help/encouragement. They are Keith B. Anderson, Robert E. Baldwin, Ke-young Chu, Cletus C. Coughlin, Gary W. Davis, J. Michael Finger, Wendy L. Hansen, Corinne Krupp, Jisoon Lee, Chung Ki Min, Michael O. Moore, Thomas J. Prusa, Dominick Salvatore, and Wendy E. Takacs. All of the authors who wrote articles adapted in this book have granted me their permissions of extracting from each of their articles for my work. Concurrently, I also gratefully acknowledge fair-use permissions granted by the editors/publishers/associations/government/organization: American Economic Association (abstracting with credit), Cambridge University Press (with a full citation on behalf of the American Political Science Association), Southern Economic Association (with the source acknowledged), Western Economic Association International (customary biographical citation), MIT Press, University of Chicago Press, University of Chicago Law School (fair use), the

Institute für Weltwirtschaft, Elsevier Science, Inc., Blackwell Publishing, the WTO (with attribution and notification), and the U.S. Government (public domain). I also extend my special thanks to Ms. Rosemary Chase, Copyright Office of George Mason University, who provided me with valuable advise and suggestions.

Periods of my leave from George Mason University in the past were extremely helpful in making significant progress on this project. I thank my former colleagues at the University of Suwon in Korea, where I served for several years, for their support.

This project, by its nature, required that I explore a large number of documents published by the Federal Government, Congress, and international organizations. I had access to relevant documents and internet databases available, especially at the Office of U.S. Trade Representative, the International Trade Administration in the Department of Commerce, the International Trade Commission, the Library of Congress, the World Trade Organization, the International Monetary Fund, and the World Bank. I thank countless staff members and reference librarians for their kind help. I would like to extend my special thanks to Ms. Emily C. Howie, Library of Congress, for her kind help through Library Question-Answer Services and Ms. Tessa Bridgeman at the WTO for valuable materials and information sent from Geneva through mail and the WTO World Wide Web Server on the Internet.

I am deeply grateful to Serena Leigh Krombach (Director, Editorial Acquisitions, Lexington Books), members of the editorial board, and anonymous viewers for their support and encouragement. My gratitude goes also to the publishing team at Rowman & Littlefield. Karen Ackermann (Associate Editor) and Kathryn Funk (Acquisitions Editor) have been invaluable contributors.

Finally, my greatest debt is to my family. I thank Soojun and my two children, Caroline and Edward, for their forbearance and help.

Jae Wan Chung
Fairfax, Virginia

Part I

U.S. TRADE LAWS AND INTERNATIONAL TRADE AGREEMENTS

Chapter 1

Constitutional Mandate of Trade Policy and Trade Protection

U.S. trade policy affects not only the U.S. economy but also economies large and small around the world. Although the United States presents itself as a free trade nation, trade policy today stresses free but fair trade. It is often referred to as managed trade policy. Since U.S. trade policy is inextricably linked to U.S. trade law, it is important to understand policy from the legislative point of view.

As a brief introduction to the legislative process, a trade bill in the United States becomes law through a long and complex process of advocacy and negotiation. This process begins with a trade bill submitted by a legislative member(s) in the House of Representatives. Although trade legislation is not the domain of the executive branch, the White House is frequently the source of a bill. In essence, a bill agreed to in identical form by the House and the Senate becomes law if both chambers pass it and the President signs it. Some economists often complain that U.S. trade policy is subject to change by lobbyists representing particular corporate or other interest groups. Once established through a complex process of legislation, however, an individual or private organization is unable to change readily a given U.S. trade policy course.

In fact, the U.S. Congress has the constitutional mandate to be responsible for American trade policy and dictates trade policy through the passage of bills into law. Although it often delegates this authority to the executive branch, Congress retains the ultimate responsibility to set the overall direction of U.S. trade policy.

Section 1 looks into the constitutional mandate of U.S. trade policy. Section 2 examines the process of trade legislation, free or protective. As it is important to know the determinants of protective trade laws, section 3 explores

the causes of protective trade legislation. The last section summarizes the
chapter and draws conclusions.

1.1 TRADE LEGISLATION AND TRADE POLICY

The United States Constitution empowers the Congress, not the President, to
set U.S. trade laws and policies. Section 8, Article I of the Constitution states:

Article I: Section 8
   "[1]The Congress shall have Power To lay and collect Taxes, Duties, Imposts
and Excises, to pay the Debts and provide for the common Defense and general
Welfare of the United States; but all Duties, Imposts and Excises shall be uniform throughout the United States;
   [2]To borrow Money on the credit of the United States;
   [3]To regulate Commerce with foreign Nations, and among the several States."
Source: U.S. House of Representatives, *The Constitution of the United States of
America* (Washington, D.C.: U.S. GPO, June 20, 2003) 4.

The House of Representatives and the Senate have equal legislative functions and powers, although the House must initiate revenue bills. In general,
most trade laws originate in the House of Representatives. Within the
House, jurisdiction over trade legislation lies with the Committee on Ways
and Means. This committee has played a central role in legislating trade
laws and governing various trade statutes throughout American history. In
the Senate, the Committee on Finance has jurisdictional responsibility for
trade acts.[1]
   Congress has increasingly delegated authority for the day-to-day management of trade policies to the executive branch. For example, the Reciprocal
Trade Agreements Act in 1934 authorized the President to negotiate international trade agreements for the reduction of tariffs. The Trade Act of 1974 extended substantially the presidential authority to include not only tariff negotiations but also NTB (nontariff barriers) negotiations. In the case of the
Omnibus Trade and Competitiveness Act of 1988, Congress required the
President to negotiate the Uruguay Round, to respond to Congressional requests for consultation on trade issues, and to formulate an annual trade policy agenda. The role of the executive branch, however, is restricted by various institutional constraints imposed by the legislative branch.[2] There is also
an element of interbranch trade politics due to the intersection between legislative and executive domains and prerogatives. In any event, it is important
to understand U.S. trade policy from the perspective of U.S. trade law because the two are generally inseparable in the United States.

1.2 PROCEDURES FOR TRADE LEGISLATION

This section outlines the legislative procedure for enacting a U.S. trade law. The procedure is exactly the same as that required for any other law. Only a member of the House of Representatives may introduce a trade bill, including the amendment or repeal of existing laws.[3] The Senate may propose a trade-related bill or amend/concur with a House bill.

Laws are often legislated, amended, or repealed under the pressure of constituents who are in pursuit of their economic or other self-interests. Constituents may be individuals or groups of individuals, bar associations, labor unions, manufacturers' associations, or chambers of commerce. In many cases, constituents are a valuable resource for legislators because they have considerable knowledge regarding the laws that will augment the economic vitality of their district. Through lobbying, however, these special interest groups often seek "economic rent" accruing from trade protection. This results in a social welfare loss due to the unproductive use of scarce resources. Such rent-seeking behavior is a key proposition of public choice theory.[4]

The executive branch can offer legislative proposals to the Speaker of the House and to the Vice-President, who presides over the Senate. Executive agencies draft bills containing the administration's programs and committee chairs of the legislative branch introduce in both chambers.

Before a member of Congress proposes a bill, it is customary for the member to consult with the Legislative Counsel of the House to frame the ideas in suitable legislative language and then submit the bill to committees with broad jurisdiction, including the House Ways and Means. The committees may hold public hearings. They then recommend the bills to the Speaker of the House and the Senate Majority Leader. The Speaker and the Majority Leader work out a compromise with assistance from their advisors and members of the majority party on the House Rules Committee. A single bill emerges from the House and proceeds to the floor for House debates. The Senate procedure is similar; the committees, especially the Finance Committee, recommend the reported bills to the Presiding Officer and the Majority Leader. They work out a single compromise before debates on the Senate floor or reconcile differences on the floor. If neither the House nor the Senate agrees to accept the other chamber's bill, the bill proceeds to the House-Senate Conference Committee. This joint committee reconciles differences and sends the final version back to each chamber for a confirmation vote. The bill finally advances to the President upon passage by the House and Senate. The President must act within ten days from the date of House or Senate delivery of the bill. If the President signs the bill, it becomes law and thus a publicly binding statute. In the event of a veto by the President, the President returns the bill, including his stated objections, to the House of Representatives or the Senate, wherever the bill originated.[5] If the House initiated the bill, the House must vote on it at once. If two-thirds of those members constituting a quorum override the veto, the bill returns with the President's objections to the Senate. Otherwise, the bill is repealed. A Senate bill takes a similar route; if the Senate overrides the veto with a two-thirds vote, the bill becomes law.

Assume that a bill has originated in the House of Representatives. The House takes the following steps:[6]

- A member of the House presents a bill to the Clerk's Office.
- The clerk assigns a legislative number.
- The bill is referred to appropriate committees by the Speaker.
- Each printed bill enters onto the committee's Legislative Calendar.[7]
- The chairperson of a committee refers the bill to the appropriate subcommittee, usually within two weeks, and sends copies of the bill to the relevant departments and agencies in the executive branch, including the General Accounting Office.[8] The departments and agencies, in turn, submit their reports to the Office of Management and Budget to find out whether or not they are consistent with the program of the President.
- The subcommittee makes a report to the committee. The committee discusses the reported bill and amends it as needed. If the committee votes for the bill under consideration and it emerges as the single bill of the House after reconciliation by the Speaker, the chairman of the committee introduces the new bill to the full House.[9]
- The committee files the approved bill with the clerk of the committee.[10]
- If a quorum is present, the House votes on passage of the amended bill. The House often expedites the consideration of bills in the Committee of the Whole House. Such a parliamentary arrangement enables the House to act with a quorum of less than the requisite majority of 218.[11]
- Upon passage with a majority of the members' votes, the House delivers the bill to the Senate. The Presiding Officer of the Senate refers the bill to the appropriate standing committee of the Senate for consideration; the committee chairperson, in turn, refers it to a subcommittee.
- The Senate passes the bill with a simple majority vote and returns the engrossed Senate amendments, if any, together with the original House bill to the House of Representatives.
- The House of Representatives either passes the Senate's amended bill or requests a conference with the Senate to resolve any disagreement.[12]
- When both the House and Senate pass a bill in *identical* form, first the Speaker and then Senate's President (either the Vice President or the President Pro Tempore) sign the bill.

• Upon receipt of the signed bill, the committee that originally reported the bill presents it to the President for signature or veto.

When a bill originates in the Senate, the Senate follows procedures similar to those listed above. The legislative process begins with a subcommittee of the appropriate standing committee of the Senate. If the Senate passes the bill, it moves to the House for consideration. The appropriate House standing committee reports the bill to the full House. If the House passes the bill without amendment, it returns to the Senate. The Senate has two options, either to concur with the House or request a conference with the House to resolve any disagreement.

1.3 CAUSES OF PROTECTIVE TRADE LEGISLATION

Table 1.1 presents the numbers of trade and trade-related bills submitted by the Committee on Ways and Means and the Finance Committee, respectively, along with major economic indicators for 1975–1992, a period of relatively high trade bill activity. Numbers in parentheses are those of protective bills. A casual observation of the data presented in this table suggests that the number of bills, total or protective, appears to have relationships with major economic variables such as trade balance, fiscal deficit, and the rate of unemployment with and without time lags. Legislative members in both chambers significantly increased the number of trade bills submitted in 1977, presumably because of the emergence of high American trade deficits. In 1983, there was a sharp increase in the fiscal deficit along with a significant rise in the trade deficit. For the period of observation, the number of trade bills submitted was the largest. Both the trade deficit and fiscal deficit remained high in 1985. That year again saw a sudden upsurge in trade bills submitted by both chambers, leading to efforts that eventually culminated in the 1988 Trade Act.

What are the factors that have motivated legislators to submit protective trade bills? Several econometric studies have been done on petitions filed mostly by interest groups, the first step of a quasi-judicial investigative process involving three of five principal U.S. trade remedy provisions: Section 701 (countervailing duty), section 731 (antidumping duty), and/or section 201 (escape clause).[13] Included are Takacs (1981), Salvatore (1987), Couglin, et al. (1989), and Krupp (1994).[14] None of these authors has attempted to explore the empirical validity of economic rent as a cause of trade protection, presumably because a method to compute rent that uses only existing data was not yet available. However, ignorance of the rent accruing from trade protection is both theoretically and empirically a serious mistake.

Table 1.1. Trade Bills and Major Economic Indicators (1975–1992)

Year	House Bill	Senate Bill	Trade Balance	Fiscal Deficit	Rate of Unemployment
1975	1	1	18.116	–53.2	8.5
1976	4 (1)	1	4.295	–73.7	7.7
1977*	62 (36)	16 (11)	–14.335	–53.7	7.1
1978	36 (21)	19 (11)	–15.143	–59.2	6.1
1979	17 (14)	3 (2)	–0.285	–40.7	5.8
1980	3 (2)	2 (1)	2.317	–73.8	7.1
1981	2 (1)	0	5.030	–79.0	7.6
1982	4 (2)	4 (2)	–11.443	–128.0	9.7
1983*	117 (40)	26 (11)	–43.985	–207.8	9.6
1984	12 (3)	4 (1)	–98.951	–185.4	7.5
1985*	19 (13)	28 (17)	–124.243	–212.3	7.2
1986	2 (2)	8 (2)	–150.859	–221.3	7.0
1987	15 (7)	7 (4)	–166.338	–149.8	6.2
1988*	1	4 (2)	–127.083	–155.2	5.5
1989	10 (4)	11 (7)	–103.839	–152.5	5.3
1990	7 (5)	4 (3)	–92.661	–221.4	5.5
1991	3 (2)	1 (1)	–7.424	–269.2	6.7
1992	5 (2)	4 (3)	–61.549	–290.4	7.4

Note: Trade bills are bills submitted by the Committee on Ways and Means in the House and trade-related bills by Finance Committee in the Senate, respectively. H.Res, S.Res, H.J.Res, S.J.Res, H.Con.Res, and S.Con.Res are not included in the number of free or protective trade bills. Numbers in parentheses represent protective trade bills.

Trade balance: Balance on Current Account, billions of dollars, seasonally adjusted,
Fiscal deficit: billions of dollars, fiscal years,
Rate of unemployment: Civilian unemployment rate, percent, monthly data seasonally adjusted.

*Years for special attention.

Sources:
(1) Trade bills from the Library of Congress, Internet Federal Legislation Data Base retrieved through the LOCIS (Library of Congress Information Service), prepared by 1995 class (spring semester) of International Economics.
(2) Trade balance and rate of unemployment from the Council of Economic Advisers, *Economic Report of the President* (Washington, D.C.: U.S. GPO, 1996).

The underlying rationale here is that laws are often legislated or amended under the pressure of interest groups. Although interest groups are a valuable information source for legislators, they usually seek economic rent through lobbying in the legislative process. Public choice theory suggests that rent-seeking results in a considerable loss of social welfare.[15] Irrespective of its statistical significance, the model to be tested is specified better with rent.

Chung (1999) later carried out a time series analysis to explore the protectionist sentiment prevailing in Congress that motivates legislative members to submit protective trade bills. Since protective trade bills, a reasonable measure of protectionism, are only subjectively identifiable from the total of trade bills submitted in each year, he uses three different petitions under sections 701, 731, and both combined, respectively, as the measures for protectionism. The postulated hypothesis is that conventional economic variables (import penetration and unemployment) and political economy variables (rent accrued from trade protection and election dummy) are the primary explanatory variables for protectionism. He focuses on the steel industry protection during the period of the 1980s and early 1990s when managed trade policy was implemented most *actively* by means of sections 701 and 731, the countervailing and antidumping duties in the Omnibus Trade and Competitiveness Act of 1988. Unlike other studies, the rent accruing from trade protection, calculated by the formula available in the aforementioned paper, is incorporated into the model as an integral component. The maximum likelihood estimates confirm the statistical significance of all explanatory variables.[16] It is notable that high unemployment is a strong factor in generating protectionism and that rent leads to protectionism, implying abuses of provisions by interest groups. The results provide us with better insights into the origins of legislative behavior for trade protection in Congress and important implications for U.S. trade policy. Chung concludes that, despite freer and more competitive trade in the WTO era and the continuation of multilateral trade negotiations, protectionism will prevail and trade management will be the policy stance in the United States as long as problems of high unemployment and high trade deficits remain unresolved.

1.4 SUMMARY AND CONCLUSIONS

Congress, not the President, has the power to lay and collect duties and to regulate international trade. Since, in principle, trade law dictates trade policy in the United States, it is important to comprehend U.S. laws prior to understanding U.S. trade policy. The legislative procedure for a trade law is the same as the procedure required for any other law. It begins with a trade bill submitted by a legislative member of an appropriate committee. Within Congress, the Committee on Ways and Means of the House of Representatives has primary jurisdictional responsibility for trade matters. A subcommittee carries out preliminary work on submitted bills.

The Speaker of the House and House Majority Leader or the Presiding Officer and Senate Majority Leader usually combine the bills submitted by committees with jurisdiction over international trade. A single bill emerges from each chamber, on which members in each chamber debate and vote. The House and Senate reconcile any differences on a submitted bill until they agree to an identical form. They vote for the bill that then becomes law after (1) the President approves it; (2) the President fails to return the bill with objections to the House or Senate, wherever it originated, within ten days while Congress is in session, or (3) each chamber overrides a Presidential veto by a two-thirds vote.

A trade act in the United States is legislated through an ostensibly democratic process. Yet this process involves private constituents, public hearings and intra- as well as interbranch politics, often resulting in rent-seeking behavior by special interest groups. Such a lengthy and complex procedure makes trade policy, once established, fairly rigid and difficult to alter. Trade policy is therefore rarely implemented in a timely manner. In addition, unless strong political undercurrents in Congress lean toward the redirection of a particular trade policy, it is very short-sighted for a foreign authority or an interest group to believe that it can influence existing policy through rent-seeking behavior.

Econometric results confirm the postulated hypothesis suggesting that protective trade legislation has conventional economic and political economy causes—import penetration, unemployment, rent accruing from trade protection, and an election dummy. These results have important policy implications. Despite ongoing multilateral and regional trade negotiations, protectionism in the United States will prevail as long as problems of high unemployment, trade deficits aggravated by import penetration, and rent accruing from trade remedy legislation remain unresolved.

NOTES

1. At present, there are twenty-two standing committees in the House and sixteen in the Senate. There are also several select committees and several standing joint committees. Members may serve on more than one committee. The majority party determines the proportion of members on the various committees from each of the two major political parties. The Committee on Standards of Official Conduct is the only exception; it requires an equiproportional membership.

2. Institutional constraints imposed by the legislative branch on the executive branch limit the autonomy of the Federal administration. See chapter 5 of this book.

3. A proposal introduced in Congress takes one of four forms: the bill, the joint resolution, the concurrent resolution, and the simple resolution. Most legislation is initiated in the form of a bill. However, if a joint resolution proposes an amendment to the Constitution and both Houses approve the amendment by two-thirds, the joint resolution is not presented to the President; it is presented directly to the National Archives and to the States for ratification. Joint resolutions may originate either in the House of Representatives or in the Senate but not jointly in both Houses. The concurrent resolution is a resolution on matters affecting the operation of both Houses, and the sim-

ple resolution applies to matters affecting one house only. Bills originating in the House of Representatives and the Senate are designated by the prefix letters H.R. and S., respectively, followed by numbers. Joint resolutions originating in the House of Representatives and the Senate are denoted by H. J. Res. and S. J. Res. followed by numbers. Concurrent resolutions of the House and the Senate are H. Con. Res. and S. Con. Res., followed by numbers, respectively. A simple resolution is designated H. Res. and S. Res., followed by numbers.

4. See James M. Buchanan and Gordon, *Calculus of Consent* (Ann Arbor, MI: University of Michigan Press, 1965), Gordon Tullock, "The Welfare Costs of Tariff, Monopolies, and Theft," *Western Economic Journal* 5 (1967): 224–32, Ann Krueger, "Political Economy of the Rent-seeking Society," *American Economic Review* 69 (1974): 291–303, Jagdish Bhagwati, "Directly-Unproductive Profit-Seeking (DUP) Activities," *Journal of Political Economy* 90 (1982): 988–1002, Gary S. Becker, "A Theory of Competition among Pressure Groups for Political Influence," *Quarterly Journal of Economics* 98 (1983): 371–400, T. A. Pugel and I. Walter, "U.S. Corporate Interests and the Political Economy of Trade Policy," *Review of Economics and Statistics* 67 (1985): 465–73, and Stephen P. Magee, William A. Brock, and Leslie Young, *Black Hole Tariffs and Endogeneous Policy Theory* (Cambridge, UK: Cambridge University Press, 1989). Also, see Dennis C. Mueller, *Public Choice* (Cambridge: Cambridge University Press, 1979) and Robert D. Tollison, "Rent Seeking: A Survey," *Kyklos* 35 (1982), 575–602. There is a view that suggests a public good character of political activity, implying that a collective action can take place if a group is small or well-organized. See Mancur Olson, *The Logic of Collective Action* (Cambridge, MA: Harvard University Press, 1965).

5. If the President fails to return a bill with objections within ten days while Congress is in session, it automatically becomes law. If Congress is in recess, the bill does not become law. Such a case is referred to as a "pocket veto."

6. See U.S. House of Representatives, *How Our Laws are Made*, revised and updated by Edward F. Willett, Jr., Esq. (Washington, D.C.: U.S. GPO, 1990) and Walter J. Oleszek, *Congressional Procedures and the Policy Process* (Washington, D.C.: Congressional Quarterly Press, 1978).

7. A public bill (one that affects the public at large) is referred to the Union Calendar if it is a bill for revenue and appropriations or the House Calendar otherwise. Most trade bills are public bills as opposed to private bill (one that affects an individual).

8. Most committees have two or more subcommittees. Except for the Committee on the Budget, each standing committee that has more than twenty members must establish at least four subcommittees.

9. It is the first reading of the bill. Today the House omits the first reading.

10. At this point, the bill is an act signifying that it is the act of one body of the Congress.

11. There are 435 members of the House, apportioned to the fifty states according to their total population, and 100 members of the Senate, two from each State.

12. The conference committee is often referred to as the "Third House of Congress."

13. See U.S. House of Representatives, *Overview and Compilation of U.S. Trade Statutes* (Washington, D.C.: U.S. GPO, 1995) for the trade remedy law. Chapter 4 will discuss it in detail.

14. There have been numerous studies done on ITC's decision-making behavior, concerning whether the ITC's final determination is based on rules or discretion (politics). These studies also indirectly address the implications of trade protection. Chapter 9 will discuss them in detail.

15. See Note 4 above. Also, see Charles K. Rowely, Willem Thorbecke, and Richard E. Wagner, *Trade Protection in the United States* (Northampton, MA: Edward Elgar Publishing, 1995) for public choice perspectives on trade protection in the United States.

16. The model applied to sections 701, 731, and both combined together is as follows:

$$\Delta NP_t = a + b1\ \Delta PEN_t + b2\ \Delta UE_t + b3\ \Delta RTP_t + b4\ DUM_t + u_t,$$

where NP = number of petitions under sections 701, 703, and both; PEN = import penetration: Imports/(Domestic Production-Exports+Imports); UE = rate of unemployment; RTP = rent accrued from trade protection; DUM = election dummy. To avoid the spurious results frequently generated from time series analysis, Chung (1999) has conducted Dickey-Fuller tests for unit roots in the first-order autoregressive equation and converted the data to first-difference form. He has also conducted cointegration tests, confirming long-run relationships among the variables retained with first differencing. Note that Salvatore (1987) measured protectionists' pressure in terms of the number of petitions. Also, note that Krupp (1994) employed the above definition of import penetration, which is the same as that of the U.S. Bureau of Labor Statistics.

Chapter 2

Primary Trade Laws in the Past

Trade acts have been legislated throughout the history of the United States. The first act dates to 1789. Periods of protectionism have alternated with movements toward trade liberalization. Table 2.1 presents the main trade laws.[1] The chief trade barrier in the past was the tariff, which was the only significant means of trade policy at that time. A figure presenting the historical trend of U.S. tariff rates looks roughly like a seismograph.[2] While the average tariff rate (primarily imposed on manufacturing goods) has gradually been reduced since the beginning of the GATT era, nontariff barriers (NTBs) such as quotas and subsidies surfaced as major protectionist devices during the 1970s.

This chapter outlines primary U.S. trade laws enacted since 1930. It is necessary to examine briefly trade laws in the past because each of the subsequent laws evolved from one or more of the preceding laws. The main components of a new law generally reflect the international trade issues and political situation at the time of legislation. The Omnibus Trade and Competitiveness Act of 1988 (hereafter referred to as OTCA) is the trade law today. Given the importance of today's law, the following two chapters are devoted to the OTCA. The laws explored in this chapter are:

1. Smoot-Hawley Tariff Act of 1930,
2. Reciprocal Trade Agreements Act of 1934,
3. Trade Expansion Act of 1962,
4. Trade Reform Act of 1974,
5. Trade Agreements Act of 1979.

Table 2.1.   Main U.S. Trade Acts[1]

Year	Act	Administration	Purpose
1789	Tariff Act of 1789	Washington (F)	Tariffs for revenue
1846	Walker Tariff Act	Polk (D)	Decrease in tariffs
1861	Morrill Tariff Act	Buchanan (D) /Lincoln (R)	Increase in tariffs
1890	McKinley Tariff Act	Harrison, B. (R)	Increase in tariffs
1894	Wilson-Gorman Act	Cleveland (D), 2nd	Decrease in tariffs
1897	Dingley Tariff Act	McKinley (R)	Increase in tariffs
1909	Payne-Aldrich Tariff Act	Taft (R)	Decrease in tariffs
1913	Underwood-Simmons Act	Wilson (D)	Decrease in tariffs
1922	Fordney-McCumber Act	Harding (R)	Sharp increase in tariffs on farm goods
1930	Smoot-Hawley Tariff Act of 1930	Hoover (R)	Strong protection
1934	Reciprocal Trade Agreements Act of 1934	Roosevelt (D)	Free trade
1962	Trade Expansion Act of 1962	Kennedy (D)	Free trade
1974	Trade Reform Act of 1974	Nixon/Ford (R)	Free trade
1979	Trade Agreements Act of 1979	Carter (D)	Free trade
1988	Omnibus Trade and Competitiveness Act of 1988	Reagan (R)	Protection

1. Among the acts legislated in the past, those unlisted in this table are: Tariff of 1816, Tariff of 1824, Tariff of Abominations in 1828, Tariff of 1832, Tariff of 1833, Tariff of 1842, Tariff of 1857, Tariff of 1872, Tariff of 1875, Mongrel Tariff of 1883, and Emergency Tariff of 1921, Trade Act of 1968, and Trade and Tariff Act of 1984.

D = Democrat, R = Republican, and F = Federalist.

Souces: Allen and Walter (1971), Baldwin (1983), Pugel and Walter (1984), and Magee et al. (1989), <www .u-s-history.com>, and <http://shelby.senate.gov>.

2.1 THE SMOOT-HAWLEY TARIFF ACT OF 1930

The Smoot-Hawley Tariff Act of 1930 (hereafter referred to as S-H), also known more formally as Public Law No. 361 and the Tariff Act of 1930, was legislated

> To provide revenue, to regulate commerce with foreign countries, to encourage the industries of the United States, to protect American labor, and for other purposes.[3]

This act raised the average tariff rate from 38.2 percent in 1930 to 55.3 percent in 1931. Tariffs hit all-time highs on some 70 agricultural products and 900 manufactured goods.

Protectionist sentiment was widespread in America during the years following World War I. The Republican Party was in favor of a protective tariff as it had been since its founding in the 1850s and drew significant support from manufacturing interests in the Midwest and Northeast. Although the Democratic Party, which represented southern agricultural interests, was nominally against high tariffs, many Democratic members of Congress supported the Republican Party. After President Herbert Hoover (Republican) took office in March 1929, Congress began to work for a measure to impose tariffs on agricultural surplus that threatened to destabilize the price structure in the United States. Logrolling among Congressional members facilitated to generate a single bill of elevated tariff rates on both farm products and manufactures.[4] The bill passed the Senate on June 13, 1930 and the House on June 14. *Congressional Record* has a breakdown of roll call votes of both chambers. Among 86 votes cast in the Senate, 44 votes were in favor of passage of the bill and 42 votes were against it. Among 422 votes cast in the House, 245 were in favor (of which Republican votes—230 and Democratic votes—15) and 177 votes were against (of which Republican votes—27 and Democratic votes—150), respectively. Ignoring a petition of 1028 economists to veto the bill and formal protests by more than thirty countries, President Hoover signed it into law on June 17, 1930. This law is referred to as the Smoot-Hawley (S-H) Act because of its joint sponsorship by Representative Willis C. Hawley (Republican, Oregon; Chairman, Committee on Ways and Means) and Senator Reed Smoot (Republican, Utah; Chairman, Committee on Finance).

The S-H provided a key foundation for the current tariff system by establishing a uniform U.S. tariff schedule; it became the legislative basis for trade remedy law in effect today. Section 303 relates to countervailing duties imposed against foreign subsidies.[5] Title VII of S-H reinstated the Antidumping Law of 1921 and the Antidumping Act of 1916, the first U.S. statute to impose antidumping duties. Provisions on petitions and case investigations are also included in the S-H.

The tariff escalation mandated by S-H drew widespread retaliation against the United States from approximately sixty foreign countries. They levied similar increases in their tariff barriers. As illustrated by his contracting spiral diagram, Kindleberger (1973) suggested that world trade in March 1933 was only approximately one-third of the level in January 1929. U.S. exports decreased by two-thirds, dropping the U.S. share of world trade from 16 percent to 11 percent in 1933. The S-H symbolizes protectionist sentiment in the United States even today. A majority of economists nowadays regard the S-H legislation as the worst mistake ever made in the history of U.S. trade policy.

Two questions arise: One is concerned with the causes of the S-H and the other with its effect on the Great Depression. The first question requires that we examine the economic situation prior to the passage of the bill. Table 2.2

Table 2.2.　Cyclical Phases in the 1920s and 1930s

Expansion	July 1921–May 1923
Contraction (mild and brief)	May 1923–July 1924
Expansion	July 1924–October 1926
Contraction (mild and brief)	October 1926–November 1927
Expansion	November 1927–August 1929
Economic Collapse[1]	August 1929–1933

1. NBER's date for the stock market crash is August 1929, whereas Gordon's date is October of the same year.

Source: Information available in Gordon (1974), 41 and 43.

presents cyclical phases during the 1920s. This period, excluding the last one, is characterized by three expansions and two contractions. Since the two contractions were mild and brief, the 1920s is generally regarded as a boom period. Table 2.3 presents major macroeconomic series during the five years before and after 1930. Prior to 1930, none of these series shows a notable irregularity. Economic growth was steady, the rate of unemployment was low, and inflation and wage rates remained stable. Private savings (except in 1928), government spending, and tax revenue remained almost the same. The current account surplus continued with no radical changes in exports and imports throughout the period. While bond prices remained stable, stock prices increased steadily up to 1929. The Federal Reserve maintained a steady money supply, although the expansion prior to 1929 resulted in moderate increases in interest rates and speculative demand for money. Although published data for private investment is available only for one year, it is widely known that the 1920s was a period of investment boom, especially in automobiles, electric power, chemical products, oil, rubber products, natural gas, and airplanes. Technical changes in these products with no substantial changes in input combinations raised worker productivity. There were no inflationary expectations to increase wages. Overall, the U.S. economy was prosperous and stable.[6] It is difficult to understand why such a strong protectionist sentiment emerged amid the boom of the 1920s.

Several suggested causes of the S-H legislation are presented in the literature; most are controversial.

(1) Pressure from Interest Groups in the Agricultural Sector

Technological innovations in the United States resulted in large-scale farming that decreased the price of U.S. farm goods. As a result, the parity ratio turned against farmers. Agricultural interest groups lobbied the government and encouraged logrolling among legislators in order to restore a parity ratio favor-

Table 2.3. Major Macroeconomic Indicators before and after the Smoot-Hawley Tariff Act of 1930

Year	GNP[1]	u	B/P	X	M	D	I[2]	S	G	T	MS	w	Ps	p
1925	179.4	3.2	1.1	6.4	5.3	37.6		10.7	2.9	3.6	42.1	0.5	11.2	13.7
1926	190.0	1.8	0.8	6.4	5.6	39.3	18.0	10.1	2.9	3.8	43.7	0.5	12.6	-10.7
1927	189.8	3.3	1.1	6.5	5.4	38.8		10.1	2.8	4.0	44.7	0.5	15.3	-6.3
1928	190.9	4.2	1.4	6.8	5.5	38.8		6.1	2.9	3.9	46.4	0.6	20.0	1.8
1930	183.5	8.7	1.0	5.5	4.4	44.7		5.6	3.3	4.1	45.7	0.6	21.0	2.5
1931	169.3	15.9	0.5	3.6	3.1	53.2	16.8	2.5	3.6	3.1	42.7	0.5	13.7	-8.8
1932	144.2	23.6	0.4	2.5	2.1	59.1		-3.3	4.7	1.9	36.1	0.4	6.9	-10.3
1933	141.5	24.9	0.4	2.4	2.0	53.6		-3.8	4.6	2.0	32.2	0.4	9.0	-5.1
1934	154.3	21.7	0.6	3.0	2.4	46.7		-1.0	6.7	3.0	34.4	0.5	9.8	3.4
1935	169.5	20.1	0.1	3.3	3.1	42.9		2.4	6.5	3.7	39.1	0.5	10.6	NA3

Notations:

GNP in billions of dollars in 1958 prices,

u = rate of unemployment in percent of civilian labor force, fourteen years old and over, annual average,

p = rate of inflation in terms of CPI (1967 = 100),

B/P = the balance of payments on goods and services in billions of dollars,

X = exports of goods and services, in billions of dollars,

M = imports of goods and services, in billions of dollars,

D = duty, per cent,

I = gross capital formation, private and public, five-year annual period averages for 1922–1926 and 1927–1931, respectively, billions of dollars,

S = personal savings, billions of dollars,

G = government expenditure, billions of dollars,

T = tax revenue, billions of dollars,

w = average hourly earnings for production workers in manufacturing, dollars,

Ps = stock price, Standard and Poor's index of common stocks, 1941–1943 = 10.

MS = M2 in billions of dollars, annual average.

1. The official figures of the Department of Commerce begin at 1929. Figures for GNP and its components before 1929 are the figures estimated by Simon Kuznets, *Capital in American Economy: Its Formation and Financing*, Appendix A, NBER (New York, 1961).

2. Only two figures are available. The series estimated by Simon Kuznets are 20.3, 20.9, 19.9, 19.4, and 21.1 billions of dollars in 1929 prices for the five years before 1930.

3. NA = Not available.

Source: U.S. Department of Commerce, Bureau of the Census, *Historical Statistics of the United States, Colonial Times to 1970* (Washington, D.C.: U.S. GPO, 1969).

able to them.[7] Apart from this, U.S. exports of cotton, cotton manufactured goods, wheat, wheat flour, and meat decreased significantly. Table 2.4 shows U.S. exports and imports of major farm goods selected by volume for five years before and after 1930. The agricultural industry was a much larger proportion of the American economy in the 1920s than it is today. It accounted for nearly 25 percent of total employment in the mid-1920s. Hoover wanted to keep his campaign promise to farmers and announced his intention of reviewing not only the agricultural tariff schedule but also others. Members of Congress took this occasion to overhaul the entire schedule of tariffs. Tariff rates drastically amended at that time reminded one of protectionism inherited from the Fordney-McCumber Tariff Act of 1922 (a strongly protective act passed during the Republican Harding Administration).

A recent econometric analysis of Senatorial votes for the S-H by Cupitt and Elliott (1994) offers poor support for a pressure group model of policy making. Apart from the above argument, many also believe that the S-H was politically designed to institute permanent agricultural protection, especially against imports from Europe and Australia. Observe that such imports decreased dramatically after 1930.

Table 2.4.   Exports and Imports of Farm Goods (millions of dollars)

	Exports						Imports			
Year	Cotton Manufact.	Cotton	Tobacco	Wheat	Wheat Flour	Meat	Coffee	Sugar	Silk	Fruits
1925	1060	149	153	149	234	127	286	246	396	89
1926	814	129	137	202	285	107	323	233	393	88
1927	826	133	139	240	325	71	264	258	390	85
1928	920	135	154	120	194	68	310	207	368	90
1929	771	135	146	112	192	79	302	209	427	87
1930	497	89	145	88	157	66	209	130	263	75
1931	326	60	110	50	84	36	175	113	191	60
1932	345	46	65	33	51	19	137	97	114	44
1933	398	39	82	5	19	26	124	105	103	37
1934	373	43	125	10	27	35	133	118	72	46
1935	391	39	134	NA[1]	15	28	137	133	96	55

1. NA = Not available.

Source: U.S. Department of Commerce, Bureau of the Census, Historical Statistics of the United States, Colonial Times to 1970 (Washington, D.C.: U.S. GPO, 1969).

(2) Workers' Demand for Higher Wages and Collective Bargaining

Prices were stable throughout the 1920s. There were no inflationary expectations tempting workers to demand higher wages. The United States was more concerned about low wages due to massive unemployment in Europe after World War I. Given the Stolper-Samuelson theorem (suggesting that protection increases the real wage of a scarce factor), one might suspect that the Wagner Act (supporting workers' rights to collective bargaining) was the chief reason for passage of the S-H. However, the Wagner Act was not passed until 1935.[8]

(3) Instability in the World Economy

The collapse of the gold standard (1880–1914) destabilized the international financial system. Denmark, Finland, Norway, Sweden, and the United Kingdom devalued their currencies, whereas France, Germany, Italy, and the Netherlands maintained a fixed exchange rate. The relative devaluation of the former countries enabled them to recover from the Great Depression quickly by raising exports. Political leaders in the United States worried about the future of the global economy and competition with European countries. The general sentiment in the United States favored the need to protect American industries. Lake (1988) suggests that the emergence of unilateral protectionism would inevitably lead to higher tariffs. However, it is hard to believe that the United States actually felt threatened by most European countries that recovered from the Great Depression (with the exception of Great Britain).

In any event, considering the lengthy procedure required by Congress to pass a bill, the political and economic forces set in motion for the Smoot-Hawley Act might have arisen long before the U.S. economy began to show symptoms of the Great Depression.

We now turn our attention to the second question, that is, effect of the S-H on the Great Depression. The stock market crashed on "Black Tuesday," when the Dow Jones Industrial Average fell from an all-time high of 381 to 326 on October 22, 1929 and then to 230 over the following six trading days.[9] Immediately after the crash, some economists, such as Irving Fisher, were optimistic about a quick recovery. However, the U.S. economy experienced the most severe contraction in its business cycle history during the period of 1929 to 1933. Real GNP in 1933 fell by 30 percent (45 percent in current prices) in comparison with that in 1929. The rate of unemployment rose from 3 percent in 1929 to 25 percent in 1933, the highest rate ever reached. The Consumer Price Index (1967 = 100) decreased by 10 percent in 1932. Stock prices in terms of the Standard and Poor's Index (1941–1943 = 10) dropped from 26.0

in 1929 to 6.9 in 1932. The Depression dispersed to the rest of the world. Despite the recovery that began since 1934 under the New Deal employed by the Roosevelt administration, the rate of unemployment remained as high as 17 percent for the subsequent ten years.[10]

After seven decades have passed, economists continue to debate the causes of the Great Depression. There are economists who focus on *the real sector* (i.e., a contractionary shift of the IS curve: a graphical representation of the real sector of economy). Some blame an exogenous fall in consumption as household wealth declined and uncertainty rose following the stock market crash. Other economists point to the large decrease in investment in residential housing presumably because of excess supply during the boom of the 1920s coupled with reduced immigration. Still others argue that government fiscal policy dealing with the traumatic economic decline was inadequate. They charge that politicians, especially Democrats, rigidly adhered to a balanced budget at a time of massive unemployment. The Revenue Act of 1932, for instance, increased various taxes, reinforcing the cyclical downturn.

There are economists who suggest that *the monetary sector* (i.e., a contractionary shift of the LM curve: a graphical representation of the monetary sector) was responsible for the Depression. The rationale here is that the U.S. stock market was booming in the 1920s as the result of optimism stemming partly from technological progress that rapidly raised the standard of living. The Federal Reserve, newly born in 1914, employed a tight money policy to cool off the speculative bubble in the stock market in 1928 and 1929. The bubble in the market burst suddenly. Widespread bank failures (more than nine thousand banks), caused by insolvency, sharply reduced public confidence in the banking system that resulted in massive withdrawals of demand deposits. Banks, in turn, responded to lower reserves by tightening credit to investors. Such interactive behavior between depositors and banks reduced the banking multiplier. Hence, the money supply decreased by about 30 percent during the period from 1929 to 1933. This policy increased the rate of interest and decreased investment, pushing the U.S. economy into the Depression. Friedman and Schwartz (1963) argued that the Fed's "passive, defensive, and hesitant" policy allowing a large decrease in nominal money supply caused the "great contraction."[11] Bernanke (1983) asserted that there was evidence that the series of bank closings helped start and aggravate the Great Depression. Field (1984) confirmed a close correlation between the Fed's tight policy in the late 1920s and the subsequent economic downturn.

Related to this argument is the suggestion that the deflation in the early 1930s was responsible for the Depression because such a prolonged deflation was possible only with a contractionary monetary policy. This view is subject to criticism. Although the nominal money supply decreased, there is evidence that the real money supply increased and nominal interest rates fell continuously from 1929 to 1933.

Was the S-H Act responsible for the Great Depression? Many economists believe so. However, the S-H was not actually enacted until more than eight months (ten months according to the National Bureau of Economic Research—NBER) after the collapse in October 1929. Another view suggests that, although U.S. net exports decreased substantially as a result of foreign retaliations following the S-H, the U.S. foreign sector in terms of the volume of trade (7 billion dollars of exports and 5.4 billion dollars of imports in 1929) was too small to make such a big negative contribution to its GNP (203.6 billion dollars) at that time. There are economists such as Eichengreen (1986) and Crucini (1994), who report that the S-H's impact on the economy was negligible. On the other hand, there are also economists who suggest that the S-H was a key contributor to the propagation of the Great Depression. Recent studies include Crucini and Kahn (1996), McDonald, O'Brien, and Callahan (1997), and Irwin (1998). Bhagwati (1988) suggests the increase in tariffs by the S-H and foreign retaliations against the United States was disaster. Romer (1986) even suggests that macroeconomic data of such variables as unemployment and real GDP before World War I are not reliable to assess the performance of macroeconomic policy.

The S-H was nevertheless partially responsible for exacerbating and prolonging the Great Depression for at least three reasons: First, almost all macroeconomic series show significant deterioration after 1930. Second, much of the political and legislative activity creating the S-H took place in 1929. Third, the foreign trade retaliation against the United States and worldwide protective measures led Americans to speculate negatively on an uncertain future for the U.S. economy.

2.2 THE RECIPROCAL TRADE AGREEMENTS ACT OF 1934

From the beginning of the Roosevelt Administration in 1933, the seemingly disastrous effect of the S-H on U.S. exports was a serious concern in both legislative and executive branches. The Depression was at its peak and the New Deal was just beginning. Congress was dominated by the Democratic Party. Appointed as Secretary of State, Senator Cordell Hull from Tennessee called for opening new foreign markets for U.S. goods by reversing high tariff barriers. He was instrumental in the passage of the Reciprocal Trade Agreements Act by Congress in March 1934. Enacted in June 1934 upon signing by the President, the Reciprocal Trade Agreements Act (hereafter referred to as the RTAA), also known as Public Law 73–316, was basically an amended ver-

sion of the S-H; it added at the end of Title III the following: Part III—Promotion of Foreign Trade, marking the end of one era of American protectionism.[12]

The main objective of the RTAA was to authorize the President to enter
into *bilateral* agreements with other countries for reciprocal tariff reductions
without Congressional approval and to extend a most-favored-nation status to
other countries, although periodic renewals were required (Section 350). The
RTAA also granted authority for the United States to participate in the first
five rounds of GATT trade negotiations, from 1947 to the Dillon Round (the
trade negotiations that took place under the GATT from 1960–1962, named
after the then U.S. Undersecretary of State, who proposed the negotiations).[13]
The authority granted to the President by Congress includes the mutual need
for close cooperation between the legislative and executive branches in order
to avoid the disastrous fallout from the S-H.[14]

This act was renewed eleven times (in 1937, 1940, 1943, 1945, 1948,
1949, 1951, 1953, 1954, 1955, and 1958), eight of which were extended after World War II and four during the Eisenhower Administration
(1953–1961). The authority in most renewals included the reduction of tariff
rates up to 50 percent of the existing duty prior to each renewal. The exten-
sions of RTAA in 1955 (P.L. 84–86) and 1958 (P.L. 85–686) in particular
were made in an attempt to expand foreign markets for U.S. goods. However,
there were also Congressional attempts to restrict Presidential authority by
special provisions. Four notable ones are the provisions on peril point, escape
clause, national security, and reduced period of renewals. The first three are
briefly explained here.

The peril point is a hypothetical limit beyond which a reduction in tariff
imposed on the items designated for negotiation would imperil domestic producers. The President could still reduce tariff rates below the peril point but
was obliged to inform Congress and to explain the action. The escape clause
is the provision that allows an industry to apply for relief from increased imports resulting from a tariff cut to the Tariff Commission. This clause permitted withdrawal of a concession if a concession was harmful to the domestic
industry. The peril point was introduced in 1948 and eliminated in 1949; the
escape clause and peril point were introduced in 1951. The provision on national security was introduced in 1954. The Administration entered into
thirty-two bilateral trade agreements with twenty-seven countries by 1945.

In conclusion, the RTAA is significant in that issues regarding U.S. tariffs
have fallen largely to the executive branch since 1934, and that bilateral
agreements for reciprocal tariff reductions have drastically changed the
method for establishing future tariff levels. In addition, the RTAA paved the
way toward multilateral agreements under $GATT_{1947}$ by authorizing U.S. par-

ticipation in GATT negotiations, which remains the principal framework of the world trading system today.

The RTAA was superseded by the Trade Expansion Act of 1962.

2.3 TRADE EXPANSION ACT OF 1962

There was considerable erosion in U.S. economic superiority during the 1950s as foreign economies damaged by World War II gradually recovered. Many U.S. industries felt increasingly threatened especially by industries in the EEC.[15] Meanwhile, the 1934 Act, after being extended eleven times, was expiring in June 1962. President Kennedy believed that it was time for the administration to have flexible bargaining power for trade expansion. He asked not for renewal, but for replacement of the twenty-eight-year-old law by a new law. The President sought two basic types of tariff-cutting authority for use over the next five years: 1) general authority to reduce tariffs by 50 percent in exchange for concessions from other countries and 2) special authority to reduce or eliminate all tariffs on those products where the United States and the EEC dominate world trade by 80 percent or more of their exports combined.

The Trade Expansion Act of 1962 (TEA), Public Law 87–794, was enacted in the form requested by the administration. This act has been known as the law authorizing the Kennedy Round (1962–1967), the sixth round, of the GATT. It was a substantive round in GATT history in terms of tariff reductions, especially for manufactured goods. Tariffs were reduced on the average by about 35 percent and were subject to gradual reductions continuing until 1972. The TEA also authorized the Adjustment Assistance Program for firms and industries to enhance their competitiveness, ranging from technical assistance (Section 313 (a)) and employee training (Section 326 (a)) to trade adjustment allowances (Section 602).[16] The intent of the assistance program was to help workers and firms or industries adjust to more liberalized trade practices. It authorized the President to appoint a Special Representative for Trade Negotiations, at the rank of Ambassador, as the chief U.S. trade negotiator, upon confirmation by the Senate (Section 241). Congress was concerned about U.S. concessions for trade agreements that might inflict damages on U.S. industries through excessive imports. An escape clause was inserted into the act to deal with such circumstances.

There are several other notable provisions of the TEA. Section 252 concerned foreign import restrictions. Under Subtitles (a) and (b), the President was authorized to retaliate against foreign import restrictions in violation of the GATT. Subtitle (c) authorized the President to increase duties or restrict imports from any countries that had burdensome restrictions against U.S.

agricultural imports. Section 231 authorized the President to withdraw trade concessions from a communist country, whereas Section 402 gave the President power to provide MFN status to any communist country subject to U.S. interests.

The Trade Act of 1974 succeeded the TES.

2.4 TRADE REFORM ACT OF 1974

Although the Kennedy Round achieved some of the largest tariff cuts in the history of the United States, it did not lead to an open, competitive, non-discriminatory, and fair world trading system, to reform trade institutions, and to deal with nontariff barriers (NTBs) that were becoming increasingly prevalent worldwide during the 1970s. In addition to problems of trade deficits, unprecedented peacetime inflation in the United States, and a relative decline in manufacturing employment, there were also major complaints about foreign unfair trade practices using NTBs that were filed by American industries such as footwear, textiles, clothing, television, and steel.

As it had done periodically in the past (e.g., cases of the RTAA and TEA), Congress again delegated to the President specific and limited authority to negotiate with foreign countries for reciprocal tariff concessions by legislating the Trade Act of 1974 (Public Law 93–618). It was H.R. 10710 amended by the Senate, enacted on January 3, 1975, often referred to as the Trade Reform Act of 1974 (TRA). The TRA authorized the President, during the five-year period beginning on the date of enactment, to enter into trade agreements with foreign countries, including the Tokyo Round (1973–1979, the seventh multilateral trade negotiations) for further tariff cut beyond the level of the Kennedy Round by about 30 percent. Other authorizations include assurance of reciprocal trade benefits; fair treatment and equitable market access for U.S. exports; trade agreements to harmonize, reduce, or eliminate NTBs; to relieve firms, industries, and workers from serious injury by import competition; improvement of procedures for responding to unfair trade practices in the United States and abroad; extended MFN treatment; and extension of preferential tariff treatment to exports of LDCs. Such a close cooperation between Congress and the President in the negotiation and implementation of trade agreements was reflected first in the RTAA of 1934 and has remained a part of U.S. trade legislation for over sixty years; this was the origin of fast track authority.[17] The TRA is known as the act that reduced the average tariff rate by one-third during the Tokyo Round and that laid the basis for today's trade remedy laws by systematically compiling and elaborating provisions included in previous laws. It was indeed this law that turned the overall direction of U.S. trade policy from simply *free* trade to *fair* trade.

The TRA consists of six titles. The provisions cited most frequently in the literature are as follows:

1. In Title I (Negotiating and Other Authority), Sections 101–102 authorized the President to negotiate trade agreements with foreign countries during the five-year postenactment period in order to modify duty rates and to take all appropriate and feasible steps to harmonize, reduce, or eliminate NTBs and other distortions. The TRA passed with a provision requiring the President to determine whether any major industrial countries had failed to make concessions equivalent to U.S. concessions. Section 141 established a new Office of the Special Representative for Trade Negotiations. As the chief representative of the United States for each trade negotiation, he reports to the President and Congress on the administration of trade agreements and advises them with respect to NTBs.
2. Sections 201–203 in Title II (Relief from Injury Caused by Import Competition) are concerned with the escape clause that deals with relief from injury due to competing imports, including investigation, presidential actions, and import relief by offsetting duties, import duties, and orderly marketing arrangements with foreign countries.[18]
3. Title III (Relief from Unfair Trade Practices), Sections 301–302, contains the primary statutory authority requiring the President to respond to unjustifiable or unreasonable tariff and other import restrictions, discriminatory acts or policies, and export subsidies of foreign governments against the United States.[19] Section 321, an amended version of Section 201 of the Antidumping Act of 1921, is concerned with investigations of injury due to dumping by foreign countries. Section 331, containing amendments to Sections 303 and 516 of the Tariff Act of 1930, deals with the imposition of countervailing duties and the procedures for petition and injury determination.
4. Sections 501 and 504 in Title V (Generalized System of Preferences) authorized the President to extend or limit the GSP. The United States was the last developed country to extend the GSP.

2.5 TRADE AGREEMENTS ACT OF 1979

The Trade Agreements Act of 1979 (Public Law 96–39; H.R. 4537 passed by Congress on July 26, 1979, hereafter TAA) was legislated primarily to authorize the administration to implement all agreements negotiated under the Trade Act of 1974, specifically the Tokyo Round. The objective of the authorization was to improve an open world trading system, the expansion of opportunities for U.S. trade, and enforcement of the rules of international trade.

Among the eleven titles included in the TAA, the most important is Title I, which is concerned with countervailing and antidumping duties. This section addressed a growing concern in the United States with two types of foreign unfair trade practices—subsidy and dumping. In accordance with section 101 in Title I of the TAA, the S-H was amended by adding at the end new countervailing and antidumping duties, Subtitles A through D of Title VII. This amendment resulted in substantial changes to the S-H and the TRA, in Section 701 (countervailing duties imposed) and Section 731 (antidumping duties imposed). Section 701 requires the administering authority to impose a countervailing duty (CVD) equal to the amount of net subsidy as determined by judicial processes, if the authority determines that there is a material injury or retardation of U.S. industry by subsidized imports.[20] In addition, Section 771(5) of the TAA redefined subsidy to mean "bounty or grant." This definition is much broader than in the S-H. In the TAA, a countervailing subsidy includes the provision of capital, loans, or loan guarantees on terms inconsistent with commercial consideration, the provision of goods and services at preferential rates, grants of forgiveness on debt covering operating losses, the assumption of any expenses of manufacture, production, or distribution, tax credits, pre- or postexport financing, excessive tax rebates, accelerated depreciation for exporters, preferential working capital finance, reduced duties on materials incorporated in exports, and preferential tax treatment tied to exports. Section 731 requires an antidumping duty (AD) to be imposed on imports at less-than-fair value if a U.S. industry is determined to be materially injured or retarded.

U.S. antidumping practices in the past, established in the Antidumping Act of 1921, were inconsistent with the GATT in several respects. Some of these are: 1) the GATT required "material injury," whereas the United States did not; 2) the United States did not adopt the requirement that the sales at less-than-fair value (LTFV) standard be the principal, major, or substantial cause of injury to domestic industry. The TAA mandated formal time limits for assessments.

The growing number of petitions claiming foreign unfair trade practices persuaded Congress to restructure the international trade functions of the executive branch. As a result, the authority for implementing the CVD and AD provisions was transferred from the Department of Treasury to the Department of Commerce. In addition, the Department of Commerce became responsible for trade adjustment assistance and monitoring compliance with international trade agreements. The Office of Special Trade Representative was responsible for trade negotiations to resolve petitions filed by U.S. exporters who alleged foreign import restrictions.

Title IV of the TAA is another important part of the agreements negotiated during the Tokyo Round related to technical barriers to trade or standards-related barriers. The functions of federal agencies and judicial proceedings regarding standards-related activities are described in this title. Section 413, in particular, requires the Secretaries of Commerce and Agriculture to gather information on the adequacy of representation in international standards-related activities, to identify any activities that might substantially affect U.S. commerce, and to coordinate with the Special Trade Representative.

Other parts of this act include Customs Valuation (Title II), an amended version of the relevant part of S-H, which deals with the valuation of imported merchandise; and Government Procurement (Title III), which provides authority to modify discriminatory purchasing requirements, to encourage reciprocal competitive procurement practices, and monitoring and enforcement.

2.6 SUMMARY AND CONCLUSIONS

The Smoot-Hawley Tariff Act of 1930 was the most protective law in the history of U.S. trade policy. The tariff escalation drew widespread retaliation against the United States. U.S. exports decreased dramatically, dropping the U.S. share of world trade. Although the S-H was not the direct cause of the Great Depression, it was partially responsible for exacerbating and prolonging the Great Depression. This act was drawn up when the American economy was enjoying a boom period and the balance of payments was in (a current account) surplus. There are numerous causes of the S-H legislation cited in the literature, including agricultural interest but they are controversial.

The purpose of the Reciprocal Trade Agreements Act of 1934 was to authorize the President to enter into bilateral agreements for reciprocal tariff reductions without Congressional approval and to extend to other countries on a most-favored-nation basis. The RTAA also granted authority for the United States to participate in the first five rounds of GATT from 1947 to the Dillon Round to expand foreign markets. This act was renewed eleven times.

The Trade Expansion Act of 1962 replaced twenty-eight-year-old RTAA of 1934. It was legislated primarily to provide the President with a flexible bargaining power for trade expansion and initiatives for trade liberalization. The Kennedy Round was the substantive round in GATT history in terms of tariff reductions.

The Trade Reform Act of 1974 authorized the President to enter into other trade agreements with foreign countries. It is best known as the act for the Tokyo Round and the basis of today's trade remedy provisions.

The Trade Agreements Act of 1979 was legislated mainly to authorize the administration to implement all agreements negotiated under the Tokyo Round. In accordance with a provision in the TAA, the S-H was amended by adding at the end thereof the new countervailing and antidumping duties. The

TAA restructured the international trade policy functions of the executive branch in response to the growing number of petitions claiming foreign unfair trade practices.

NOTES

1. For trade laws passed during the earlier history of the United States, see Frank W. Taussig, *The Tariff History of the United States*, 8th ed. (New York, NY: G. P. Putnam's Sons, 1931), and Percy W. Bidwell, *Tariff Policy in the United States* (New York, NY: Putnam,1933).

2. The figure presented by the U.S. Bureau of the Census is widely known in the literature and thus not presented here.

3. The statement in the quotation is the preamble of the Smoot-Hawley Tariff Act of 1930.

4. Logrolling is a process of legislative vote trading for mutual political benefit.

5. It is notable that the provision on the countervailing duty in today's trade remedy law existed already in the 1930 tariff act.

6. See Robert A. Gordon, *Economic Instability and Growth: The American Record* (New York, NY: Harper and Row Publishers, 1974), 17.

7. See E. E. Schattschneider, *Politics, Pressures and the Tariff* (Englewood Cliffs, NJ: Prentice Hall, 1935). Standard historical pattern of raising tariffs for special interest of every legislative member is a public choice perspective.

8. The right of collective bargaining was allowed by the Wagner Act legislated in 1935.

9. The time between 1929 and 1933 was the period of the *great contraction*, the most severe depression ever experienced by the United States. See Milton Friedman and Anna Jacobson Schwartz, *A Monetary History of the United States, 1896–1960* (Princeton, NJ: Princeton University Press, 1963), 299.

10. See N. Gregory Mankiew, *Macroeconomics*, 2d ed. (New York, NY: Worth Publishers, 1994) for a good reference to the information in this paragraph.

11. See Milton Friedman and Anna Jacobson Schwartz, *A Monetary History of the United States, 1896–1960* (Princeton, NJ: Princeton University Press, 1963), 411.

12. See U.S. Congress, *The Statute at Large of the United States of America from March 1933 to June 1934* 48, Part I (Washington, D.C.: U.S. GPO, 1934), 943.

13. The Dillon Round (1960–1962) achieved offsetting effects against European Common Market tariffs on trade with nonmember countries. It also produced a reciprocal 20 percent overall tariff reduction for a two-year period.

14. See note 16 below.

15. The European Common Market was formed in 1958, and the European Free Trade Area (EFTA) was formed in 1960. A free trade area and a common market remove all trade barriers among members. But the former lets each member to retain its own tariff rates against nonmembers, whereas the latter harmonizes trade policies, including a common tariff schedule. Members of the European Common Market were

West Germany, France, Italy, the Netherlands, Belgium, and Luxembourg. Members of the EFTA were England, Sweden, Denmark, Switzerland, Norway, Austria, and Portugal. Both existed until the European Union (EU) was formed in 1993.

16. The Act amended Section VII of the 1951 Trade Act. The amended version required the USTC to determine industrial injury from increased imports as the result of trade concessions and to recommend an appropriate amount of tariffs, quotas, or any other import relief to the President. The President would then provide the requested relief and adjustment assistance or reject the USTC's findings and recommendations.

17. The Ford Administration and Congress explicitly created the "fast track authority" to expedite procedures for Congressional consideration of trade agreements within mandatory deadlines, including a limitation on debate and the omission of amendment. It is a tight schedule for a bill that permits no further amendments but only one up-or-down votes. The authority was first used in the Trade Act of 1974 to deal with the Tokyo Round negotiations. Congress renewed fast track authority for negotiation of trade agreements in 1979, 1983, 1984, 1988, 1991, 1993, 1998, and 2001 and for implementation of trade agreements in 1979, 1985, 1988, 1993, and 1994. For additional information, see Carolyn C. Smith, "Fast-Tack Negotiating Authority for Trade Agreement and Trade Promotion Authority: Chronology of Major Votes," *CRS Report for Congress* received through the CRS Web (December 2001): 1–5.

18. Today's version of Section 201 will be discussed in chapter 4 in detail.

19. Today's version of Section 301 will be discussed in chapter 4 in detail.

20. Material injury is defined as harm that is not inconsequential, immaterial, or unimportant.

Chapter 3

Trade Law of the Present Era: An Overview

The Omnibus Trade and Competitiveness Act of 1988 (hereafter referred to as the OTCA) is the primary U.S. trade law of the present era. After several years of intense debate during a period of mounting trade and fiscal deficits, the one hundredth Congress, under unified Democratic control, passed H.R. 4848 that was signed by President Reagan in August 1988 to become the OTCA (Public Law 100–418).[1] The OTCA is a comprehensive law that encompasses a broad spectrum of components, ranging from presidential authority to many substantive and procedural changes dealing with unfair trade practices of foreign countries. The OTCA focuses on opening foreign markets to U.S. trade and providing relief from both fair and unfair trade practices. A significant portion of this Act is amended versions of provisions from many earlier laws.

The most important elements of the OTCA include:

1. Section 301
2. Super 301
3. Special 301
4. Antidumping Actions
5. Countervailing Duty Actions
6. Safeguard Actions
7. Telecommunications
8. Government Procurement
9. Unfair Trade Practices
10. Trade Adjustment Assistance for Workers
11. Trade Adjustment Assistance for Firms and Industries
12. International Textile Arrangements
13. Generalized System of Preferences.

The first six of them are the "principal trade remedy provisions." This chapter discusses the OTCA's recent history and purpose, analyzes Congressional votes on the OTCA bill, and outlines the main features of the law. The trade remedy provisions of the OTCA constitute the main part of today's managed trade policy. In light of their importance, the trade remedy provisions will be separately discussed in detail in chapter 4.

The remaining seven are concerned with area-specific statutes invoked when circumstantial changes in a specific area against U.S. trade policy warrants tactical maneuvers by the United States. They are outlined here.

The provision on telecommunications requires the USTR to review the operation and effectiveness of U.S. telecommunications trade agreements each year and to determine whether or not a foreign country is in violation due to any act, policy, or practice implemented as a result of the trade agreement. In case of government procurement, the executive order mandates the U.S. authority to identify countries that are in violation of the relevant provisions of the WTO and the NAFTA against U.S. products and services and to take appropriate countermeasures if necessary. The provision on unfair trade practices is based on Section 337 of the Trade Act of 1930. It is the provision that prohibits unfair acts or unfair methods of competition when importing or selling imported goods. Trade Adjustment Assistance for Workers is also based on the 1974 Trade Act. Title II of this act authorizes the U.S. Department of Labor to provide worker assistance such as trade adjustment assistance, training, job search, relocation allowances, and reemployment services for workers. Further, it authorizes the U.S. Department of Commerce to provide the Trade Adjustment Assistance Program for Firms and Industries. There is an international agreement for textiles and clothing. This agreement went into force on January 1, 1995 as part of the WTO agreements. It provides for gradual and complete integration of textiles and clothing into the WTO regime over a ten-year transition period. This agreement supersedes the Multifiber Arrangement. OTCA also includes the Generalized System of Preferences (GSP), a program that grants duty-free treatment to specified products imported from over 140 designated developing countries in order to provide more trade opportunities. Growing importance of these area-specific statutes in connection with the future U.S. trade policy merits further explanation and chapter 7, which is dedicated to U.S. trade policy in action, provides details.

This specific chapter outlines the OTCA of 1988 including both the principal trade remedy provisions and the area-specific trade remedy provisions. Section 1 discusses the background and purpose of enactment of this law. Section 2 is concerned with the OTCA legislation in the House and the Senate. Section 3 presents statutory composition of the OTCA. Section 4 draws conclusions.

3.1 BACKGROUND AND PURPOSE OF OTCA

Congressional dissatisfaction with the massive fiscal deficit, combined with its macroeconomic connection to the trade deficit, led to a strong undercurrent of protectionism that began in 1983. As shown in table 1.1, numbers of trade bills submitted by both House and Senate increased sharply in that year. Meanwhile, foreign countries had become increasingly competitive, and some were moving toward expanding existing trade blocs or creating new ones. The original bill (H.R. 3) for the Trade Act of 1988 (OTCA) was submitted in 1986, when political turbulence over increasing trade deficits and fiscal deficits was at its peak. Figure 3.1 exhibits U.S. trade deficits and fiscal deficits that began to show notable trends in the early 1980s and reached three-digit numbers in billions of dollars in 1985 ($124 and $212, respectively).

As the first comprehensive trade law since the Smoot-Hawley Tariff Act of 1930, the OTCA derives from numerous sources. It has linkages to almost every previous law in the long history of U.S. trade policy, especially those passed since 1930.

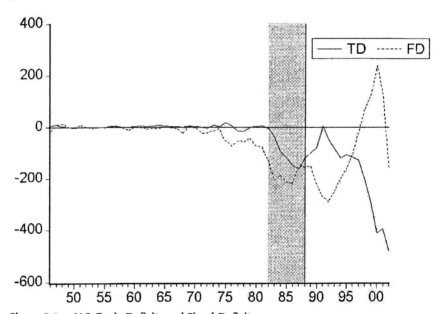

Figure 3.1.   U.S. Trade Deficits and Fiscal Deficits.
TD: Balance on Current account, seasonally adjusted
FD: Fiscal deficits (federal), fiscal years (October 1–September 20) 1946–2002; billions of dollars

For the statistical data, see Council of Economic Advisers, *Economic Report of the President* (Washington, D.C.: U.S. GPO, 2004) 379 and 402. Source: Constructed by the author.

The overall purpose of this act is described in its powerful preamble:

"To enhance the competitiveness of American industry and other purposes."

In essence, the OTCA attempts to establish more open, fair and equitable access for U.S. exporters to foreign markets in order to reduce or eliminate trade barriers and other trade-distorting practices. It also aims to set up a more effective system of international trading discipline and procedures. The OTCA mandates U.S. responses to foreign unfair trade practices, improves the enforcement of antidumping and countervailing duty laws, amends the escape clause to alleviate the damage due to imports by means of a new program of trade competitiveness assistance, and defends and expands intellectual property rights in international trade.

The OTCA required the President to negotiate multilateral (Uruguay Round), regional (NAFTA), and bilateral trade negotiations; to respond to Congressional requests for consultation and advice on trade issues; and to formulate an annual trade policy agenda. The Uruguay Round was completed soon thereafter in 1994; the NAFTA was formed in 1992; and countless bilateral agreements have been made since the mandate was issued. Chapter 5 details the Uruguay Round, the NAFTA, and subsequent movements for other regional agreements, and bilateral agreements.

In summary, the OTCA:

- requires the President to retaliate against foreign trade abuses but allows him to choose the form of retaliation, either tariffs or quotas;
- expands the definition of unfair trade practices that can trigger retaliation;
- transfers the authority to decide whether a foreign trade practice is unfair from the President to the U.S. Trade Representative (USTR);
- requires the U.S. Trade Representative to take retaliatory action if foreign countries deny U.S. intellectual property rights;
- limits access to American telecommunications products and services, streamlines export licensing rules, reduces controls on low-technology equipment, and enhances enforcement of U.S. and multilateral export controls of high-technology items;
- enhances government programs to remedy industrial injuries inflicted by import competition and expands the trade adjustment assistance program for workers who lose their jobs;
- protects American companies against takeovers by foreign firms if national security is threatened;
- expands U.S. export promotion activities, providing greater opportunities for small business; and
- expands U.S. subsidies in order to reduce agricultural export prices.

3.2 LEGISLATION

The Committee on Ways and Means (headed by Rep. Daniel D. Rostenkowski, Democrat, Illinois) introduced the original bill for the OTCA, H.R. 3, in 1986. The House of Representatives passed the bill on April 30, 1987, and the Senate passed it on July 21, 1987. However, then President Reagan vetoed the bill on May 24, 1988. He opposed the provision that required employers to notify workers of plant shutdowns and layoffs resulting from injuries from imports and the limiting of exports of petroleum from Alaska. The House overrode the President's veto the same day, but the Senate sustained the President's veto on June 8, 1988.[2] After much negotiation, the House passed the final version of the bill (H.R. 4848) on July 13, 1988, the Senate passed it on August 3, 1988, and the President signed the bill into law (P.L. 100–418) on August 23, 1988.[3] Appendices 3.1 and 3.2 to this chapter show the results of House and Senate roll calls on the Omnibus Trade Bill (H.R. 4848). The House passed the bill by 376 yeas to 45 nays, with a breakdown of 243–4 for Democratic votes and 133–41 for Republican votes. The Senate passed the bill by 85 yeas to 11 nays, with 50–1 by Democrats and 35–10 by Republicans.

Marks (1993) conducted an econometric analysis of the votes on five main amendments to the omnibus trade bills of the House of Representatives and Senate in 1987. Using the probit estimation technique, he confirmed the relationship between economic interests and congressional voting on the trade bill of 1987.[4]

3.3 STATUTORY COMPOSITION AND TRADE REMEDY LAWS

The OTCA consists of ten titles that act as direct countermeasures to foreign competition believed to be in violation of trade agreements with the United States or unfairly based trade agreements against the United States. These range from provisions on trade, customs, and tariff laws to provisions on ocean and air transportation. For a full list, see table 3.1. Most of the main provisions that are central to today's U.S. trade policy are in Title I. Some of the other titles may become increasingly important in future U.S. trade policy.

Table 3.2 presents Subtitles C and D of Title I that list trade remedy provisions. Subtitle C is concerned with the U.S. response to foreign unfair trade practices, while Subtitle D covers adjustment to import competition. The main provisions in Subtitle C are Section 1301 (often referred to as Section 301), Section 1302 (Super 301), Section 1303 (Special 301), Section 1312 (Section 701), and Section 1316 (Section 731). The main provision in Subtitle D is section 1401 (Section 201).

Table 3.1. Statutory Composition of the Omnibus Trade and Competitiveness Act of 1988

Title I	*Trade, Customs, and Tariff Laws*
Title II	Export Enhancement
Title III	International Financial Policy
Title IV	Agricultural Policy
Title V	Foreign Corrupt Practices Amendments; Investment; and Technology
Title VI	Education and Training for American Competitiveness
Title VII	Buy American Act of 1988
Title VIII	Small Business
Title IX	Patents
Title X	Ocean and Airtransportation

Source: U.S. House of Representatives, Committee on Ways and Means, *Trade Legislation Enacted into Public Law,1981 through 1988* (Washington, D.C.: U.S. GPO, 1989).

Section 301, along with Super 301 and Special 301, constitute "unilateralism" in U.S. trade policy in response to foreign unfair trade practices.

- Section 301 is Chapter 1 of Title III of the Trade Act of 1974, as amended by Section 1301 of the OTCA of 1988. It provides the authority and procedures for the President to enforce U.S. rights under international trade agreements and to mandate retaliation to certain unfair foreign practices. The authority to make a determination of either fair or unfair practices was transferred to the USTR.
- Super 301 is Section 310 of the Trade Act of 1974, as added by Section 1302 of the OTCA. This provision is the version enacted by a revision of Section 301 worked out by Senators Donald W. Riegle, Jr. and John C. Danforth after the substitution of the Senate's revision of Section 301 for the Gephardt amendment.[5, 6] It requires the USTR to identify trade liberalization priorities within the statutory period.
- Special 301 is Section 182 of the Trade Act of 1974, as added by Section 1303 of the Omnibus Trade and Competitiveness Act of 1988. It requires

Table 3.2. Trade Remedy Laws in the Omnibus Trade and Competitiveness Act of 1988

Title I–Trade, Customs, and Tariff Laws
    Subtitle C–Response to Unfair International Trade Practices
        Part 1–Enforcement of United States Rights under Trade Agreements and Responses to Foreign Trade Practices
        Part 2–Improvement in the Enforcement of the Antidumping and Countervailing Duty Laws
    Subtitle D–Adjustment to Import Competition
        Part 1–Positive Adjustment by Industries Injured by Imports

Source: U.S. House of Representatives, Committee on Ways and Means, *Trade Legislation Enacted into Public Law, 1981 through 1988* (Washington, D.C.: U.S. GPO, 1989).

the USTR to identify countries that deny adequate and effective protection of American intellectual property rights.

Sections 701 and 731 are two provisions of the Tariff Act of 1930, as amended by Sections 1312 and 1316 of the OTCA respectively.

- Section 701 provides the provision for a countervailing duty (equal to the amount of net subsidy) to be imposed under certain conditions, in addition to any other applicable duties.
- Section 731 provides the provision for antidumping duty to impose under certain conditions.
- Section 201 is Chapter 1 of Title II of the Trade Act of 1974, as amended by Section 1401 of the OTCA of 1988. It is the provision that sets forth the authority and procedures for the President to take action, including providing import relief, to aid a domestic industry seriously injured by import competition. Note that this provision concerns relief from "fair" trade, whereas all the other provisions above deal with relief from "unfair" trade practices by foreign countries.

These six provisions are referred to as the trade remedy provisions. U.S. trade policy based on these provisions is referred to as *managed* or *administered* trade policy. They will be discussed extensively in chapter 4.

There are several other important provisions in the OTCA, including agricultural imports sold below U.S. prices, and provisions on trademark and patent infringement. During the 1990s, the Clinton administration worked toward passage of a Fair Trade in Financial Services Act, which seeks to open overseas markets for U.S. banks and financial firms and to block the expansion in the United States of those foreign institutions whose own governments restrict American operations. This act has been stalled in Congress for years, in part because of opposition from the Federal Reserve Board.

The OTCA is widely viewed as a protectionist act because of its unilaterally aggressive Section 301 and Super 301, where the threat of import barriers by the United States exists if an identified nation does not comply with U.S. trade laws. For details of the frequently invoked provisions discussed above and their effectiveness, the reader should consult chapters 4 and 9.

3.4 SUMMARY AND CONCLUSIONS

The Omnibus Trade and Competitiveness Act of 1988 defines today's U.S. trade law. The impetus for this legislation was the continued growth of the U.S. trade deficit after 1982. Given the large trade deficit and its macroeconomic link with the fiscal deficit, there arose a strong push for protectionism in the United States during the Reagan era. Both the House and Senate, irritated by mounting trade deficit, passed the Omnibus Trade Bill (H.R. 4848) by absolute majorities in 1988.

The OTCA is a comprehensive law. It includes ten titles; each title is broken down into subtitles, parts, and sections. Title 1 includes trade remedy provisions. It focuses on opening foreign markets to U.S. trade and providing relief from both fair and unfair trade practices. The main elements of the trade remedy law are Section 301, Super 301, Special 301, Section 701, Section 731, and Section 201. These provisions represent the core of current U.S. trade policy and will be extensively discussed in the subsequent chapter.

The OTCA is widely viewed as a protectionist law because of the provisions regarded as unilateral. This chapter highlights legislative background and statutory composition of the OTCA.

APPENDIX 3.1:
HOUSE VOTES ON H.R. 4848: OMNIBUS TRADE BILL

State	Representative's Vote
Alabama	Callahan(Y) Dickinson(Y) Nichols(Y) Bevill(Y) Flippo(Y) Erdreich(Y) Harris(Y)
Alaska	Al Young(Y)
Arizona	Rhodes(Y) Udall(Y) Stump(N) Kyl(N) Kolbe(N)
Arkansas	Alexander(Y) Robinson(Y) Hammerschmidt(Y) Anthony(Y)
California	Bosco(Y) Herger(Y) Matsui(Y) Fozio(Y) Pelosi(Y) Boxer(Y) Miller(Y) Dellums(Y) Stark(Y) Edwards(Y) Lontos(Y) Konnyu(Y) Mineta(Y) Shumway(Y) Coelho(Y) Pannetta(Y) Pashayan(Y) Lehman(Y) Lagomarsino(Y) Thomas(Y) Gallegly(Y) Moorhead(Y) Beilenson(Y) Waxman(Y) Roybal(Y) Berman(Y) Levine(Y) Dixon(Y) Hawkins(Y) Martinez(Y) Dymally(Y) Anderson(?) Dreier(N) Torres(Y) Lewis(N) Brown(Y) McCandless(N) Dornan(N) Dannemeyer(N) Badham(N) Lowery(Y) Lungren(N) Packard(N) Bates(Y) Hunter(N)
Colorado	Schroeder(Y) Skaggs(Y) Campbell(Y) Brown(Y) Hefley(Y) Schaefer(Y)

State	Representative's Vote
Connecticut	Kennelly(Y) Gejdensop(Y) Morrison(Y) Shays(Y) Rowland(Y) Johnson(Y)
Delaware	Carper(Y)
Florida	Hutto(Y) Grant(Y) Bennet(Y) Choppell(Y) Mccollum(N) MacKay(NV) Gibbons(Y) Young(Y) Biliakis(Y) Ireland(Y) Nelson(Y) Lewis(Y) Mack(Y) Mica(NV) Shaw (Y) Smith(Y) Lehman(Y) Pepper(Y) Fascell(Y)
Georgia	Thomas(Y) Hatcher(Y) Swindall(Y) Lewis(Y) Gingrich(Y) Darden(Y) Bowland(Y) Jenkins(Y) Barnard(Y)
Hawaii	Saiki(Y) Akaka(Y)
Idaho	Craig(Y) Stallings(Y)
Illinois	Hayes(Y) Savage(Y) Russo(Y) Davis(Y) Lipinski(Y) Hyde(Y) Collins(Y) Rostenkowski(Y) Yates(Y) Porter(Y) Annunzio(Y) Crane(N) Fawell(N) Hastert(Y) Madigan(N) Martin(N) Evans(Y) Michel(N) Bruce(Y) Durbin(Y) Vacancy Gray(Y)
Indiana	Visclosky(Y) Sharp(Y) Hiler(Y) Coats(Y) Jontz(Y) Burton(N) Myers(Y) McClosky(Y) Hamilton(Y) Jacobs(Y)
Iowa	Leoch(Y) Tauke(Y) Nagle(Y) Smith(Y) Lightfoot(Y) Grandy(Y)
Kansas	Roberts(Y) Slattery(Y) Meyers(Y) Glickman(Y) Whittaker(Y)
Kentucky	Hubbard(Y) Natcher(Y) Mazzoli(Y) Bunnings(Y) Rogers(Y) Hopkins(Y) Perkins(Y)
Louisiana	Livingston(NV) Boggs(NV) Tauzin(Y) McCrery(Y) Huckaby(Y) Baker(Y) Hayes(Y) Hollowway(Y)
Maine	Brennan(Y) Snowe(Y)
Maryland	Dyson(Y) Bentley(Y) Cardin(Y) McMillen(Y) Hoyer(Y) Byron(Y) Mfume(Y) Morella(Y)
Massachusetts	Conte(Y) Boland(Y) Early(Y) Frank(Y) Atkins(Y) Marvroules(Y) Markey(Y) Kennedy(Y) Moakley(Y) Studds(Y) Donnelly(Y)
Michigan	Conyers(Y) Pursell(Y) Wolpe(Y) Upton(Y) Henry(Y) Carr(Y) Kildee(Y) Traxler(Y) Vander Jagt(Y) Schuette(Y) Davis(Y) Bonior(Y)

State	Representative's Vote
	Crockett(Y) Hertel(Y) Ford(Y) Dingell(Y) Levin(Y) Broomfield(Y)
Minnesota	Penny(Y) Weber(N) Frenzel(Y) Vento(Y) Sabo(Y) Sikorski(Y) Stangeland(Y) Oberstar(N)
Mississipi	Whitten(Y) Espy(?) Montgomery(Y) Dowdy(Y) Lott(Y)
Missouri	Clay(Y) Buschner(N) Gephardt(N) Skelton(Y) Wheat(Y) Coleman(Y) Taylor(Y) Emerson(Y) Volkmer(Y)
Montana	Willams(Y) Marlenee(N)
Nebraska	Bereuter(Y) Doub(N) Smith(Y)
Nevada	Bilbray(Y) Vocanovich(N)
New Hampshire	Smith(N) Gregg(Y)
New Jersey	Florio(Y) Hughes(Y) Vacancy Smith(Y) Roukema(Y) Dwyer(Y) Rinaldo(Y) Roe(Y) Torricelli(Y) Rodino(Y) Gallo(Y) Couter(N) Saxton(Y) Guarini(Y)
New Mexico	Lujan(Y) Skeen(Y) Richardson(Y)
New York	Hochbruekner(Y) Downey(Y) Mrazek(N) Lent(Y) McGrath(Y) Flake(Y) Ackerman(Y) Scheuer(Y) Manton(Y) Schumer(Y) Towns(Y) Owens(Y) Solarz(Y) Molinari(Y) Green(N) Rangel(Y) Weiss(Y) Garcia(Y) Bioggi(?) DioGuardi(Y) Fish(Y) Gilman(Y) Stratton(?) Solomon(Y) Boehlert(Y) Martin(Y) Wortley(N) McHugh(Y) Horton(Y) Slaughter(Y) Kemp(N) LaFake(Y) Nowak(Y) Houghton(Y) Morrison(Y)
North Carolina	Jones(Y) Valentine(Y) Lancaster(Y) Price(Y) Coble(Y) Rose(Y) Hefner(Y) McMillan(Y) Ballenger(Y)
North Dakota	Dorgan(Y)
Ohio	Luken(Y) Gradison(N) Hall(Y) Oxley(Y) Latta(Y) McEwen(Y) DeWine(N) Lukens(Y) Kaptur(Y) Miller(Y) Eckart(Y) Kasich(Y) Pease(Y) Sawyer(Y) Wylie(Y) Regula(Y) Traficant(Y) Applegate(Y) Feighan(Y) Oakar(Y) Stokes(Y)
Oklahoma	Inhofe(Y) Synar(Y) Watkins(Y) McCurdy(Y) Edwards(Y) English(Y)

State	Representative's Vote
Oregon	Aucoin(Y) Smith, R.(N) Wyden(Y) Defazio(Y) Smith, D.(N)
Pennsylvania	Foglietta(Y) Gray(Y) Borski(Y) Kolter(Y) Schulze(Y) Yatron(Y) Weldon(Y) Kostmayer(Y) Shuster(Y) MaDade(Y) Konjorski(Y) Murtha(Y) Coughlin(Y) Coyne(Y) Ritter(Y) Walker(N) Gekas(Y) Walgren(Y) Goodling(Y) Gaydos(Y) Ridge(Y) Murphy(Y) Clinger(Y)
Rhode Island	St. Germain(Y) Schneider(Y)
South Carolina	Ravenel(Y) Spence(?) Derrick(Y) Patterson(Y) Spratt(Y) Tallon(Y)
South Dakota	Johnson(Y)
Tennessee	Quillen(Y) Vacancy Lloyd(Y) Cooper(Y) Clement(Y) Gordon(Y) Sudquist(Y) Jones(Y) Ford(Y)
Texas	Chapman(Y) Wilson(Y) Bartlett(Y) Hall(Y) Bryant(Y) Barton(Y) Archer(Y) Fields(Y) Brooks(Y) Pickle(Y) Leath(Y) Wright(Y) Boulter(Y) Sweeney(Y) de la Garza(Y) Coleman(Y) Stenholm(Y) Leland(Y) Combest(Y) Gonzalez(Y) Smith(Y) DeLay(N) Bustamante(Y) Frost(Y) Andrews(Y) Armey(Y) Ortiz(Y)
Utah	Hansen(Y) Owens(Y) Nielson(Y)
Vermont	Jeffords(Y)
Virginia	Bateman(N) Pickett(Y) Bliley(Y) Sisisky(Y) Payne(Y) Olin(Y) Slaughter(Y) Parris(Y) Baucher(Y) Wolf(Y)
Washington	Miller(Y) Swift(Y) Bonker(Y) Morrison(Y) Foley(Y) Dicks(Y) Lowry(Y) Chandler(Y)
West Virginia	Mollohan(Y) Staggers(Y) Wise(Y) Rahall(Y)
Wisconsin	Aspin(Y) Kastenmeier(Y) Gunderson(Y) Kleczka(Y) Moody(Y) Petri(N) Obey(N) Roth(Y) Sensenbrenner(Y)
Wyoming	Cheney(?)

Note: Y = Yeas, N = Nays, and ? = Not voting.

Source: U.S. House of Representatives, *Congressional Quarterly Almanac*, and *CQ Weekly* (Washington, D.C.: U.S. GPO, 1988).

APPENDIX 3.2:
SENATE VOTES ON H.R. 4848: OMNIBUS TRADE BILL

State	Senator's Vote
Alabama	Heflin(Y) Shelby(Y)
Alaska	Murkowski(Y) Stevens(N)
Arizona	DeConcini(Y) McCain(N)
Arkansas	Bumpers(?) Pryor(Y)
California	Cranston(Y) Wilson(Y)
Colorado	Wirth(Y) Armstrong(Y)
Connecticut	Dodd(Y) Weiker(Y)
Delaware	Biden(?) Roth(Y)
Florida	Chiles(Y) Graham(Y)
Georgia	Fowler(Y) Nunn(Y)
Hawaii	Inouye(Y) Matsunaga(Y)
Idaho	McClure(N) Symms(N)
Illinois	Dixon(Y) Simon(Y)
Indiana	Lugar(Y) Quayle(Y)
Iowa	Harkin(Y) Grassley(Y)
Kansas	Dole(Y) Kassebaum(Y)
Kentucky	Ford(Y) McConnell(Y)
Louisiana	Breaux(Y) Johnston(Y)
Maine	Mitchell(Y) Cohen(Y)
Maryland	Mikulski(Y) Sarbanes(Y)
Massachusetts	Kennedy(Y) Kerry(Y)
Michigan	Levin(Y) Riegle(Y)
Minnesota	Boschwitz(N) Durenburger(Y)
Mississippi	Stennis(?) Cochran(Y)
Missouri	Bond(Y) Danforth(Y)
Montana	Baucus(Y) Melcher(Y)
Nebraska	Exon(Y) Karnes(Y)
Nevada	Reid(Y) Hecht(Y)
New Hampshire	Humphrey(N) Rudman(Y)
New Jersey	Bradley(Y) Lautenberg(Y)
New Mexico	Bingaman(Y) Domenici(Y)
New York	Moynihan(Y) D'Amato(Y)
North Carolina	Sanford(Y) Helms(N)
North Dakota	Burdick(Y) Conrad(Y)
Ohio	Glenn(Y) Metzenbaum(Y)
Oklahoma	Boren(Y) Nickles(Y)
Oregon	Hatfield(N) Packwood(Y)

State	Senator's Vote
Pennsylvania	Heinz(Y) Specter(Y)
Rhode Island	Pell(Y) Chafee(Y)
South Carolina	Hollings(Y) Thurmond(Y)
South Dakota	Daschle(Y) Pressler(Y)
Tennessee	Gore(Y) Sasser(Y)
Texas	Bentsen(Y) Gramm(Y)
Utah	Garn(Y) Hatch(Y)
Vermont	Leahy(Y) Stafford(Y)
Virginia	Trible(Y) Warner(Y)
Washington	Adams(Y) Evans(N)
West Virginia	Byrd(Y) Rockfeller(Y)
Wisconsin	Proxmire(N) Kasten(Y)
Wyoming	Simpson(Y) Wallop(Y)

Note: Y = Yeas and N = Nays.

Source: U.S. House of Representatives, *Congressional Quarterly Almanac*, and *CQ Weekly* (Washington, D.C.: U.S. GPO, 1988).

NOTES

1. See U.S. House of Representatives, Committee on Ways and Means, *Trade Legislation Enacted into Public Law*, 1981 through 1988 (Washington, D.C.: U.S. GPO, January 27, 1989), 221–688. Reciprocal Trade Agreement Authorities Act of 1997 (H.R. 2621) and Bipartisan Trade Promotion Authority Act of 2001 (H.R. 3005) are the two acts that emerged on the floor for enactment after the OTCA of 1988. The former failed to pass the House and the latter passed the House on December 6, 2001 with votes 215–214.

2. The House passed the bill over President Reagan's veto, by 308–113, with 248–1 of Democratic votes and 60–112 of Republican votes. The Senate, however, rejected the bill (supporting the President) by 61–37, with 51–2 of Democratic votes and 10–35 of Republican votes.

3. For the chronology of votes in legislation authorizing fast track negotiating authority of the OCTA, see Carolyn C. Smith, "Fast-Track Negotiating Authority for Trade Agreements and Trade Promotion Authority: Chronology of Major Votes," *CRS Report for Congress* received through the CRS Web (December 2001).

4. See Note 5 of Chapter 9 for the probit technique.

5. Democratic Representative Richard Gephardt, then the majority leader and a member of the House Ways and Means Committee, attached an amendment to the Senate bill. While the Senate approach focused on foreign unfair trade barriers, Gephardt's approach linked "excessive and unwarranted" trade surpluses to unfair

trade practices conducted with the United States and required countries with the bilateral imbalance to reduce a specified amount of surplus or face trade sanctions. His bill required the imposition of a 25 percent tariff on countries that had a worldwide trade export surplus of 150 percent or a bilateral surplus of 165 percent. He took his fight to the floor of the House where his bill passed by a narrow margin of 218 to 214.

6. There are mixed reactions to Super 301. It "conjured up the spectacle of the world's supreme superpower subjecting its trading partners to public humiliation. . . . These fears later proved to be exaggerated." See Pietro Nivola, *Regulating Unfair Trade* (Washington, D.C.: The Brookings Institution, 1993), 104.

Chapter 4

Principal Trade Policy Instruments

American trade remedy laws provide a broad range of legal bases for the implementation of trade policy and enforcement activities. There are six principal trade remedy provisions:

- Enforcement of U.S. rights and responses to foreign unfair trade practices,
- Identification of trade liberalization priorities,
- Identification of intellectual property rights priorities,
- Export subsidies and the countervailing duty,
- Dumping and the antidumping duty,
- Import relief by safeguard actions.

The first five are concerned with unfair trade practices by foreign countries, whereas the last deals with relief from injury caused by fair import competition. Most trade disputes between the United States and the rest of the world have arisen and still arise in connection with U.S. trade remedy laws. Many other laws are involved as well, including telecommunications, government procurement, unfair import practices, and trade adjustment assistance.

The trade remedy laws represent the core of current U.S. trade policy. This chapter focuses on the main U.S. trade remedy provisions included in the Omnibus Trade and Competitiveness Act of 1988 (OTCA), which is the primary U.S. trade law of the present day.

Table 4.1 summarizes the six principal trade remedy laws. The USTR is responsible for Section 301 (unfair trade practices and enforcement of U.S. rights), Super 301 (identification of trade liberalization priorities), and Special 301 (identification of countries that deny adequate and effective protection of intellectual property rights). Both the ITA and ITC are responsible for

Table 4.1. Principal U.S. Trade Remedy Provisions

Section	Focus	Criteria for Action	Remedy	Administrative Authority
Section 301	Foreign trade practices violating trade agreement or injurious to U.S. trade	Unjustifiable, unreasonable, or discriminatory practices, burdensome to U.S. commerce	All appropriate and feasible actions	USTR, subject to Presidential direction
Super 301	Foreign trade barriers and distorting practices	Unfairly high and excessive protection	Identification of priority country	USTR, subject to Presidential direction
Special 301	Inadequate protection of intellectual property rights and inequitable market access to the United States	Excessive protection and denial of adequate and and effective protection of intellectual property rights	Identification of intellectual property rights priority	USTR, subject to Presidential direction
Section 701	Foreign subsidy	Material injury or threat	Countervailing duty	ITC and ITA
Section 731	Foreign dumping	Material injury or threat	Antidumping duty	ITC and ITA
Section 201	Increasing imports	Serious injury or threat	Any appropriate and feasible actions, such as duties, quotas, adjustment assistance, and OMA	ITC and USTR, subject to presidential direction

Source: Modified by the author the version available in the Council of Economic Advisers, *Economic Report of the President,* 1988 (Washington, D.C.: U.S. GPO), 152. Also, see Coughlin (1991), 5.

Section 701 (countervailing duty) and Section 731 (antidumping duty). The USTR and ITC are responsible for Section 201 (escape clause), providing relief for industrial injuries caused by fair import competition covered by trade agreements.

The first six sections of this chapter examine each of the trade remedy provisions listed above along with the statutory processes for dealing with trade disputes between domestic and foreign firms/interest groups. Section 7 explores the origins of the trade remedy provisions. Section 8 discusses briefly other provisions/areas that become increasingly important. The last section summarizes and draws conclusions.

4.1 ENFORCEMENT OF U.S. RIGHTS AND RESPONSES TO FOREIGN UNFAIR TRADE PRACTICES

Section 301 (of the Trade Act of 1974, as amended; Section 1301 of the OTCA), is the provision that deals with foreign unfair practices affecting U.S. exports of goods and services. It enforces U.S. rights under international trade agreements and to respond to unreasonable, unjustifiable, or discriminatory foreign government practices that burden or restrict American commerce. This provision also outlines the procedures for negotiating with foreign countries to eliminate their trade barriers. The following excerpt is the statement for mandatory or discretionary action taken by the USTR against various types of unfair trade practices:

Mandatory Action
    If the USTR determines that the rights of the United States under any trade agreement are being denied; or an act, policy, or practice of a foreign country violates, is inconsistent with any trade agreement, is unjustifiable and burdens, or restricts United States commerce, it is mandatory for the USTR, within the power of the President, to enforce the trade agreement act or to obtain the elimination of foreign act, policy, or practice.

Discretionary Action
    If the USTR determines that an act, policy, or practice of a foreign country is unreasonable or discriminatory and burdens or restricts United States commerce, the USTR has discretionary authority, within the power of the President, to take all appropriate actions to obtain the elimination of foreign act, policy, or practice.
    Source: U.S. House of Representatives, Committee on Ways and Means, *Overview and Compilation of U.S. Trade Statutes* (Washington, D.C.: U.S. GPO, 1995), 503–508.

The principal amendments were made in 1988 to strengthen Section 301 of the 1974 Trade Act by:

- Transferring the authority from the President to the USTR, who now decides whether a foreign trade practice is unfair (subject to the specific direction, if any, of the President),
- Making Section 301 mandatory in the event of an obvious trade agreement violation or unjustifiable practice,
- Tightening time limits imposed on all investigations and actions.

Other sections, related to Section 301, deal with the initiation of investigations; consultation upon the initiation of an investigation; Trade Representative determination; the implementation of action; monitoring foreign compliance; and the modification and termination of action.

Any interested party may file a petition with the USTR or the USTR may itself initiate an investigation. As shown in figures 4.1 and 4.2, the USTR reviews the allegations and determines the need for investigation in accordance with the statutory schedule. The USTR can decide to investigate a case within forty-five days from the receipt of the petition and provides the opportunity for a public hearing within thirty days. The foreign country in question undergoes consultation for ninety days.[1] The USTR makes either an affirmative or negative deter-

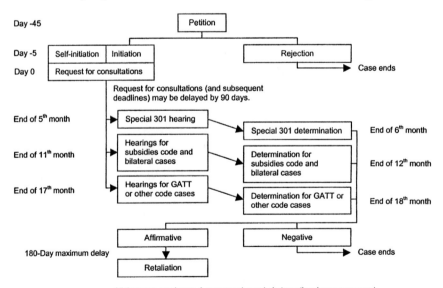

All times are maximum. A case may be ended at any time by an agreement.

Figure 4.1.   Statutory Investigation Procedure and Timetable for Section 301
Source: Office of the USTR; U.S. House of Representatives, Committee on Ways and Means, *Trade Legislation Enacted Into Public Law, 1981 Through 1988* (Washington, D.C.: U.S. GPO, 1989), 289–90 for a more complete description.

mination within eighteen months after the investigation begins in cases involving formal WTO dispute settlement procedures, six months in cases of Special 301, and twelve months otherwise. The maximum period for delaying retaliation is 180 days, subject to specific direction, if any, by the President.

4.2 IDENTIFICATION OF
TRADE LIBERALIZATION PRIORITIES

Super 301 (Section 310 of 1974 Trade Act, as added by Section 1302 of the 1988 Trade Act) requires the USTR to determine those nations that maintain the most pervasive system of trade barriers and designate them as "priority foreign countries." The USTR also lists the most significant trade barriers and designates them as "priority practices." The USTR then initiates Section 301 investigations into the trade barriers. The Constitution and Sections 141 and 301–310 of the Trade Act of 1974 vested this authority in the President. Super 301 has often been called as a "hit list" of the worst trade offenders, providing the President and the USTR with the legal basis to retaliate unilaterally against any nation conducting trade considered unfair to the United States. An excerpt from the provision is as follows:

> Super 301 requires the USTR to identify U.S. trade liberalization, including 1) priority practices and countries of major trade barriers and distorting practices, and 2) level of U.S. exports of goods and services, and potential U.S. exports to each priority country in the absence of need to be identified.
> *Source:* U.S. House of Representatives, Committee on Ways and Means, *Overview and Compilation of U.S. Trade Statutes* (Washington, D.C.: U.S. GPO, 1995), 516–17.

The USTR must submit the lists of priority countries, priority practices, and the trade amounts to the House Ways and Means Committee and the Senate Finance Committee, and they must publish the lists in the *Federal Register* no later than thirty days after Super 301 is issued. After submission of the report, the USTR must initiate investigations pursuant to Section 301 within twenty-one days.

In identifying priority foreign country practices, the USTR takes into account all relevant factors, including:

- The major trade barriers and distorting practices described in the *National Trade Estimates Reports,*
- Compliance with trade agreements by the country in question,
- The medium-term and long-term implications of foreign government procurement plans,

- The international competitive position and export potential of U.S. products and services.[2]

The procedures for Super 301, including initiation of investigations and consultations, determination of the USTR, implementation of actions, and monitoring of foreign compliance, etc., are stated in Section 1301 of OTCA (Sections 302–309) in detail.[3]

The following is an approximate summary of the procedures:

1. The USTR must identify foreign trade barriers to include them in the *National Trade Estimate Report*. This must include an inventory of trade practices that affect output of goods and services and investment.
2. The USTR must identify priority countries and practices and submit the list to the House Ways and Means Committee, the Senate Finance Committee, and the Federal Register. In identifying foreign trade practices, the USTR takes into account comments and advice received from firms, Congress, and private sector advisors on the potential to increase U.S. exports, the likelihood that investigations would have eliminated these practices, and compatibility with the U.S. objectives in the Uruguay Round agreement.[4]
3. The USTR must begin an investigation. An investigation takes twelve months in the event of barrier and eighteen months in the event of breach of agreement.
4. The USTR begins to negotiate with priority countries to eliminate priority practices or to provide compensation within three years.
5. The USTR must estimate the total amount of increase in U.S. exports and publish this in the annual report.
6. After making determination, the USTR takes section 301 action, subject to the direction, if any, of the President within thirty days.

Figure 4.2 (also see figure 4.1) shows the statutory period required for implementation and procedures for Super 301 and Section 301.

4.3 IDENTIFICATION OF INTELLECTUAL PROPERTY RIGHTS PRIORITIES

Special 301 (Section 182 of the Trade Act of 1974, as by Section 1303 of the OTCA) mandates that the USTR identifies priority foreign countries that deny adequate and effective protection of U.S. intellectual property rights (copyrights, patents, and trademarks, etc.) or deny fair and equitable market access. The priority countries are potentially subject to an investigation under

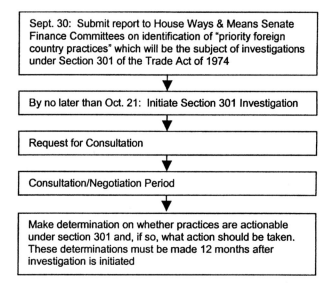

Figure 4.2. Procedures for Section 301 amd Super 301
Source: Office of the USTR; U.S. House of Representatives, Committee on Ways and Means, *Trade Legislation Enacted Into Public Law, 1981 Through 1988* (Washington, D.C.: U.S. GPO, 1989), 289–90 for a more complete description.

Section 301. Congress believes that denial of adequate and effective protection of intellectual property rights by foreign countries is not only harmful to U.S. economic interests in foreign markets but also undermines the creativity and investment that are the main engines of economic growth. The provision is summarized as follows:

> Special 301 requires the USTR to identify foreign countries that deny adequate and effective protection of intellectual property rights and deny fair and equitable market access to the United States.
> *Source:* U.S. House of Representatives, Committee on Ways and Means, *Trade Legislation Enacted into Public Law, 1981 through 1988* (Washington, D.C.: U.S. GPO, 1989), 293–95.

No later than thirty days after the date on which the annual report listing priority countries is submitted to the Committee on Ways and Means and to the Committee on Finance, the USTR must identify those foreign countries. See figure 4.1 for the statutory period for implementation.

4.4 COUNTERVAILING DUTIES

Subsidies are direct and indirect government grants for the production or exportation of goods. The countervailing duty (hereafter referred to as CVD) is a duty imposed on a countervailable subsidy for offsetting certain foreign government subsidies benefiting imports into the United States, if it causes material injury to a U.S. industry.[5] The rationale for the CVD is that a countervailing duty case involves "less-than-fair value" (LTFV) conduct because it deals with the selling of goods at less than their "fair value" in foreign markets. The United States prohibits subsidies as a kind of nontariff barrier.

Table 4.2 shows the history of the countervailing duty. This law dates back to legislation authorizing the imposition of CVDs on subsidized sugar imports in 1897. It remained substantially the same until 1979 when the United States revised the CVD law to make it consistent with the trade agreement reached in the Tokyo Round. One addition was an injury test requirement in all CVD cases involving imports from countries that are signatories to the GATT/Uruguay Round agreement and are thus subject to the Subsidy Code.[6]

Section 701 (Subtitle A of Title VII of the Tariff Act of 1930, as amended by section 1312 of the OTCA) is the main provision for a CVD. Other provisions related to this provision are the procedures for initiating a countervailing duty investigation, preliminary determinations, termination or suspension of investigation, final determinations, and assessment of duty. The chief elements of section 701 are stated in the excerpt below:

> Section 701 requires the authority to impose, in addition to any other duty, equal to the amount of net subsidy if (1) the ITA determines that a subsidy is being provided, directly or indirectly, with respect to the manufacture, production, or

Table 4.2.   History of Section 701: Countervailing Duty

1897	The first U.S. statute of a CVD Act was legislated.
1922	Congress amended the provision.
1930	The Smoot-Hawley Tariff Act included a provision for CVD.
1974	The Trade Act of 1974 extended the application of the CVD law to duty-free imports and many procedural matters.
1979	Congress approved the GATT Subsidies Code.[1]
1984	The Trade and Tariff Act of 1984 modified the CVD law for application to upstream subsidies.[2]
1988	The Omnibus Trade and Competitiveness Act of 1988 clarified the USTR to revoke the injury test for countries who dishonored their obligations in connection with export subsidies.

1. An injury test is required for all CVD cases involving imports from countries who are signatories to the GATT agreement. Section 101 of the Trade Agreement Act of 1979 added a new title VII to the Tariff Act of 1930, containing the new provisions of the CVD law.
2. Subsidies bestowed on inputs that are incorporated into the manufacture of final products imported into the United States.

Source: Compiled by the author from information available in U.S. House of Representatives, Committee on Ways and Means, *Overview and Compilation of U.S. Trade Statutes* (Washington, D.C.: U.S. GPO, 1993, 1994, and 1995).

exportation of a class or kind of merchandise imported, or sold (or likely to be sold) for importation, into the United States, (2) the ITC determines that an industry in the United States is materially injured or is threatened with material injury.

Source: U.S. House of Representatives, Committee on Ways and Means, *Overview and Compilation of U.S. Trade Statutes* (Washington, D.C.: U.S. GPO, 1995), 361–63.

Once a petition against a foreign subsidy is filed by any U.S. complainant, the ITA determines the amount, if any, of the subsidy, and the ITC determines if an industry in the United States is materially injured or is threatened with material injury in accordance with statutory processes. The statutory process for the ITC is quasi-judicial, involving a domestic firm as the plaintiff, a foreign firm as the defendant, and the ITC as the judge. The formula used to calculate a net subsidy is as follows:

Net Subsidy = Gross Subsidy
–Application Fee, Deposit, or Similar Payment
–Loss in the Subsidy Value Resulting from Deferred Receipt
–Export Taxes, Duties, or Other Charges on Exports to the United States specifically intended to offset the subsidy.

Figure 4.3 is the timetable for CVD investigations. It is self-explanatory.

Any affected or interested party files a petition with the ITA or ITC. The ITA and the ITC may also self-initiate an investigation. If a petition is filed with the ITA, the ITA should make either an affirmative or a negative preliminary determination within twenty days as to whether an investigation is warranted. If a petition is filed with the ITC, the ITC has forty-five days for an investigation. If the ITA or the ITC makes a negative determination, the case is terminated. In the event of ITC's preliminary affirmative determination, the ITA makes either an affirmative or a negative preliminary determination within forty days for a simple case or 105 days for a complicated case. At this stage, the ITA announces a preliminary estimate of the export subsidy, and importers are required to make a cash deposit or post a bond equal to the estimated subsidy. If the preliminary ITA decision is negative, no deposit is required. The ITA makes its final determination within seventy-five days for all cases, affirmative or negative and simple or complicated. If the final ITA decision is affirmative, the ITA must determine the final subsidy margin. If it is negative, the case is terminated at this stage. In the event of an affirmative final determination by the ITA, an ITC hearing takes place. If the ITC finds no material injury, the case is dismissed; otherwise, the ITC's final determination leads to an ITA order of a CVD against the imported merchandise.

The total numbers of days required to complete the statutory process (if the ITC's and ITA's preliminary and final determinations are affirmative throughout

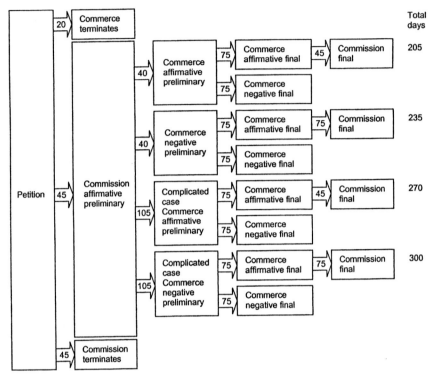

Figure 4.3.   Statutory Timetable for Section 701
Source: USITC, *Annual Report* (Washington, DC: U.S. GPO, 1991), 35.

the four stages) are 205 for simple cases and 270 for complicated cases. If the ITC's and ITA's determinations are inconsistent with each other at stages III and IV, however, the total number of days increases to 235 for a simple case and 300 for a complicated case. Once the ITC's determination on material injury is final, the ITA directs the U.S. Customs Service to assess CVDs equal to the amount of the net subsidy.

4.5 ANTIDUMPING DUTIES

The theory of price discrimination suggests that, if a monopolist can separate consumers into groups in terms of the price elasticity of demand, he can charge different prices for the same product in different markets to maximize his profit. Such price discrimination is referred to as dumping when merchandise is sold at a LTFV in a foreign market. Dumping is a non-tariff barrier because it restricts foreign prices to a floor. The United States regards dumping as an unfair trade practice and thus imposes antidumping duties (hereafter referred to as AD) up to the amount of the dumping margin if the dumping causes material injury to a domestic industry. Table 4.3 presents a history of the antidumping duty. The Antidumping Act of 1916 was the first AD act that provided for civil action in a Federal Court against dumping performed with the intention of destroying or injuring an American industry. It was followed by the Antidumping Act of 1921, which provided the statutory guidelines for investigation into alleged dumping practices and for the imposition of duties by the Department of the Treasury. The provisions of AD law were incorporated into Title VII of the 1930 Tariff Act and have been substantially amended by the 1979 Trade Act, the 1984 Trade Act, the 1988 Trade Act, and the 1994 UR Agreements Act. Also, under the Trade Agreements Act of 1979, Congress approved the revised GATT Antidumping Code.[7] This 1979 Act added a new Title VII to the Tariff Act of 1930.

Section 731 (Subtitle B of Title VII of the Tariff Act of 1930, as amended) is the provision for assessment of antidumping duties. Other related provisions are investigations, preliminary determinations, termination, or suspension

Table 4.3.   History of Section 731: Antidumping Duty

1916	Congress enacted the first Antidumping Act.
1921	The Antidumping Act of 1921 authorized the U.S. Treasury to investigate dumping practices and impose duties.
1930	The Smoot-Hawley Tariff Act (Title VII, Subtitle B, Sections 731–739) specified procedures for assessment and collection of ADs.
1954	The function of determining injury was tranferred from the Treasury Department to the U.S. Tariff Commission (now the ITC), while the Treasury Department kept the authority to determine sales at less than fair value.
1967	The GATT's Antidumping Code broadened the scope of Article VI of the original GATT agreement which had specifically addressed dumping remedies.
1979	Congress approved the revised GATT Antidumping Code, repealed the Antidumping Act of 1921, and added a new title VII to the Tariff Act of 1930, including section 731. This act moved fair market value determination duty from the Department of the Treasury to the Department of Commerce.
1984	The antidumping law was amended by the Trade and Tariff Act of 1984.
1988	The antidumping law was further amended by Title I, Subtitle C, Part 2 of the Omnibus Trade and Competitiveness Act of 1988.

Source: Compiled by the author from information available in U.S. House of Representatives, Committee on Ways and Means, *Overview and Compilation of U.S. Trade Statutes* (Washington, D.C.: U.S. GPO, 1993, 1994, and 1995).

of investigations, final determinations, and assessments of duty. The main
provision is stated below.

> Section 731 requires
> ITA to determine if a class or kind of foreign merchandise is being, or is likely
> to be, sold in the United States at LTFV, and
> ITC to determine if an industry in the United States is materially injured or
> is threatened with material injury. If the authority's decision is affirmative, then
> such a merchandise is subject to an antidumping duty, in addition to any other
> duty, imposed in an amount equal to the amount by which the foreign market
> value exceeds the United States price for the merchandise.
> *Source:* U.S. House of Representatives, Committee on Ways and Means,
> *Overview and Compilation of U.S. Trade Statutes* (Washington, D.C.: U.S.
> GPO, 1995), 385.

The ITA first determines the fair value by three different methods. They are, in
order of preference, the home market sales (HMS), third-country sales (TCS),
and constructed value (CV) methods. The HMS method is the weighted average of prices in the home market of the exporting country for goods similar to
those exported to the importing country during the period of investigation. The
TCS method is the weighted average of prices for goods similar to those exported to a third country. This method is used if home sales for these goods in
the exporting country are small or do not exist. If the first two methods cannot
be used, the fair value is constructed. The formula for CV is the sum of cost of
production, 10 percent for operating expenses and 8 percent for profit. Any
price below the fair value is dumping. Congress transferred the authority to investigate the dumping margin from the Department of Treasury to the Department of Commerce in 1979 and encouraged use of the CV method.

Figure 4.4 shows the statutory timetable for AD investigations. The entire
process is similar to that for the CVD procedure, except that an injury test is
automatic. The ITC is responsible for making the final injury determination.
The standard of material injury under the AD law is the same as that under
the CVD law. However, the time period for investigation and determination
is longer in antidumping cases. The total number of days required to complete the entire statutory process is 280 for a simple case if the ITC's and
ITA's determinations are consistently affirmative (preliminary and final)
throughout the four stages. An extended case takes 340 days. If the ITC's and
ITA's determinations are inconsistent at stages II and III, however, the total
number of days increases to 310 for a simple case and 370 for an extended
case. The ITA's preliminary affirmative determination for a complicated case
at stage II takes 330 days; for an extended case, the total number of days can
reach 390. For the ITA's preliminary negative determination in a complicated
case, the total number of days is 360, for an extended case 420 days. Once the
ITC's determination on material injury is final, the ITA directs the U.S. Cus-

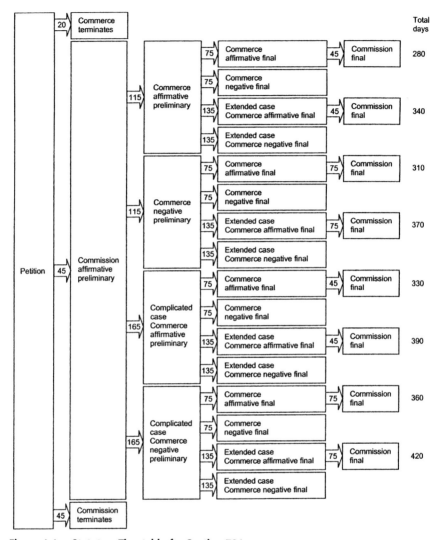

Figure 4.4.   Statutory Timetable for Section 731
Source: USITC, *Annual Report* (Washington, DC: U.S. GPO, 1991), 36.

toms Service to assess ADs equivalent to the amount by which the foreign market value exceeds the price in the United States.

4.6 SAFEGUARD MEASURE

The provisions examined so far in this chapter are concerned with "unfair" and "illegal" trade practices that adversely affect U.S. commerce. Unlike these provisions, Section 201 (provision of the Trade Act of 1974, as amended) provides U.S. industries with temporary relief from fair but injurious import competition if the ITC determines that the industrial damage inflicted by foreign imports is serious.[8] The provision is often referred to as an "escape clause," meaning that it permits a country to escape temporarily from its international obligations under the GATT/WTO. The main provision is as follows:

> Section 201 provides authority for the President to take any appropriate and feasible actions which will facilitate efforts by the domestic industry to make a positive adjustment to import competition, if the ITC determines that increased amounts of U.S. imports of a particular commodity are regarded as to be a substantial cause of serious injury or the threat to the import-competing domestic industry.
> *Source:* U.S. House of Representatives, Committee on Ways and Means, *Overview and Compilation of U.S. Trade Statutes* (Washington, D.C.: U.S. GPO, 1995), 543.

The procedures for implementation of section 201 include investigations, determinations, and recommendations by the ITC; action by the President; and monitoring, modification, and termination of action. Relief may be granted for an initial period of up to four years, with the possibility of extending the action to a maximum of eight years.

Trade associations, firms, unions, or groups of workers file petitions with the ITC or the USTR. Upon receipt of a petition, the ITC investigates the case and makes a determination of import injury within 180 days. Criteria for import relief are based on Article XIX of the GATT and the UR Agreement on Safeguards. Sixty days after receiving a report from the ITC, the President usually takes one of the following actions:

- Increase or imposition of a duty on the imported article,
- Quantitative restriction, or
- Rearrangement of orderly marketing agreements with foreign countries that limit imports into the United States.

The President then submits legislative proposals to Congress for assistance in making a positive adjustment.

Chapter 7 dives into the six principal trade remedy policies in action.

4.7 ANTECEDENTS OF TRADE REMEDY STATUTES

Most of the trade remedy provisions have evolved over time to their present amended versions. The origins of some provisions date back as far as trade

Table 4.4.   Chief Sources of U.S. Trade Remedy Provisions in Brief

Provisions	Chief Sources
Section 301	Trade Reform Act of 1974
Super 301	OTCA of 1988
Special 301	OTCA of 1988
Section 701	SHTA of 1930
Section 731	Antidumping Act of 1921
Section 201	Trade Reform Act of 1974

Source: Author's compilation on the basis of (1) U.S. House of Representatives, Committee on Ways and Means, *Overview and Compilation of U.S. Trade Statutes* (Washington, D.C.: U.S. GPO, 1993, 1994, and 1995) and (2) U.S. House of Representatives, Committee on Ways and Means, *Trade Legislation Enacted into Public Law, 1981 through 1988* (Washington, D.C.: U.S. GPO, January 27, 1989).

laws passed before 1930. Table 4.4 shows the origins of Section 301, Super 301, Special 301, Section 701, Section 731, and Section 201. Their corresponding sections in the OTCA are Sections 1301, 1302, 1303, 1312, 1316, and 1401, respectively.

Their chief sources are summarized as follows:

1. Section 301

This is a section of Chapter 1 (Sections 301–309), Title III of the Trade Act of 1974, amended by sections in Part I, including Section 1301, Subtitle C of Title I, the OTCA. The Tariff Act of 1930 already included a similar section. However, note that Section 337 in the 1930 Act is concerned with unfair trade practices in "import" trade.

2. Super 301

This is a new section added at the end of Section 301 of Chapter 1, Title III of the Trade Act of 1974, amended by section 1301 and included in Section 1302 of the OTCA.

3. Special 301

This is a new section added at the end of Section 182 of Chapter 8, Title I of the Trade Act of 1974, amended by Section 1303 and included in Section 1303 of the OTCA.

4. Section 701

This section is a part of Subtitle A of Title VII of the Tariff Act of 1930 (the earliest provision dates back to 1897), as added by the Trade Agreement Act of 1979 and amended by the Trade and Tariff Act of 1984 and the OTCA (Part 2, Subtitle C of Title I).

5. Section 731

The origin of this section is the Antidumping Act of 1916. Section 731 is Subtitle B of Title VII of the Tariff Act of 1930, as amended by Part 2, Subtitle C of Title I, the OTCA.

6. Section 201

This section has existed since the Trade Agreement Extension Act of 1951. Congress has attempted to introduce the current section 201 for many years. It is in Chapter 1 of Title II of the Trade Act of 1974, as amended by section 1401 of the OTCA.

Sections 701 and 731 have a longer history than other trade remedy provisions. As introduced in earlier sections in this chapter, tables 4.2 and 4.3 present their history in detail.

4.8 OTHER PROVISIONS

There are other trade provisions that also play important roles in U.S. trade enforcement activities. They are summarized in this section.

1. Section 1337 of OTCA—Telecommunications

This provision requires the USTR to review the operation and effectiveness of the U.S. telecommunications trade agreement by the end of March of each year and to determine if a foreign country that has made a telecommunications-related agreement with the United States complies with its terms.

2. Executive Order 13116 of 1999, reinstituted certain elements of Title VII of the OTCA—Government Procurement

This order requires the USTR to identify countries that are not in compliance with their obligations under the WTO Government Procurement Agreement, Chapter 10 of the NAFTA, or other agreements and enables the USTR to take appropriate countermeasures.

3. Section 337 of the Smoot-Hawley Tariff Act of 1930—Unfair Import Practices

It is illegal to partake of unfair acts or unfair methods of competition in the importation or sale of imported goods, especially those that deal with U.S. intellectual property rights. The investigations are conducted by the ITC.

4. Trade Adjustment Assistance (TAA)

There are two different assistant programs: Assistance for workers and assistance for firms and industries. Both provide assistance for workers and firms/industries affected by imports.

• *Assistance for Workers*

This program was authorized under Title II, Chapter 2, of the Trade Act of 1974, as amended, and by the NAFTA Implementation Act. Assistance programs include job training, trade adjustment allowances, job search, relocation, and other employment services. The Department of Labor administers the program.

• *Assistance for Firms and Industries*

This program was authorized under Title II, Chapter 3, of the Trade Act of 1974, as amended. In order to be eligible for the assistance, a firm or an industry must prove that increased imports contributed importantly to declines in its sales, production, or both, and to the separation or threat of separation of a significant portion of workers. The Department of Commerce administers the program.

4.9 SUMMARY AND CONCLUSIONS

The objective of the U.S. trade remedy laws included in the OTCA is to provide American industries with the legal basis for relief from fair and unfair import competition primarily by means of provisions in six different areas: Section 701, Section 731, Section 201, Section 301, Super 301, and Special 301. Each provision has its own statutory process and timetable for quasi-judicial investigations, determinations, and retaliatory policy actions. In general, the entire process is lengthy, complex, and thus costly to both the plaintiff country (the United States) and defendant countries. Since it is an interagency statutory process, trade policy decisions are not readily reversible by a government authority or agency.

The U.S. trade remedy laws have been highly controversial in both the United States and foreign countries. Among them, Super 301 has been most controversial. The GATT has no explicit provisions relating to Super 301. Foreign countries view Super 301 as an aggressive, unilateral device to penalize countries that have a large trade surplus with the United States. The United States retains the right to retaliate against unjustifiable, unreasonable, or discriminatory foreign trade practices, to levy countervailing or antidumping duties, and to provide positive adjustment assistance. Each of the provisions corresponding to these cases is largely consistent with those in the GATT/UR. The controversies are not about the principles but about the actual processes for injury determination and the specific methods of determining amounts of foreign subsidy and dumping.

Other trade laws that play important roles in U.S. trade enforcement activities include provisions on telecommunications, government procurement, unfair import practices, and trade adjustment assistance for workers and for firms and industries.

NOTES

1. The USTR may delay consultation with the foreign country for up to ninety days. If a trade agreement is involved, the consultation period either depends on the period specified in the agreement or is 150 days.

2. See Office of Federal Register, *Federal Register*, Presidential Documents 59, no. 45, (Washington, D.C.: U.S. GPO, March 8, 1994), 107–27.

3. See U.S. House of Representatives, Committee on Ways and Means, *Trade Legislation Enacted into Public Law, 1981 through 1988* (Washington, D.C.: U.S. GPO, 1989), 282–90; also see chapter 7.

4. See U.S. House of Representatives, Committee on Ways and Means, *Hearing: USTR Identification of Priority Practices and Countries Under Super 301 and Special 301 Provisions of the Omnibus Trade and Competitiveness Act of 1988*, Serial 101-28 (Washington, D.C.: U.S. GPO, June 8, 1989), 11.

5. Contervailable subsidies correspond to "red light" subsidies in the Uruguay Round term because they are prohibited at all times. They include grants, loans at a lower interest rate or loan guarantees, equity infusion, forgiveness of debt, export insurance at a low premium, transportation and freight at low rates, fiscal incentives such as tax credits, governmental transactions of goods and services other than general infrastructure, and governmental payments to a funding mechanism for the private sector. There are also subsidies that are not countervailable. Noncountervailable subsidies are referred to as "green light" subsidies in the Uruguay context. These include subsidies for R&D, subsidies to disadvantaged regions, and subsidies to adapt existing facilities to new environmental standards; they are noncountervailable sub-

ject to specific requirements and limitations. See Rossidies and Maravel (1992), chapters 13 and 38, for specific requirements and conditions in details.

6. The Subsidy Code is a multinational agreement on subsidies and countervailing measures. See Articles VI, especially Section 5, XVI, XVI, and XXIII of the GATT in appendix I.

7. GATT's Antidumping Code brings all GATT signatory countries into conformity with Article VI of the GATT, including appropriate procedural requirements for antidumping investigations. See Article VI, especially Section 5 of the GATT in Appendix I at the end of this book.

8. This provision was initially included in the GATT primarily at the request of the United States.

Chapter 5

The World Trade Framework

Congress has authorized the President to negotiate international agreements for the reduction of trade barriers through trade laws. Examples include the Reciprocal Trade Agreements Act of 1934, the Trade Act of 1974, and the Omnibus Trade and Competitiveness Act of 1988. Trade acts such as these have required that U.S. trade policy should incorporate with international trade agreements at all levels. As a result, the coordinated use of multilateral agreements, regional negotiations, and bilateral initiatives constitutes the driving force of U.S. trade policy today.[1] Such a multifaceted policy means that one needs to be familiar with international trade agreements to understand systematically U.S. trade policy.

On October 23, 1947, twenty-three countries including the United States began trade negotiations under provisional rules that have been known as the General Agreement of Tariffs and Trade (GATT). The purpose of this multilateral trade agreement was for all sides to reduce tariffs and other barriers to free trade and eliminate discriminatory treatment in international commerce for the global welfare concurrently. Under free trade that is dictated only by competitive market forces, a country specializes and exports a good produced relatively cheaply in exchange for a good specialized by another country. The GATT, not an organization but an agreement, required contracting parties (not member countries) to conduct trade within the frameworks of the agreement.[2] U.S. trade policy faithfully and consistently followed the GATT for about half a century. In 1994, the Uruguay Round (UR), the eighth round of the GATT, was completed and established the World Trade Organization (WTO). Since then, American trade policy has been based on the UR agreement. Since the mid-1980s, the United States has also had regional interests in trade with countries in the American continent, the EU, and Asia. At present, the most notable regional agreement is the North American Free Trade Agreement (NAFTA) formed in 1992. During the 1980s and 1990s, the United States made a large number of bilateral agreements with almost all of its trading partners and has continued to expand its bilateral approach.

American trade policy under the UR agreement is significantly different from that under the $GATT_{1947}$. In contrast with a more general and defensive policy in the past, the United States follows a more specific and offensive policy in view of negotiating many issue-oriented problems with foreign countries, monitoring the adherence of foreign countries to the trade agreements, and enforcing all levels of these agreements. The objective of U.S. trade policy at present is to open virtually all foreign markets for U.S. export of goods, services, and investment, as opposed to that to reduce primarily tariff barriers in connection with goods trade. Naturally, countries participating within the schema of the WTO have a similar objective for their own trade policies.

Current U.S. trade policy is characterized by a broad array of multilateral, regional, and bilateral agreements. Future trade policy will no doubt maintain the same pattern for the time being, although it is expected to be somewhat modified and expanded by post-Uruguay developments at all levels, including the Doha Round, the ninth round of the GATT, and the Free Trade Area of the Americas (FTAA), the most ambitious regional trade agenda. However, the future is not entirely promising because of two difficult areas for negotiation among countries. One is the agricultural sector that has long been protected by subsidies in most countries. It is highly unlikely that countries will eliminate the subsidies provided to this often politically-charged sector in the near future. The other is the financial sector. Newly emerging markets in East Asia experienced severe financial crises in the late eighties and early nineties. The U.S. Treasury and the IMF believed that full capital account liberalization would help the region grow even faster. However, many economists, including Stiglitz (2002), believe that IMF and U.S. Treasury policies to liberalize capital markets in East Asian countries, where their high saving rates require no desperate need for additional capital, was the single most important factor leading to the financial crisis.[3] Financial crises in Latin American countries, following upon debt crises experienced in the 1980s, are also a recurring problem. Argentina has been on the verge of a complete economic breakdown as it faced difficulty with the IMF in rolling over some $10 billion in debt, while Brazil has received a $30 billion loan from the IMF to stabilize its economy. Even worse, global trade imbalances (related to trade policy in each country and capability of the WTO) and financial crises appear to be correlated. The future path of the FTAA depends on endeavors of the United States and other member countries for successful negotiations of the long list of trade agenda.

Sections 1, 2, and 3 outline multilateral, regional, and bilateral agreements, respectively. Section 4 discusses recent development of multilateral agreements. Section 5 draws conclusions.

5.1 MULTILATERAL AGREEMENTS[4]

I. GATT

After World War II, twenty-three industrial countries publicly recognized that obstacles to trade hindered economic development and growth. They set out rules for international trade conduct on October 23, 1947, primarily aimed at reducing tariff barriers. These rules, known as the GATT or $GATT_{1947}$, reigned over member countries' trade policies for almost half a century until the Uruguay Round was concluded in 1994, the eighth round under the GATT. Each of the first seven rounds has gradually reduced tariff rates across countries under the leadership of the Geneva-based Secretariat. The full nine rounds, including the Doha Declaration, are listed in Table 5.1. The first five

Table 5.1.   GATT Rounds

Round	Year	Place	Objective	Members
1	1947	Geneva	Tariffs	23
2	1949	Annecy, France	Tariffs	13
3	1951	Torquay, U.K.	Tariffs	38
4	1956	Geneva	Tariffs	26
5	1960–1961	Geneva (Dillon Round)	Tariffs	26
6	1964–1967	Geneva (Kennedy Round)	Tariffs and Antidumping Measures	62
7	1973–1979	Geneva (Tokyo Round)	Tariffs, nontariff measures and framework agreements	102
8	1986–1994	Geneva (Uruguay Round)	Tariffs, nontariff measures, rules, services, intellectual property rights, dispute settlement, textiles and clothing, agriculture, establishment of the WTO, etc.	148*
9	2001–	Doha (Doha Round)	Lowering barriers, especially in the areas of services and agriculture	

Note: Fifth, sixth, and seventh rounds are often referred to as the Dillon Round, the Kennedy Round, and the Tokyo Round, respectively.

*The number is subject to change.

Source: WTO, *WTO* (France: St. Juste-la-Pendue), 9 updated.

rounds, especially the fifth round, took the bilateral form for reciprocal agreements. As discussed in chapter 2, the Kennedy Round (the sixth round, completed in 1967) and the Tokyo Round (the seventh round, completed in 1979) significantly reduced tariff rates. Expansions of trade through tariff reductions among countries greatly benefited the entire world. As of May 1994, there were 123 member countries, accounting for over 80 percent of world trade.

The original version of the GATT had three parts that contained thirty-four articles. The last version had four parts that comprised thirty-eight articles. Part I is concerned with nondiscrimination and tariff concessions; Part II deals with NTBs and dispute settlement; Part III covers customs unions; and Part IV contains provisions on the GSP that were added in 1965. The GATT's three main features are:

- Most-Favored-Nation (MFN) Treatment (Article I),
- Elimination of trade barriers other than duties (Articles XI and XVI), and
- Consultation and dispute settlement (Articles XXII and XXIII).

In light of the GATT's objective, Article I is the key provision. Any tariff imposed by one member country on an imported good must be applied equally to all member countries. Article XI calls for the elimination of quantitative restrictions. Article XVI is concerned with the stringent use of subsidies. In the event of trade disputes, the GATT first encourages bilateral consultation (Article XXII), and the settlement process begins in accordance with Article XXIII, if consultation fails. In addition to the three main features of the GATT, it is notable that Article VI is concerned with antidumping and countervailing duties. Article XIX is the escape clause. It is necessary to explain briefly the settlement process of trade disputes. Disputes related to any of the following are subject to GATT settlement:

- the operation of customs regulations and formalities
- antidumping and countervailing duties
- quantitative and exchange regulations
- subsidies
- state-trading operations
- sanitary laws and regulations for the protection of human, animal, or plant life and health.

Article XXIII (Nullification or Impairment) rules that (1) in cases where the benefit accruing to a contracting party is nullified or impaired by another party's negligence of its GATT obligations, it may direct its concern to the other party's attention by writing a proposal; (2) if the contracting parties fail to reach a satisfactory agreement for adjustment within a reasonable time (normally twelve months), the matter may be referred to a panel of three experts from third countries established by the GATT Council for Investigation and Recommendation; (3) after consultation with the contracting countries, the Economic and Social Council of the United Nations, and any appropriate intergovernmental organization, GATT authorizes the contracting party or parties to suspend the application of GATT obligations or concessions; and (4) no later than sixty days after the suspension, the contracting party is free to advise the Secretary-General of the U.N., in writing, of its intention to withdraw from this agreement.

The GATT was often criticized for its lack of an enforcement mechanism in the dispute settlement system because the panel's ruling was *not binding* on the parties. In cases where the GATT permits the plaintiff (complaining) country to retaliate against the defendant (complained) country, the latter could veto the retaliation. An Appellate Body without success, often followed by cross-retaliation, heard appeals of panel decisions. Consequently, disputes dragged on for years or disputants did not often have their differences settled through the GATT. The GATT Council has established panels over 100 times since 1947 and did so more frequently than ever while the Uruguay Round was negotiated.[5] The lack of an enforcement mechanism was one of the main reasons for a new multilateral trade negotiation and led eventually to the successful completion of the Uruguay Round. Appendix I to this book presents components of $GATT_{1947}$.

II. The Uruguay Round

Every country benefited from trade liberalization under the GATT. Meanwhile, the world economy was rapidly globalizing, international investment was exploding, and trade in intellectual property services was becoming increasingly important. However, the GATT did not cover many of these areas of trade. It also failed to provide meaningful rules for important aspects of agricultural trade that constituted the main loophole in the multilateral system. The textile and clothing sector was excluded from normal GATT discipline. In addition, the GATT did not bring about prompt dispute settlement.

For the purpose of further trade liberalization and administrative reform, trade ministers of 117 participating countries agreed to begin new multilateral trade negotiations at a meeting held in Punta del Este, Uruguay, on September 20, 1986. It took more than seven years (1986–1994) to complete the often-contentious negotiations. They agreed on the contents of the Final Act of the Uruguay Round in Geneva on December 15, 1993 and signed the historic

Final Texts of the GATT Uruguay Round Agreements Including The Agreement Establishing The World Trade Organization in Marrakech, Morocco, on April 15, 1994. It was the eighth round of negotiations under the auspices of the GATT and resulted in the most comprehensive multilateral trade agreement in history. The Marrakesh Declaration affirmed that the Uruguay Round (UR) would strengthen the world economy and lead to more trade, investment, employment, and income growth throughout the world. For the chronology of the UR, see table 5.2.

The Marrakesh texts consist of

- Final Act Embodying the Results of the Uruguay Round of Multilateral Trade Negotiations,
- Agreement Establishing the World Trade Organization,
- Ministerial Decisions and Declarations, and
- Understanding on Commitment in Financial Services.

Among the four annexes in the agreement establishing the WTO, the substantive achievement of the UR, Annex 1 contains Multilateral Agreements

Table 5.2.   Chronology of the Uruguay Round

November 1982	Work Program formed at the Ministerial meeting of GATT members in Geneva after the attempt to launch a major new negotiation on agricultural trade without success
September 20, 1986	Official announcement for a new MTN by about 150 countries at Punta del Este, Uruguay
January 28, 1987	First trade negotiation council (TNC) meeting held in Geneva
1988	Midterm review at the Ministerial meeting in Montreal, Canada; launched the second stage of the Uruguay Round; early results of agreements reached are concessions on market access for tropical products, a dispute settlement system, and trade policy review mechanism
December 7, 1990	TNC meeting held at Brussels to discuss agricultural subsidies but failed to reach an agreement, extending the round
December 20, 1991	A proposal for the Final Act submitted by Arthur Dunkel, GATT Secretariat
November 20, 1992	The Blair House Agreement for reductions of agricultural subsidies between the United States and the E.C.
July 7, 1993	Agreement to reduce tariffs on manufactures by four countries, the United States, Japan, E.C., and Canada at the G7 meetings held in Tokyo
August 30, 1993	Agreement to set the deadline for completion of the MTN at TNC
December 15, 1993	Uruguay Round agreed to by 117 countries
April 12, 1994	Ministerial meeting agreed to complete the UR
April 15, 1994	The Final Texts signed by 127 countries in Marrakech, Morocco

Source: Author's compilation from various sources.

on Trade in Goods, General Agreement on Trade in Services, and Agreement on Trade-Related Aspects of Intellectual Property Rights. In Annex 1A, there are thirteen agreements, including General Agreement Tariffs and Trade 1994 (GATT$_{1947}$). Annex 2 deals with the Understanding on Rules and Procedures Governing the Settlement of Disputes. Annexes 3 and 4 are concerned with the Trade Policy Review Mechanism and Plurilateral Trade Agreements, respectively.[6]

The primary agreements included in Annex 1A are:

- General Agreement of Tariffs and Trade (GATT$_{1994}$)
- Agreement on Agriculture
- Agreement on Trade-Related Investment Measures (TRIMS)
- General Agreement on Trade in Services (GATS)
- Agreement on Trade-Related Intellectual Property Rights (TRIPS)

The Final Agreement was subject to ratification by individual member country governments before January 1, 1995. In the United States, the House ratified it on November 29, 1994 (H.R. 5110; Title: To approve and implement the trade agreements concluded in the Uruguay Round of multilateral trade negotiations, sponsored by Representative Richard A. Gephardt) and the Senate on December 1, 1994 (S. 2467; Title: The same as that for the House bill, sponsored by Senator George J. Mitchell), respectively, after each held extensive public hearings, including testimony from the U.S. DOC's private sector industrial advisory committees, labor unions, and the agricultural sector. Appendices 5.1 and 5.2 in this chapter show the final vote results for roll calls in the House (288 yeas and 146 nays) and the Senate (76 yeas and 24 nays). The UR agreement came into force on January 1, 1995, with the phase-in of different provisions starting from July 1, 1995. It replaced the GATT with far more power over member countries.

The UR effectively created a new world trade order. Below are the main features characterizing the UR:

1. Trade Liberalization

Tariff and NTB negotiations on industrial products continue to be the dominant agenda of multilateral trade negotiations (MTNs). Only this part of the UR agreements corresponds to the existing GATT, which may therefore be referred to as GATT$_{1994}$ as opposed to GATT$_{1947}$. More than 120 countries have made commitments to reduce tariffs, for the most part phased out over five years. These are expected to result in a 30 percent cut in tariffs on industrial products imposed by developed countries, leaving tariff levels between 6.3 percent and 3.8 percent. However, trade liberalization of the agricultural and clothing sectors and government procurement is likely to be controversial. In fact, trade liberalization in the agricultural sector has been very sluggish. For example, Japan's import quotas on agricultural products and the EU's massive export subsidies under the Common Agricultural Program (CAP) are the most difficult areas to negotiate. Both Japan and Korea decided to terminate long-standing import quotas of rice. The EU and the United States compromised to allow the UR to complete the agreement. The UR agreement required member countries to replace import quotas by tariffs and to reduce subsidies by 36 percent over a six-year period. The textiles and clothing sector has been protected by the Multi-Fiber Agreement (MFA) that assigns import licenses to exporting countries. Nevertheless, the UR agreement will phase out the MFA over a ten-year period. Government procurement is still another protected area. The UR agreement established a rule to open up the market for government contracts. $GATT_{1947}$ applied only to trade on goods. Trade in services of about one-fourth the size of world merchandise trade and trade-related intellectual property are now subject to the General Agreement on Trade in Services (GATS) and the Trade-related Aspects of Intellectual Property Rights (TRIPS), respectively, set up under the UR agreement. These agreements also provide the bases for future negotiations in the aforementioned areas.

2. The World Trade Organization (WTO)

The UR has substantially improved and strengthened the operational and organizational aspects of the $GATT_{1947}$ trading system. As the embodiment of the UR results and the successor of the $GATT_{1947}$, it established the WTO on January 1, 1995. The WTO based in Geneva is the legal and institutional foundation of the multilateral trading system. It includes the institutional structure of $GATT_{1947}$ but extends it to new disciplines, such as trade in services, intellectual property, and trade-related investment. The WTO ensures full, effective implementation of UR agreements and facilitates the "cross-retaliation." In principle, the WTO requires member countries (148 members as of February 16, 2005) to participate fully by adhering to all of the UR agreements with two exceptions: customs union and the Generalized Scheme of Preference (GSP) and by submitting schedules of market access commitments for manufacturing goods, agricultural goods, and services.[7] The WTO maintains the GATT tradition of decision-making not by voting but by *consensus*. If consensus is not possible, decisions are made by a majority of votes of *one country, one vote*.[8] Its primary functions are:

- to administer the Uruguay Round agreements
- to provide a forum for trade negotiations

- to settle trade disputes
- to oversee national trade policies
- to provide technical assistance and training for developing countries and
- to cooperate with other international organizations.

There are four fundamental principles of the trading system:

First, the WTO not only maintains the Most-Favored-Nation (MFN) clause and national treatment, as stipulated in Articles I and III of $GATT_{1947}$ but expands the MFN boundary. Other nondiscrimination provisions include the ones on intellectual property rights, services, rules of origin, trade-related investment, and sanitation.

Second, the WTO ensures predictable and growing access to markets through nondiscriminatory tariff reductions and increased transparency of domestic laws, regulations, and practices. A country cannot increase the *bound* tariffs without compensation negotiations with its main trading partners (Article XXVIII of $GATT_{1994}$).

Third, the WTO is a system of rules dedicated to open, fair, and undistorted competition. Rules applied to unfair trade practices (especially dumping and subsidies) were extended and clarified in WTO agreements designed to promote *fair* competition.

Fourth, $GATT_{1994}$ contains three articles in Part IV, including the GSP, that encourage economic development and transition as in the case of $GATT_{1947}$.

The Ministerial Conference (MC) is the primary decision-making authority for all WTO matters. It consists of representatives from all WTO members and meets at least once every two years. The MC appoints a Secretariat headed by the Director-General, who is responsible for the WTO's day-to-day administration and operation. As shown in figure 5.1, there are one council and two subsidiary bodies under the MC:

- General Council (GC)
- Trade Policy Review Body (TPRB)
- Dispute Settlement Body (DSB).

The GC, the principal unit, is composed of representatives of all the members. It conducts the WTO's functions between meetings of the MC and meets as appropriate. The GC has three main councils: the Council on Trade in Goods, Council on Trade in Services, and Council on Trade-Related Aspects of Intellectual Property Rights. It is also assisted by four additional committees, which also assist the MC directly.[9] The first council has twelve committees and the second has five committees.[10]

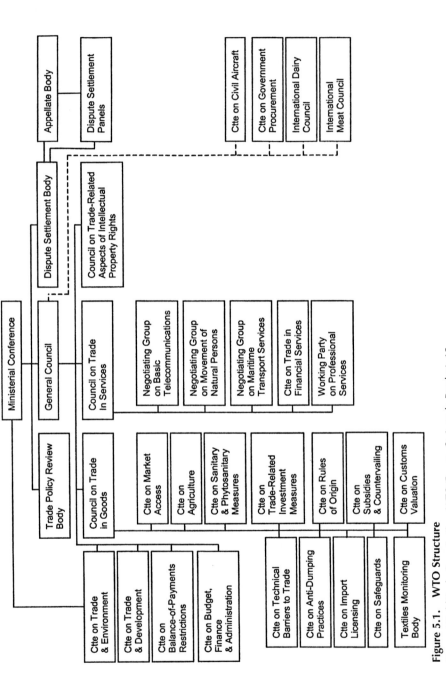

Figure 5.1. WTO Structure
Source: World Trade Organization, *WTO* (France: St. Juste-la-Pendue), 15.

The TPRB is responsible for improving the transparency and understanding trade policies on a regular basis; annually reviewing the operation of the trading system; overseeing the establishment of a central registry of notifications that are made under various agreements (for example, standards and subsidy); and calling for a complementary global trade policy to ensure a healthy basis for world trade.[11]

The DSB is responsible for the formal settlement of trade disputes. It consists of the Dispute Settlement Panels (DSP) and the Appellate Body (AB). Settlement of trade disputes is an important function of the WTO. This function will be discussed separately in the following section.

3. Dispute Settlements under the WTO

For improvement of the transparency in dispute settlement procedures, the Dispute Settlement Understanding (DSU) has established a single system that adopts the findings of panels charged with settling trade disputes and a new Appellate Body to hear appeals of panel findings in all areas (goods, services, and intellectual property rights). The single system is expected to result in a more effective and expeditious resolution of disputes and to enable members to enforce their rights more strongly.

There are twenty-seven provisions in the DSU. The main features are: stringent time limits on each stage of the process, transparency, right to appeal, no blocking of the adoption of panel reports, cross-retaliation, and effective procedures for authorizing retaliation. Members of the WTO are not supposed to take unilateral action against perceived violations of the trade rules but instead seek recourse to the multilateral dispute settlement system and to abide by its rules and findings.

How does the WTO settle trade disputes? The panel process is basically quasi-judicial.

- The first step requires consultation. Should consultations fail, and if both parties agree, the case can be brought to the WTO Director-General who, acting in an *ex officio* capacity, will attempt to resolve the dispute.
- If consultations fail to arrive at a solution after sixty days, the complainant can ask the DSB to establish a panel to examine the case. The Director-General must set up a group of three qualified panelists who serve in their individual capacities.
- The panel submits its final report to the parties within six months (three months in urgent cases) and, three weeks later, it is circulated to all WTO members.
- The panel reports are adopted by the DSB within sixty days of issuance.

- If one party decides to appeal, the DSB establishes a standing Appellate Body (AB) of seven persons who serve four years (three of seven sit at any one time to hear appeals).
- The DSB adopts the AB's report thirty days later. The parties must unconditionally accept the AB's report unless there is a consensus against its adoption.[12]
- The parties negotiate compensation for up to twenty days.
- In the absence of a satisfactory compensation agreement between the parties after thirty days, the DSB authorizes retaliation by the complainant.

Figure 5.2 exhibits the panel process for dispute settlements.

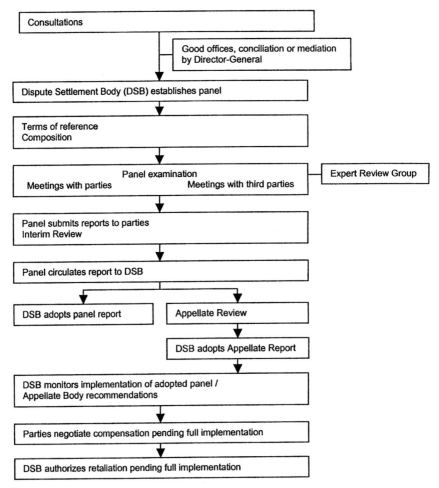

Figure 5.2. Panel Process
Source: WTO, *WTO* (France: St. Juste-la-Pendue), 18.

III. Main Differences between the GATT and the WTO

The chief differences between the GATT$_{1947}$ and the WTO are as follows:

* The GATT was a set of rules, whereas the WTO is a permanent institution.
* The GATT was applied on a provisional basis, whereas the WTO commitment is permanent.
* The GATT covered primarily trade in merchandise, whereas the WTO encompasses trade in goods, services, and intellectual property rights.
* The GATT dispute settlement was not binding, whereas WTO's settlement is.

Appendix II at the end of the book lists components of the UR agreement.

5.2 REGIONAL AGREEMENTS

The main regional agreements involving the United States which are either completed or in progress are the North American Free Trade Agreement (NAFTA), the Free Trade Area of the Americas (FTAA), the Asia Pacific Economic Cooperation (APEC), and the New Transatlantic Market Place (NTMP).[13] These trade agreements cover regions around the world, showing the seriousness of American interest in world trade. This section summarizes each of the aforementioned regional agreements.

I. The NAFTA

1. Background

The origin of the NAFTA is the U.S.-Canada Free Trade Agreement (CFTA) completed in 1987.[14] In the 1980s, Mexico's economy was on the brink of collapse, primarily because of its huge amount of external debt. Mexico realized that oil exports and commercial loans could no longer finance its economic growth. As a radical reform of economic policy, Mexico had to shift from oil exports to exports of manufactures and to inducement of foreign investment. Since it was difficult for Mexico to penetrate European and Asian markets, access to the U.S. market was critical. In August 1990, Mexico formally proposed negotiations for the NAFTA with the United States. In September 1990, Canada was concerned about possible erosion of its gains from the trade creation effect of the CFTA and a trade diversion effect of the NAFTA.[15] Canada therefore requested to be included in the NAFTA negotiations, which both the United States and Mexico accepted.

Formal negotiation for the NAFTA began on June 12, 1991 and was completed on August 12, 1992. The NAFTA entered into effect on January 1,

1994 and was scheduled to phase out in fifteen years. Under the supervision of the NAFTA Commission, NAFTA's central oversight body chaired jointly by the three countries, the three member countries should gradually remove nearly all tariffs and NTBs within fifteen years. It is a free trade bloc, certainly the largest one ever formed by the United States, Canada (the largest export market of the United States as of 2001) and Mexico (the fourth largest export market of the United States).

A free trade area, by definition, removes all trade barriers between members, but each country retains its own tariff rates against nonmembers. It does not allow for the free movement of productive factors among the member countries. Although trade-related travel on a temporary-entry basis is facilitated by the NAFTA, workers are not freely mobile within the free trade area. Some economists argue that a regional trade arrangement is based on protectionism and thus the NAFTA is in conflict with the GATT. However, the GATT and the UR recognize the value of economic integration for freer trade as an exception to the general rule of MFN treatment (Article I in the GATT) because regional economic integration complements the multilateral trading system. Also, Article XXIV permits a customs union unless they raise trade barriers against outsiders. The rationale for such a preferential trade agreement is that regional integration reduces trade barriers among member countries and thus the trade creation effects expand world trade (if it exceeds trade diversion), so it is consistent with the principle of the GATT. There are also the dynamic gains to countries through increased competition, economies of scale, and stimulation of investment resulted from preferential trade agreements.

At the initial stage of the NAFTA negotiations, there were numerous arguments for or against the NAFTA in the United States. Most economists, business, and mass media supported the passage of the NAFTA for benefits from more open trade and investment opportunities, whereas labor unions and environmental groups voiced strong opposition to the NAFTA. Proponents suggested that the NAFTA would:

- make North American companies more competitive with Asian rivals by taking advantage of lower wages in Mexico.
- open previously closed Mexican markets to automobiles, computers, telecommunications, financial services, etc.
- strengthen Mexico economically, giving Mexicans more financial resources to purchase U.S. products and therefore creating more jobs in the United States.

However, critics voiced that the NAFTA would:

- result in the loss of U.S. manufacturing jobs to low-wage Mexican workers.

- produce unfair competition with fruit and vegetables growers in Mexico, where the growing season is the same but wages are significantly lower.
- increase environmental degradation along the U.S.-Mexico border.

The first argument against the NAFTA especially by H. Ross Perot, a leading political opponent to the NAFTA, was possible loss of American jobs to Mexico. However, his argument was not convincing because comparative advantage is not only determined by wages alone (the Ricardian law) but also other factors that enhance productivity of workers such as capital (the Heckscher-Ohlin model), technology, education for skilled labor and managerial skills, and increasing returns to scale and intra-industry trade (the trade theory under imperfect competition). Environmental problems continued to be a serious issue threatening the NAFTA until the last stage of negotiations. In process of negotiations for the NAFTA, however, this issue was reconciled by allowing the United States to maintain its health, safety, and environmental standards on the one hand and to prohibit imports that do not meet these standards on the other hand. It was also decided that the NAFTA preserves the right to enforce and to enact tougher standards such as limiting trade involving endangered species or ozone-depleting substances or restricting investment if strict standards are not met. As the first step, the border plan was to clean up rivers, hazardous waste, and air pollution. A long-term cooperative program to enhance environmental protection and conservation includes plans to control pesticides, hazardous waste, energy resources, and soil, air, and water pollution.

In May 1991, Congress extended fast track authority to the President for agreements signed by May 31, 1993.[16] A ninety-day period for congressional review began on September 18. The NAFTA was ratified by Congress on November 18, 1993. The House approved the NAFTA by 234 to 200 votes. A bipartisan coalition of 132 Republicans and 102 Democrats prevailed over the opposition of 156 Democrats, 43 Republicans, and 1 independent. The NAFTA marked its tenth anniversary as of December 2003.

The history of the NAFTA is summarized in table 5.3.

Table 5.3. Chronology of the NAFTA Negotiations

June 12, 1991	NAFTA negotiations began. Trade ministers of the United States, Canada, and Mexico met in Toronto, Canada.
August 18, 1992	Negotiations were successfully completed.
September 18, 1992	President George Bush notified Congress under fast-track procedures of his intent to enter into NAFTA.
November 18, 1993	The NAFTA was ratified by Congress.
January 1, 1994	The NAFTA went into effect.

Source: Author's compilation from various sources.

2. Highlights of the NAFTA[17]

Consistent with GATT/WTO, the NAFTA eliminates trade barriers to agriculture, manufacturing, services, and investment within the free trade area. The NAFTA includes provisions that deal with:

- market access by eliminating all tariffs and many nontariff barriers such as import licenses
- rules of origin by which the NAFTA reduces tariffs for goods made in North America measured only in terms of North American parts and labor
- safeguards, bilateral within the NAFTA and global in the multilateral agreement, which provides timely, effective relief from surges in injurious imports
- investment barriers to be eliminated, domestic and foreign investors to be fairly treated, and governmental regulations to be eliminated
- all services markets to open, except aviation transportation, maritime, and basic telecommunications
- intellectual property rights to be protected: patents, copyrights, trademarks, trade secrets, and integrated circuit designs
- access to government procurement contracts in Canada and Mexico for U.S. supplies of petroleum equipment and services, heavy electrical equipment, communication and computer systems, electronics, steel products, pharmaceuticals, and construction equipment
- standard-related measures to prohibit the use of standard and technical regulations as obstacles to trade
- dispute settlement by procedures to be completed in no more than eight months by a (bilateral or trilateral) panel created by the NAFTA Commission.

II. Other Regional Trade Agreements

The United States is active in reaching other regional free trade accords. At the December 1994 Summit of the Americas held in Miami, thirty-four democratic countries within the hemisphere agreed to conclude negotiations for the creation of the Free Trade Area of Americas (FTAA) by the year 2005 in preparation for succession to the NAFTA when it expires. Issues negotiated at various meetings include: Market access, customs procedures, and rules of origin, investment, standards, and technical barriers to trade, sanitary and phytosanitary measures, subsidies, antidumping and countervailing duties, smaller economies, government procurement, intellectual property rights, services, competition policy, and dispute settlement. Once completed, it is expected that the hemispheric FTAA will eliminate tariffs and nontariff barriers on goods and services and establish a single set of rules for fair trade in the region. Discussion regarding extension of the NAFTA to the FTAA continues. The latest meeting of leaders from North and South America was held in Quebec in April 2001. As of November 2003, however, trade talks ended in vague accord. Meanwhile, the administration reached a free trade pact with six Central American countries (CAFTA) in December 2003. There are two other regional trade agreements involving the United States.

The United States has strong interests in trade with the Asia-Pacific region. Regional negotiations in Asia have been or are expected to be in progress through the Asia-Pacific Economic Cooperation (APEC) and the Association of South East Asian Nations (ASEAN).[18] Issues include the opening of markets, normalizing trade, and strengthening the rule of law in this area. The APEC is a regional forum aimed at achieving free and open trade and investment in the region by the year 2010 for industrialized countries and the year 2020 for developing countries. It consists of eighteen countries on both sides of the Pacific. Considerable progress has been made since leaders of eighteen countries held the first meeting at Blake Island, Washington, in 1993. In 1995, they established a plan to achieve APEC's objectives in fourteen substantive trade and trade-related areas, known as the Osaka Action Agenda: tariffs, nontariff measures, services, investment, standards and conformance, customs procedures, intellectual property rights, competition policy, deregulation, government procurement, rules of origin, disputes mediation, mobility of businessmen, and implementation of UR outcomes. During the period from 1996 to 1998, APEC members continued to make further progress by establishing (1) Individual Action Plan; (2) Information Technology Agreement; (3) Early Voluntary Sectoral Liberalization in nine sectors, including environmental goods and services, chemicals, energy sector, medical equipment, forest products, fish and fish products, and telecom MRA (Mutual Recognition Agreement), and six additional sectors for further proposals, including oilseeds, food, automobiles, civil aircraft, fertilizer, and natural and synthetic rubber; (4) Updating and Improving Individual Action Plans; and (5) Trade and Investment Facilitation Measures on the improvement of customs systems, transparent technical regulations, transparent governmental procurement, dispute mediation, completion of an APEC internet tariff database, and alignment of national standards with international standards.

The United States and the EU have worked for a New Transatlantic Market Place (NTMP) since 1995. Together with seventeen specific trade agreements that the United States negotiated with the EU, the MRA and the TEP (the U.S.-EU Transatlantic Economic Partnership) have considerably enhanced trade between the two. The former has improved market access for telecommunications and information technology equipment, network, and electromagnetic compatibility for electrical products, safety for electrical and electronic products and recreational craft, manufacturing practices, pharmaceutical products, and evaluation of medical devices. The latter has reduced barriers to bilateral trade and improved U.S.-EU cooperation on a range of trade issues, especially in the areas of technical standards, agriculture, intellectual property, government procurement, services, electronic commerce, and trade-related labor and environmental issues. In the future, the United States will attempt to expand the MRA/TEP areas, including maritime safety equipment, insurance, architect services, and engineering services.

5.3 BILATERAL AGREEMENTS

Bilateral agreements are another way for ensuring greater market access for U.S. exports of goods, services, and investment. The United States has been steadily making bilateral agreements more and more with trading partners in recent years and monitoring them closely. The numbers of bilateral agreements with the EU (the largest two-way trade and investment relationship in the world with the United States), Japan (United States's third merchandise export market), Korea (United States's fifth largest export market), and China (United States's fourteenth largest market but increasingly large) are exceedingly high.[19] The total volumes of U.S. goods and services trade with these countries are $880.6 billion in 1999 and $930 billion in 2002, respectively. Although American complaints directed to Canada (United States's foremost export market and single largest trading and investment partner) and Mexico (United States's second largest export market) are considerably less than those to the aforementioned countries, presumably because these two counties are members of the NAFTA, there are bilateral agreements with them that are hoped formally to mitigate any trade disputes or complaints.[20]

Japan has always been the prime concern of the United States. However, the single most important U.S. trade policy issue in the recent past was China's admission to the WTO. Henceforth, this section focuses on bilateral agreements with China and Japan. Agreements for other countries will be discussed in chapter 7 in detail.

1. The main objectives were to open China's markets to U.S. exports, to support Chinese domestic economic reform, and to integrate China into the Pacific and world economies. After many years of negotiation, the bilateral agreement, which covers tariff and nontariff barriers to U.S. exports of industrial goods, agricultural products, and services, was completed in November 1999, and China's accession was agreed to by the United States. Bipartisan supports for market-opening policy (dating to the lifting of the trade

embargo in 1972), the Bilateral Commercial Agreement in 1980, and seventeen specific agreements mostly in the 1990s all contributed to the bilateral agreement in 1999. Among the most significant ones are the agreements on intellectual property rights in 1995 and 1996 that led China to close the vast majority of pirated production facilities of CDs and CD-ROMs and cease the exports of those products. The agreement on textiles in 1994 and 1997 reduced China's exports to the United States, and the Agreement on Agricultural Cooperation in April 1999 lifted bans on U.S. exports of citrus, meats, and wheat. Given its growing weight in world output (12 percent in 1998), China became finally a member of the WTO after thirteen years of negotiations.

2. Japan, as the largest Asian trading partner and the world's second-largest economy, has been the major U.S. competitor in trade. The primary objective of U.S. trade policy has always been to reform trade institution, market-opening, and deregulation. The U.S.-Japan Framework Agreement in 1993 addresses sector-specific barriers and underlying structural obstacles and macroeconomics in Japan. The forty-four bilateral agreements made so far (see Table 7.3) are concerned primarily with market-opening in such sectors as telecommunications, medical technology, autos, flat glass, agricultural products, and insurance. The U.S.-Japan Enhanced Initiative on Deregulation and Competition Policy in 1997 has made substantial progress in deregulating and market-opening in key sectors such as telecommunications, housing, energy, financial services, pharmaceuticals, and medical devices.

5.4 RECENT DEVELOPMENT OF MULTILATERAL AGREEMENTS

At the conclusion of the Uruguay Round, it was agreed to begin new multilateral trade negotiations no later than January 1, 2000. The purpose of the negotiations was to expand the scope of trade liberalization and to improve a number of key WTO agreements. The third Ministerial Conference of the WTO was held in Seattle in 1999 (November 30–December 4) for the initiation of new trade negotiations, referred to as the New Round. However, many countries complained about the lack of internal transparency of the WTO, the difficulty of effective participation in the WTO process, and moral (labor standards in LDCs), cultural, and environmental issues in connection with trade. Activists of Nongovernmental Organizations (NGOs) associated with the United Nations protested against the New Round because of disagreement on the agenda between developed countries and poor countries and the developed country-oriented proceedings of the conference. This protest has delayed the target period of formal, comprehensive negotiations of the New Round.

Immediately after the failure of the Seattle Conference, the WTO worked on two issues: transparency and negotiations for the New Round. On the first issue, the WTO tried to improve public relations with NGOs by providing more information and transparency on its activities. On the second issue, the WTO determined to resume negotiations for the New Round under the endorsement of the G-7 meeting (held in Tokyo in January 2000), the G-8 meeting (held in Okinawa in July 2000), the ASEM third meeting (held in Seoul in October 2000), and the APEC eighth meeting (held in Brunei in November 2000).

The United States was in favor of an immediate move toward the New Round toward reducing cross-border barriers to agricultural products and services, a top priority for many U.S. businesses and a built-in agenda that WTO members agreed upon in 1995. Market access, export subsidies, and domestic support in agriculture, and restrictions on services trade and nondiscriminatory treatment in services were the primary issues for intense negotiations. Despite strong opposition to any broad new trade liberalization by many Democrats in Congress, some Perot-type Republicans and a number of industries (textiles, citrus fruits, vegetables, and sugar beats) on the grounds that free trade had cost Americans too many jobs, the United States pursued reform aimed at improving the governance of trade institutions. This goal was crystallized by reconciliation of major trade issues especially with the EU and LDCs, the faithful implementation of commitments and concessions agreed to in the Uruguay Round by WTO members, efforts to ensure compliance through dispute settlement, flexible review of complaints on antidumping regulations, market access in nonagricultural products and electronic commerce, consideration of LDC concerns with labor and environment in connection with trade, and greater interactions with the NGO community for transparency.

The EU was also interested in prompt pursuit of the New Round but only after building up confidence with underdeveloped countries and making progress with the United States on the agenda. Japan continued to contact the United States and the EU to have the New Round launched as early as possible. An emerging country like Korea preferred the immediate start of a comprehensive New Round rather than a gradual approach to it. However, less-developed countries such as India and Brazil were more interested in dealing with LDC concerns such as the improvement of WTO procedures and the observance of WTO agreements prior to the New Round.

The fourth Ministerial Conference of the WTO was held in Doha, Qatar on November 1–13, 2001 for the purpose of resuming the New Round negotiations, the ninth round of the GATT. Two key areas of the built-in agenda for the New Round were the liberalization of trade in agriculture and services, two most fractious areas. Others were concerned with implementing current WTO agreements that included reviews of the Agreements on Trade-Related Aspects of Intellectual Property Rights (TRIPs), Trade-Related Investment

Measures (TRIMs), and the Dispute Settlement Understanding (DSU). The list for negotiation also included market access; that is, negotiations on tariffs and NTBs on all nonagricultural products, trade and competition policy, government procurement, trade facilitation, electronic commerce, trade and the environment, and LDC issues.

Details include:

1. Services

Trade in commercial services is already substantial. In light of the significant proportion of services in world output, however, it is desirable for all countries to trade services more actively.[21] The New Round aims at improving the quality of existing commitments made in the WTO Agreement on Trade in Services (GATS). It deals with further liberalization in basic telecommunications and financial services, and the latter includes distribution, construction, education, health services, maritime transport, air transport, safeguard measures, subsidies, and government procurement.

2. Agriculture

Agriculture is largely regarded as a sector protected chiefly by means of subsidies that have escaped multilateral negotiation during the past fifty years. Currently, agriculture-specific NTBs such as subsidies, import quotas, and minimum import prices are outlawed. The New Round attempts to improve access to agricultural markets in line with comparative advantage. The area of most serious disputes is agriculture. Despite successful completion of the Doha Development Agenda on July 2004 after Cancún Ministerial Conference deadlock on September 2003, protests of farmers in food-importing countries are expected to be strong at the later stage for negotiations on details for tariff/subsidy cuts. Their comparative disadvantage of food protection and prices of farm goods likely to be manipulated by food-exporting countries in the future result in ultimate dependence of food on food exporting countries, which is a matter of survival to them.

3. Trade-Related Aspects of Intellectual Property Rights

This agreement would allow better access in patent protection for drugs to promote the public health of developing countries.

4. Trade-Related Investment Measures

The interruption of OECD negotiations on a Multilateral Agreement on Investment (MAI) has resulted in the need for more comprehensive rules, e.g., a WTO-based investment code incorporating WTO's work on the Relationship between Trade and Investment and the Agreement on Trade-Related Investment Measures.

5. DSB

The Dispute Settlement Body conducted a major review of the dispute settlement procedure, but there was no consensus for specific changes to the process.

6. Market Access

Tariffs imposed on industrial products have been substantially reduced under the GATT and the UR. The New Round intends not only to reduce tariffs and NTBs to industrial products further but also to simplify WTO members' tariff structures and to convert specific duties (tariffs equal to a fixed amount of money per unit) to *ad valorem* duties (tariffs equal to a given percentage of selling price). It also attempted to alleviate LDC's obligation from reciprocating tariff reductions.

7. Transparency in Government Procurement

The absence of transparency in this area is one of the major barriers to market access and the cost of procurement decisions to trading partners. The New Round aims at an agreement on transparency of government procurement.

8. Accession

The total number of member countries in the WTO has been steadily increasing. Accession of a particular country has usually taken three to four years.[22] The WTO attempted to accelerate the admission.

9. LDC

Issues include: a slow-down in timetable for or exclusion from implementation of the UR on LDCs, clarification of the obligations of LDCs in agriculture, subsidies, textiles, technical barriers to trade, trade-related investment measures, and rules of origin.

10. Environment

Negotiations focus on reconciliation between existing WTO rules for trade and environmental agreements.

The Doha Round set the schedule for further negotiations to be concluded by May 2003. It was necessary for the WTO to reconcile different views on the scope and method of negotiations, interests, internal and external positions, and schedules among countries, especially major trading nations and LDCs like India and Brazil. The WTO called on all countries to play their roles in this renewed effort at the fifth Ministerial Conference of the WTO held in Cancún, Mexico in September 2003. However, negotiations set forth at the Doha Conference, broke down amid accusations by developing countries that developed countries refused to make significant concessions. Given the contagion phenomenon of financial crises repeated over time and their apparent relation to trade policies in developed countries, urgent progress should have been made in the above-mentioned areas, including agriculture and service (especially finance) sectors, by the self-imposed deadline of January 1, 2005. At present, however, the Doha Round approaches deadlock in the face of farm subsidy impasse. Table 5.4 presents the chronology of the WTO Ministerial Conference.

5.5 SUMMARY AND CONCLUSIONS

The $GATT_{1947}$ was the long-standing set of rules for contracting nations to conduct international trade and reigned over the multilateral trade system for nearly half a century. Trade policy in every member country was largely dictated by this multilateral trade agreement. Its three main features are MFN, discouragement or elimination of nontariff barriers, and dispute settlement. Its success in promoting and securing trade liberalization is incontestable.

Table 5.4. Chronology of the WTO Ministerial Conferences

Conference	Year	Place	Main Agenda
1st	December 9–13, 1996	Singapore	Roles of the WTO; performance evaluation of WTO agreement and development of world trade; Ministerial Declaration
2nd	May 18–20, 1988	Geneva	GATT-WTO's 50th Anniversary; Ministerial Declaration on electronic business
3rd	November 30–December 3, 1999	Seattle	New Round; failure to reach Ministerial Declaration
4th	November 8–13, 2001	Doha	New Round launched
5th	September 2003	Cancún	Negotiation failed

Source: Author's compilation from various sources.

However, GATT's narrow scope and limited role resulted in the Uruguay Round, the most comprehensive multilateral trade agreement that has devoted to further trade liberalization and administrative reforms. The WTO created under the UR agreement is responsible for full and effective implementation of the UR agreement. Unlike the settlements by $GATT_{1947}$, the WTO ensures binding dispute settlements. Under the Doha Round, countries still intend to make greater achievement in many areas, especially agriculture, toward multilateral trade liberalization. Nevertheless, Cancún deadlock that led LDCs to abandon WTO negotiations may be a sign of the limits to globalization.

Regionalism emerged in the United States in the 1980s and the 1990s, which resulted in the creation of NAFTA in the early 1990s. Other post-NAFTA free trade agreements are in progress. Countless bilateral agreements made during the two decades came into existence in an effort to promote free trade by the United States.

U.S. trade policy under the WTO is significantly different from conventional trade policy under the $GATT_{1947}$. It is a multifaceted policy characterized by multilateral agreements, regional negotiations, and bilateral initiatives, along with U.S. trade laws. In the future, the United States is likely to seek boundary expansions in the coverage of areas and regions for trade and to honor important values on trade-related environment, labor standards, and consumer protection issues in accordance with the Doha Round. However, the progress of the Doha Round is sluggish.

APPENDIX 5.1: HOUSE ROLL CALL
VOTES ON THE URUGUAY ROUND

State	Party	Representative and Vote
Alabama	Democrats:	Beville(Y) Browder(N) Cramer(N) Hilliard(N)
	Republicans:	Bachus(N) Callahan(Y) Everett(N)
Alaska	Republican:	Young(N)
Arizona	Democrats:	Coppersmith(Y) English(Y) Pastor(Y)
	Republicans:	Kolbe(Y) Kyl(Y) Stump(N)
Arkansas	Democrats:	Lambert(Y) Thornton(Y)
	Republicans:	Dickey(N) Hutchison(N)
California	Democrats:	Beccera(Y) Bilenson(Y) Berman(Y) Brown(Y) Condit(N) Dellums(N) Dixon(Y) Dooley(Y) Edwards(N) Eshoo(Y) Farr(Y) Fazio(Y)

State	Party	Representative and Vote
		Filner(Y) Hamburg(N) Harman(Y) Lantos(N) Lehman(Y) Martinez(Y) Matsui(Y) Miller(N) Mineta(Y) Pelosi(Y) Roybal-Allard(Y) Schenk(Y) Stark(N) Torres(Y) Tucker(N) Waters(Y) Waxman(N) Woolsey(N)
	Republicans:	Baker(Y) Calvert(Y) Cox(Y) Cunningham(Y) Doolittle(N) Doman(N) Dreier(Y) Gallegly(N) Herger(Y) Horn(Y) Huffingtron(Y) Hunter(N) Kim(Y) Lewis(Y) McCandless(Y) McKeon(Y) Moorhead(N) Packard(Y) Pombo(N) Rohrabacher(N) Royce(N) Thomas(Y)
Colorado	Democrats:	Schroeder(Y) Skaggs(Y)
	Republicans:	Allard(Y) Hefley(N) McInnis(N) Schaefer(N)
Connecticut	Democrats:	DeLauro(Y) Gejdenson(Y) Kennelly(Y)
	Republicans:	Franks(Y) Johnson(Y) Shys(Y)
Delaware	Republican:	Castle(Y)
Florida	Democrats:	Hastings(N) Hutto(Y) Johnston(Y) Meek(Y) Peterson(Y) Thurman(N)
	Republicans:	Bilirakis(N) Canady(Y) Diaz-Balart(N) Fowler(Y) Goos(Y) Lewis(Y) McCollum(Y) Mica(N) Miller(Y) Ros-Lehtinen(N) Shaw(Y) Steams(N) Young(Y)
Georgia	Democrats:	Bishop(Y) Darden(Y) Deal(N) Johnson(Y) Lewis(N) McKinney(N) Rowland(Y)
	Republicans:	Collins(N) Gingrich(Y) Kingston(N) Linder(Y)
Hawaii	Democrats:	Abercrombie(Y) Mink(N)
Idaho	Democrats:	LaRocco(Y)
	Republicans:	Crapo(N)
Illinois	Democrats:	Collins(N) Costello(N) Durbin(Y) Evans(N) Gutierrez(N) Lipinski(N)

State	Party	Representative and Vote
		Poshard(Y) Reynolds(Y)
		Rowstenkowski(Y) Rush(N)
		Sangmeister(Y) Yates(Y)
	Republicans:	Crane(Y) Ewing(Y) Fawell(Y)
		Hastert(Y) Hyde(Y) Manzullo(Y)
		Michel(Y) Porter(Y)
Indiana	Democrats:	Hamilton(Y) Jacobs(Y) Long(Y)
		McClosky(Y) Roemer(Y) Sharp(Y)
		Visclosky(Y)
	Republicans:	Burton(N) Buyer(Y) Myers(N)
Iowa	Democrat:	Smith(Y)
	Republicans:	Grandy(Y) Leach(Y) Lightfoot(Y)
		Nussie(Y)
Kansas	Democrats:	Glickman(N) Slattery(Y)
	Republicans:	Meyers(Y) Roberts(Y)
Kentucky	Democrats:	Baesler(Y) Barlow(N) Mazzoli(Y)
	Republicans:	Bunning(Y) Lewis(N) Rogers(N)
Lousiana	Democrats:	Fields(N) Hays(N) Jefferson(Y)
		Tauzin(Y)
	Republicans:	Bakers(Y) Livingston(N)
		McCrery(Y)
Maine	Democrat:	Andrews(N)
	Republicans:	Snowe(N)
Maryland	Democrats:	Cardin(Y) Hoyer(Y) Mfume(N)
		Wynn(Y)
	Republicans:	Bartlett(Y) Bentley(N) Gilchrest(Y)
		Morella(Y)
Massachusetts	Democrats:	Frank(N) Kennedy(Y) Markey(Y)
		Meehan(Y) Moaldey(N) Neal(Y)
		Olver(Y) Studds(Y)
	Republicans:	Blute(N) Torkildsen(Y)
Michigan	Democrats:	Barcia(N) Bonior(N) Carr(Y)
		Collins(N) Conyers(N) Dingell(Y)
		Ford(N) Kildee(N) Levin(Y)
		Stupak(N)
	Republicans:	Camp(Y) Ehlers(Y) Hoekstra(Y)
		Knollenberg(Y) Smith(Y)
		Upton(Y)
Minnesota	Democrats:	Minge(Y) Oberstar(N) Penny(Y)
		Peterson(N) Sabo(N) Vento(Y)
	Republicans:	Grams(Y) Ramstad(Y)

State	Party	Representative and Vote
Mississipi	Democrats:	Mongomery(N) Parker(Y) Taylor(N) Thompson(N) Whitten(Y)
Missouri	Democrats:	Clay(N) Danner(N) Gephardt(Y) Skelton(Y) Volmer(N) Wheat(Y)
	Republicans:	Emerson(Y) Hancock(N) Talent(Y)
Montana	Democrat:	Williams(N)
Nebraska	Democrats:	Hoaglaand(Y)
	Republicans:	Barrett(Y) Bereuter(Y)
Nevada	Democrat:	Bilbray(N)
	Republicans:	Vucanovich(Y)
New Hampshire	Democrat:	Swett(N)
	Republican:	Zeliff(Y)
New Jersey	Democrats:	Andrews(N) Hughes(Y) Klein(Y) Menendez(Y) Pallone(N) Payne(N) Torricelli(Y)
	Republicans:	Franks(Y) Roukema(Y) Saxton(Y) Smith(N) Zimmer(Y)
New Mexico	Democrat:	Richardson(Y)
	Republicans:	Schiff(N) Skeen(N)
New York	Democrats:	Ackerman(Y) Engel(N) Flake(Y) Hinchey(N) Hochbrueckener(N) LaFalce(Y) Lowey(Y) Maloney(Y) Manton(Y) McNutty(Y) Nadler(N) Owens(N) Raangel(N) Schumer(Y) Serrano(Y) Slughter(Y) Towns(N) Velasquez(N)
	Republicans:	Boehlert(Y) Fish(Y) Gilman(Y) Houghton(Y) King(Y) Lazio((Y) Levy(Y) McHugh(N) Molinari(Y) Paxon(Y) Quinn(N) Solomon(N) Walsh(Y)
North Carolina	Democrats:	Clayton(Y) Hefner(N) Lancaster(Y) Neal(Y) Price(Y) Rose(N) Valentine(Y) Watt(N)
	Republicans:	Ballenger(Y) Coble(N) McMillan(Y) Taylor(N)
North Dakota	Democrat:	Pomeroy(Y)
Ohio	Democrats:	Applegate(N) Brown(N) Fingerhut(Y) Hall(Y) Kaptur(N) Mann(Y) Sawyer(Y) Stokes(N) Strickland(N) Traficant(N)

State	Party	Representative and Vote
	Republicans:	Boehner(Y) Gillmor(Y) Hobson(Y) Hoke(Y) Kasich(Y) Oxley(Y) Portman(Y) Pryce(Y) Regula(Y)
Oklahoma	Democrats:	Brewster(Y) McCurdy(Y) Synar(Y)
	Republicans:	Istook(N) Largent(N) Lucas(N)
Oregon	Democrats:	DeFazio(N) Furse(Y) Kopetski(Y) Wyden(Y)
	Republican:	Smith(Y)
Pennsylvania	Democrats:	Blackwell(Y) Borski(Y) Coyne(Y) Foglietta(Y) Holden(N) Kanjorski(N) Klink(N) Margolis-Mezvinsky(Y) McHale(Y) Murphy(N) Murtha(Y)
	Republicans:	Clinger(Y) Gekas(Y) Goodling(Y) Greenwood(Y) McDade(Y) Ridge(Y) Santorum(Y) Shuster(Y) Walker(Y) Weldon(Y)
Rhode Island	Democrat:	Reed(Y)
	Republican:	Machtley(Y)
South Carolina	Democrats:	Clybum((Y) Derrick(Y) Spratt(N)
	Republicans:	Inglis(N) Ravenel(N) Spence(N)
South Dakota	Democrat:	Johnson(Y)
Tennessee	Democrats:	Clement(Y) Cooper(Y) Ford(Y) Gordon(Y) Lloyd(Y) Tanner(Y)
	Republicans:	Duncan(N) Quilien(Y) Sundquist(Y)
Texas	Democrats:	Andrews(Y) Brooks(Y) Bryant(Y) Chapman(N) Coleman(Y) de la Garza(Y) Edwards(Y) Frost(Y) Geren(Y) Gonzalez(N) Green(Y) Hall(N) Johnson, E. B.(Y) Laughlin(Y) Ortiz(Y) Pickle(Y) Sarpalius(Y) Stenholm(Y) Tejada(Y) Washington(Y) Wilson(Y)
	Republicans:	Archer(Y) Armey(Y) Barton(Y) Bonilla(Y) Combest(N) DeLay(Y) Fields(Y) Johnson, S.(N) Smith(Y)
Utah	Democrats:	Orton(Y) Shepherd(Y)
	Republicans:	Hansen(Y)
Vermont	Independent:	Sanders(N)

State	Party	Representative and Vote
Virginia	Democrates:	Boucher(Y) Byrne(Y) Moran(Y) Payne(N) Pickett(Y) Scott(Y) Sisisky(N)
	Republicans:	Bateman(Y) Bliley(Y) Goodlatte (Y) Wolfe(N)
Washington	Democrats:	Cantwell(Y) Dicks(Y) Foley(Y) Inslee(Y) Kreider(Y) McDermott(Y) Swift(Y) Unsoeid(N)
	Republicans:	Dunn(Y)
West Virginia	Democrats:	Mollohan(N) Rahall(N) Wise(N)
Wisconsin	Democrats:	Barca(N) Barrett(Y) Kleczka(Y) Obey(N)
	Republicans:	Gunderson(N) Klug(N) Petri(Y) Roth(N) Sensenbrenner(N)
Wyoming	Republicans:	Thomas(Y)

Note: Y =Yea and N = Nay.
Source: U.S. House of Representatives, *Congressional Quarterly Almanac*, and *CQ Weekly* (Washington, D.C.: U.S. GPO, 1988).

APPENDIX 5.2:   SENATE ROLL CALL VOTES ON THE URUGUAY ROUND

Democrats for
Akaka(Hawaii)   Biden(Delaware)   Bingaman(New Mexico)
Boxer(California)   Bradley(New Jersey)   Breaux(Lousiana)
Bumpers(Arkansas)   Conrad(North Dakota)   Dachle(South Dakota)
DeConcini(Arizona)   Dodd(Connecticut)   Feinstein(California)
Ford(Kentucky)   Glenn(Ohio)   Graham(Florida)   Kennedy(Massachusetts)
Kerrey(Nebraska)   Kerry(Massachusetts)   Kohl(Wisconsin)
Lautenberg(New Jersey)   Levin(Michigan)   Lieberman(Connecticut)
Mathews(Tennessee)   Mikulski(Maryland)   Mitchell(Maine)
Braun(Illinois) Moynihan(New York)   Murray(Washington)   Nunn(Georgia)
Pell(Rhode Island)   Pryor(Arkansas)   Riegle(Michigan)   Robb(Virginia)
Rockefeller(West Virginia)   Sarbanes(Maryland)   Sasser(Tennessee)
Simon(Illinois)   Wafford(Pennsylvania)

Republicans for
Bennett(Utah)   Bond(Missouri)   Chafee(Rhode Island)   Coats(Indiana)
Cochran(Mississippi)   Cohen (Maine)   Coverdell(Georgia)

D'Amato(New York)   Danforth(Missouri)   Dole(Kansas)
Domenici(New Mexico)   Durenberger(Minnesota)   Faircloth(North
Carolina)   Gorton(Washington)   Gramm(Texas)   Grassely(Iowa)
Gregg(New Hampshire)   Hatch(Utah)   Hatfield(Oregon)
Hutchison(Texas)   Kassebaum(Kansas)   Lott(Mississippi)
Lugar(Indiana)   Mack(Florida)   McCain(Arizona)
McConnell(Kentucky)   Murkowski(Alaska)   Nickles(Oklahoma)
Packwood(Oregon)   Pressler(South Dakota)   Roth(Delaware)
Simpson(Wyoming)   Specter(Pennsylvania)   Wallop(Wyoming)
Warner(Virginia)

Democrats Against
Baucus(Colorado)   Bryan(Nevada)   Byrd(West Virginia)
Campbell(Colorado)   Dorgan(North Dakota)   Exon(Nebraska)
Feingold(Wisconsin)   Heflin(Alabama)   Hollings(South Carolina)
Leahy(Vermont)   Metzenbaum(Ohio)   Reid(Nevada)
Wellstone(Minnestota)

Republican Against
Brown(Colorado)   Burns(Montana)   Craig(Idaho)   Helms(North
Carolina)   Inhofe(Oklahoma)   Jeffords(Vermont)   Kempthorne(Idaho)
Shelby(Alabama)   Smith(New Hampshire)   Smith(New Hampshire)
Stevens(Alaska)   Thurmond(South Carolina)

Source: U.S. House of Representatives, *Congressional Quarterly Almanac*,
and *CQ Weekly* (Washington, D.C.: U.S. GPO, 1988).

APPENDIX 5.3:   HIGHLIGHTS OF
THE U.S.-CANADA TRADE PACT

The two countries agreed:

1. Market Access
   To eliminate all tariffs and nontariff trade barriers within one, five, or ten
   years, beginning from January 1, 1989.
2. Agriculture
   To eliminate all agricultural tariffs within ten years and to eliminate license
   requirements for U.S. wheat and grain shipments to Canada. However, both
   nations agreed to exempt each other from meat-import laws.

3. Government Procurement
   To open the government procurement markets for free and fair competition.
4. Automotive
   To eliminate all automotive tariffs over the next five to ten years. The two countries agreed to allow U.S. auto makers to manufacture cars and parts in Canada for duty-free sale in the United States but denied any similar future benefits to Japanese or Koreans.
5. Services
   To establish the first comprehensive trade agreement to include trade in services, including financial service sector.
6. Investment
   To prohibit discrimination against investment from the partner country, to eliminate rules requiring an investor to export a certain percentage of production or to give preference to local inputs, to require fair compensation for exportation, and to guarantee free transfer of capital and profits.
7. Disputes
   To create a binding dispute-settlement mechanism and to resolve disagreements through arbitration.

Source: Hawkins, Jeff, "NAFTA Improves Trading Opportunities with Canada," in U.S. Department of Commerce, *Business America* (October 1992), 30–32.

NOTES

1. See USTR, *1998 Trade Policy Agenda and 1997 Annual Report* (Washington, D.C.: U.S. GPO), 7 and various other issues including the latest one.

2. See U.S. Department of State, *General Agreement on Tariffs and Trade* I (Washington, D.C.: U.S. GPO, 1949), 7. At that time, twenty-three countries agreed to draft the Charter for an International Trade Organization (ITO). The Charter was similar to the WTO today. The ITO was designed to provide not only a disciplined structure for world trade but also contained rules relating to employment, commodity agreements, restrictive business practices, international investment, and services. Although the ITO Charter was agreed to at a United Nations Conference on Trade and Development (UNCTAD) in Havana in March 1948, it fell through because the United States did not intend to seek Congressional ratification.

3. See Joseph H. Stiglitz, *Globalization and its Discontents* (New York, NY: 2002), 89–132. However, the Council of Economic Advisors (2004) suggests that foreign coun-

tries rely on U.S. financial services and that, as the world's top exporter of financial services with exports of roughly $16 billion in 2002, the United States stabilized Mexico's financial sector.

4. This section is based on U.S. Department of State, General Agreement on Tariffs and Trade I, (Washington, D.C.: U.S. GPO, 1949), USTR, *Final Texts of the GATT Uruguay Round Agreements Including The Agreement Establishing The World Trade Organization* in Marrakech, Morocco, (Washington, D.C.: U.S. GPO, April 15, 1994) and World Trade Organization, *WTO* (St. Juste-la-Pendue, France: 1995). Also, see Bernard M. Hoeckman and Michael M. Kostecki, *The Political Economy of the World Trading System from GATT to WTO* (Oxford: Oxford University Press, 1996).

5. The United States brought more cases than any other country did. See U.S. House of Representatives, Committee on Ways and Means, *World Trade Organization, Hearing before Committee on Ways and Means* (Washington, D.C.: U.S. GPO, 1994), 17.

6. Plurilateral Agreements on fair trade cover civil aircraft, open competition of government procurement, special arrangements for the dairy sector, and assistance for trade in meat.

7. The United States negotiated with China for its WTO admission for over ten years through various bilateral agreements and recently endorsed China's accession; China finally became a member in 2001.

8. Member countries in the European Community had a number of votes equal to the number of member countries. The European Union is a member in its own right as is each of its member states.

9. Four additional committees are the Committee on Trade and Environment, Committee on Trade and Development, Committee on Balance-of-Payments Restrictions, and Committee on Budget, Finance and Administration. There are four councils on plurilateral agreements. They are the International Meat Council, International Dairy Council, Committee on Government Procurement, and Committee on Trade in Civil Aircraft.

10. The committees that assist the Council on Trade in Goods are the Committee on Market Access, Committee on Agriculture, Committee on Sanitary and Phytosanitary Measures, Committee on Trade-Related Investment Measures, Committee on Rules of Origin, Committee on Subsidies and Countervailing Measures, Committee on Customs Valuation, Committee on Technical Barriers to Trade, Committee on Anti-Dumping Practices, Committee on Import Licensing, Committee on Safeguards, and Textile Monitoring Body. The committees that assist the Council for Trade in Services are the Working Party on Professional Services, Committee on Trade in Financial Services, Negotiating Group on Maritime Transport Services, Negotiating Group on Movement of Natural Persons, and Negotiating Group on Basic Telecommunications.

11. The four biggest traders—the EU, United States, Japan and Canada—are examined approximately once every two years; the next sixteen countries in terms of their share of world trade are reviewed every four years; and the remaining countries every six years or longer.

12. If the appellate body upholds the panel's finding, the defending country would have to modify its regulations or face penalties.

13. Note that both GATT$_{1947}$ and the UR recognize regional trading arrangements.

14. See appendix 5.3 for highlights of the CFTA.

15. Trade creation means the replacement of domestic production by imports from a lower-production-cost country within the preferential trade arrangement (for example, a customs union); trade diversion means the replacement of imports from a lower-production-cost country by imports from a higher-production-cost country within the same preferential trade arrangement.

16. See note 17 of chapter 2 for the history of fast-track authority.

17. See U.S. Department of Commerce, International Trade Administration, *North American Free Trade Agreement* (Washington, D.C.: U.S. GPO, 1992) and other DOC publications and documents, such as *Uruguay Round Update* (1994), *The Case for NAFTA* (1995), and *NAFTA Facts*, document nos. 1020, 4003, 8101, and 8102 (1996). See appendix III to this book for the key areas.

18. The twenty-one APEC member countries are Australia, Brunei, Canada, Chile, China, Hong Kong, Indonesia, Japan, Korea, Malaysia, Mexico, New Zealand, Papua New Guinea, Peru, Philippines, Russia, Singapore, Taipei, Thailand, the United States, and Vietnam. The ten ASEAN member countries are Brunei, Cambodia, Indonesia, Laos, Malaysia, Burma, the Philippines, Singapore, Thailand, and Vietnam.

19. See table 7.3 for numbers of bilateral agreements. The European Union grew from fifteen member countries to twenty-five on May 1, 2004, eight of which are former communist countries in Eastern Europe. Fifteen original member countries are Austria, Belgium, Denmark, Finland, France, Germany, Greece, Ireland, Italy, Luxembourg, the Netherlands, Portugal, Spain, Sweden, and the United Kingdom. Ten new members are Cypress, Czech Republic, Estonia, Hungary, Latvia, Lithuania, Malta, Poland, Slovakia, Slovenia. Bulgaria, Romania, and Turkey remain as candidate countries. Although the GDP of new members as a whole in 2002 is relatively small in comparison with that of previous fifteen member countries, the economic size of the EU is now even greater. U.S. bilateral agreements made with the EU in the future are expected to increase considerably.

20. See USTR, *Trade Policy Agenda and Annual Report* (Washington, D.C.: U.S. GPO, various issues).

21. Importance of trade in services is growing in the world economy. Worldwide services trade totaled $1.5 trillion in 2002, compared to goods trade of over $6 trillion, but services trade has been growing faster. The service sector is the largest component of the private economy in the United States. It provides more than 86 million jobs in the United States in 2003 and accounts for over half of GDP. In 2002, the United States exported services worth almost $300 billion, about 30 percent of total exports of goods and services. See Council of Economic Advisers, *Economic Report of the President* (Washington, D.C.: U.S. GPO, February 2004), 228.

22. The countries that recently joined the WTO are China, Russia, Taiwan, and Saudi Arabia. Other countries include most of the countries of the former U.S.S.R., some Balkan and Asian countries, and some less-developed countries.

Part II

U.S. TRADE POLICY, SOCIAL COST, AND POLICY REFORM

Chapter 6

Trade Policy Institutions

Trade legislation and trade policy are the domain of Congress. Unlike during the eighteenth and nineteenth centuries, when Congress sets tariff rates, trade policy encompasses a broad spectrum of arguments today. Congress has carried out its constitutional mandate by increasingly transferring authority to the executive branch over time, requiring many agencies in the executive branch to become involved in formulating and implementing trade policy. The U.S. trade policy formation is highly complex, and often politicized by interbranch as well as interagency decision-making processes.

This chapter examines the roles and responsibilities of each of the U.S. trade policy institutions and their interactions to develop and execute trade policy.[1] The first section discusses the roles of Congress. The second section examines major trade policy agencies in the administration, including the United States Trade Representative (USTR) and the International Trade Administration (ITA). The third section deals with the International Trade Commission (ITC). The fourth section focuses on private sector advisory committees. The fifth section explores implications of the interaction between policy institutions. The last section summarizes the chapter and draws conclusions.

6.1 THE LEGISLATIVE BRANCH

As discussed in chapter 1, Congress is responsible for making trade laws and thus ultimately trade policy. However, the Administration carries out many authorizations to it by the Congress, such as tariff and NTB negotiations for trade agreements, the administration of trade remedy laws, and trade adjustment assistance.

Congressional transfers or authorizations have generally been granted to the Administration through the enactment of trade laws listed below:

- The Reciprocal Trade Agreements Act of 1934 authorized the President to negotiate international trade agreements for the reduction of tariffs.
- By the late 1940s to the early 1950s, the U.S. Trade Commission acquired greater authority from Congress.
- The Trade Expansion Act of 1962 authorized the President to negotiate the Kennedy Round, the sixth round of the GATT.
- The Trade Act of 1974 extended substantially the presidential authority to include not only tariff but also NTB negotiations. It authorized the President to enter into the Tokyo Round, the seventh round of the GATT.
- The Administration was authorized to implement the Tokyo Round agreement by the Trade Act of 1979.
- The Omnibus Trade and Competitiveness Act of 1988 required the President to negotiate the Uruguay Round, to respond to Congressional requests for consultation on trade issues, and to formulate an annual trade policy agenda. Also, the ITC, the ITA, and the USTR carry out the vast majority of U.S. trade remedy law cases. However, Congress maintains a tracking system on the performance of the Administration by requiring the Administration to submit an annual trade policy agenda and report.

The five advisors from each chambers (from the Committee on Ways and Means and the Committee on Finance, respectively) are formally appointed under statute. The USTR keeps these advisors informed of U.S. objectives, the status of negotiations, and changes to U.S. trade laws. The USTR transmits any trade agreement to Congress and advises Congress on trade issues, and submits lists of priority countries and priority practices subject to Super 301 and Special 301. In addition, Congress requires the President to submit annual reports regarding actions taken under various trade provisions and on programs and trade policy developments. The ITC, a trade institution independent of the executive branch, must also submit annual reports to Congress regarding actions taken under various trade provisions.

6.2 THE EXECUTIVE BRANCH

1. National Economic Council

The National Economic Council (NEC; formerly the Economic Policy Council) is the ultimate economic policy-making authority, including trade policy, in the executive branch.[2] It was established in 1933 by a Presidential

Executive Order within the Office of Policy Development and is part of the Executive Office of the President. The purpose of the council is to advise the President on matters related to domestic and global economic policy. The NEC's primary functions are:

- To coordinate economic policy
- To ensure that policy decisions and programs are consistent with the President's economic goals
- To monitor implementation of the President's economic policy.
- The President is the chair of the NEC. Its members are composed of the USTR, the Secretaries of the Departments of Commerce, State, Treasury, Agriculture, Labor, Housing and Urban Development, Transportation, and Energy, the Administrator of the Environment Protection Agency, the Chair of the Council of Economic Advisers, the Director of the Office of Management and Budget, the National Security Advisor, and Assistants to the President for Economic Policy, Domestic Policy, and Science and Technology Policy.

2. The United States Trade Representative

By law, the United States Trade Representative (USTR) plays the key role in the development of U.S. policy on trade and trade-related investment and interagency coordination on trade policy matters.[3] The history of the USTR begins with the Trade Expansion Act of 1962. This law established the Office of the Special Representative for Trade Negotiations (often referred to as the Special Trade Representative: STR). Its main purpose was to implement U.S. trade policies and to negotiate all trade agreements, including the Kennedy Round, and programs under the Smoot-Hawley Tariff Act of 1930 and the Trade Reform Act of 1974. Partly for the Tokyo Round of multilateral trade negotiations, the Trade Act of 1974 expanded the role of the STR to that equivalent to the Cabinet level with the rank of Ambassador within the Executive Office of the President.

Pursuant to Section 1109 of the Trade Agreements Act of 1979, the USTR succeeded the STR under the Reorganization Plan of Executive Order in 1979 that authorized the USTR to set and administer overall trade policy. In addition to being the Chairman of the Trade Policy committee, the USTR serves as the principal advisor and chief spokesperson to the President on international trade policy. The USTR is also the chief trade negotiator and the representative of the United States in the major international trade organizations. Note that the USTR took the responsibility for the Uruguay Round, the NAFTA, and many bilateral trade negotiations. Section 1601 describes important functions and the responsibility of the USTR in further detail.[4] In addition to all the aforementioned responsibilities, the Omnibus Trade and Competitiveness Act of 1988 requires the USTR to develop and coordinate trade policy with other agencies, and to implement major U.S. trade policies. The Office of the USTR is composed of three deputy USTRs, General Counsel, Counselor, and two Special Counsels under the USTR. Two deputies are responsible for the coordination of trade policies and trade negotiations and one in Geneva is responsible for U.S. trade policy at the WTO and the UNCTAD. There are thirteen assistant USTRs. Eight of them are responsible for: dispute resolution, public affairs, congressional affairs, intergovernmental affairs public liaison, multilateral trade negotiations, GATT affairs, industry, and intellectual property and environment; and five of them are in charge of five different geographical areas. Two additional offices that support the USTR are the offices of Chief Textile Negotiator and Executive Director for Trade Policy Coordination.

Although the USTR is supposed to act subject to the specific direction of the President, the OTCA requires the USTR to report to both Congress and the President, and to be responsible to both for the administration of the trade agreements program, including advising on nontariff barriers and international commodity agreements. Note that Congress has moved the responsibility for implementing actions from the President to the USTR.

The primary responsibilities of the USTR are specifically as follows:

- Enforcement of part of the principal trade remedy provisions such as section 301, Super 301, Special 301 and section 201, and other provisions such as section 1337 of the OTCA (telecommunications) and Executive Order 13116 of 1999, which reinstated certain elements of Title II of the OTCA (government procurement).[5]
- All matters within the WTO
- Trade, commodity, direct investment managed by the OECD and the UNCTAD
- Expansion of market access for American goods and services
- Industrial and services trade policy
- International commodity agreements and policy
- Bilateral and multilateral trade investment issues
- Trade-related intellectual property protection issues
- Negotiations affecting U.S. import policies
- Generalized Scheme of Preference (GSP).

3. *Trade Policy Committee*

For the purpose of development of international trade policies and trade-related investment issues, the Trade Expansion Act of 1962 required the President to establish an interagency trade policy system.[6] The Trade Policy Committee (TPC) was formed for this exclusive purpose. Figure 6.1 shows the interagency process of trade policy formation. The Omnibus Trade and Competitiveness Act of 1988 specifically requires the USTR to be the chair of the TPC and to report directly to Congress.[7] The TPC consists of cabinet-level members. They are the Secretaries of the Departments of Commerce, State, Treasury, Agriculture, Labor, and other relevant agencies invited by the USTR. The USTR conducts interagency coordination on trade policy matters through the TPC that has two subcabinet coordination groups composed of seventeen federal agencies and agencies: the Trade Policy Review Group (TPRG) and Trade Policy Staff Committee (TPSC). The former is an interagency group of assistant secretary-level members and the latter is a working-level interagency group. In the event of a lack of consensus at the TPSC level, issues are forwarded to the TPRG. Failure to reach an agreement at the TPRG brings in review of the TPC. TPRG and TPSC consist of members from the Departments of Commerce, Agriculture, State, Treasury, Labor, Justice, Defense, Interior, Transportation, Energy, and Health and Human Services, the Environmental Protection Agency, the Office of Management and Budget, the Council of Economic Advisers, the International Development Cooperation Agency, the National Economic Council, the National Security Council, and the USITC (a nonvoting member of the TPSC and an observer at TPRG meetings). Approximately sixty subcommittees drawn from the office-director level of the member agencies and several task forces support the work of the TPSC.

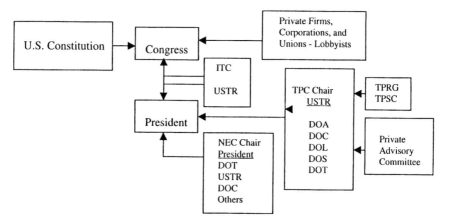

Figure 6.1. Interagency Process for Trade Policy Formation
Source: Author's compilation from U.S. House of Representatives, Committee on Ways and Means, *Overview and Compilation of U.S. Trade Statutes* (Washington, D.C.: U.S. GPO), 1995, 961–1017.

At TPC meetings, the Department of Commerce acts as the central department, addressing the U.S. trade policy agenda and key issues. Within the Department, the International Trade Administration (ITA) is the principal agency conducting U.S. trade policy, including the countervailing and the antidumping duties. The ITA will be separately discussed in the subsequent section of this chapter. Another trade-related agency in the Department is the Economic Development Administration (EDA) and the Bureau of Economic Analysis (BEA). The EDA administers the trade adjustment assistance program for firms and industries in accordance with Title II, Chapter 3, of the Trade Act of 1974, as amended. The Balance of Payments Division in the BEA produces statistics on international trade and feeds into GDP estimates. The State Department typically provides a long-range policy perspective on foreign economic matters, including policies on foreign investment, natural resources and food, international trade, and international finance and development. Within this Department, the Bureau of Economic and Business Affairs, headed by the Undersecretary for Economic and Agricultural Affairs, has overall responsibility for these issues.

The Secretary of the Treasury Department serves as the principal economic advisor to the President, the U.S. Governor of the IMF, the World Bank, other area development banks, and the Chairman of the National Advisory Council on International Monetary and Financial Policies. The Treasury Secretary also plays a key role in formulating and overseeing economic and financial policy, tax policy, public debt management, and various law enforcement functions. The Office of Assistant Secretary for International Affairs in the Treasury Department is responsible for international monetary affairs, developing nations, and international trade and investment. The U.S. Customs Service, a separate agency under the Treasury, collects import duties and enforces more than four hundred laws or regulations relating to international trade. Its responsibilities include assessing and collecting antidumping duties (AD) and countervailing duties (CVD).

The objective of the Agriculture Department is to expand foreign markets for U.S. agricultural products. The Department ensures that trade policy decisions take into account agricultural interests. The Secretary advises the President on foreign markets for U.S. agricultural products, enforces and administers certain elements of cheese quotas and meat imports, and coordinates negotiations with foreign governments on standard-related matters in agricultural trade and monitoring activities. Within the Department, the Foreign Agricultural Service, with support from agricultural attachés at U.S. embassies and other specialists, conducts international trade functions. They include lowering foreign trade barriers to U.S. farm goods and managing both the Public Law 480 program and the Commodity Credit Corporation Export Credit Sales Program.[8]

The Department of Labor is primarily concerned with the employment of U.S. workers and the improvement of wage earners' income in connection with U.S. trade policies. Within the Department, the Bureau of International Labor Affairs headed by the Deputy Undersecretary for International Labor Affairs is in charge of the formulation of international economic and trade policies affecting U.S. workers, while the Employment and Training Administration (ETA) is responsible for administration of the trade adjustment assistance program for workers. This program was authorized under both Title II, Chapter 2, of the Trade Act of 1974, as amended, and the NAFTA Implementation Act.

The two different positions of the USTR exemplify interbranch politics between Congress and the President. Congress receives reports on the trade agenda and policy issues directly from the USTR, who is the chair of the TPC by the Trade Act of 1988. The President, who is the chair of the NEC, retains the USTR as a member of the NEC. Such interbranch politics results in inefficiencies in U.S. trade policy formation and implementation including timing problems and the wasteful use of scarce resources.[9]

4. International Trade Administration

The International Trade Administration (ITA) is the main trade policy agency in the Department of Commerce. Headed by the Undersecretary for International Trade, the ITA helps U.S. businesses participate fully in the growing world market. Specifically, operations of ITA's four units are:[10]

- Trade Development Unit identifies trade opportunities for specific products or services, supports trade negotiations, and conducts market analysis. The unit reaches out to U.S. businesses through its Industry Sector Advisory Committees, President's Export Council, and Advocacy Center.
- Market Access and Compliance Unit ensures whether foreign countries comply with trade agreements in order to keep world market open to U.S. products.
- Import Administration is responsible for enforcement of sections 701 and 731 to protect American companies from less-than-fair value (LTFV) trade practices conducted by foreign countries.
- Commercial Service provides American firms with market information, trade leads, overseas business contacts, and promotional opportunities through its global network of Commercial Offices. The U.S. Foreign Commercial Service (USFCS) in the ITA provides counseling and marketing assistance to U.S. exporters through 100 domestic offices and 140 overseas posts.

6.3 THE INTERNATIONAL TRADE COMMISSION

The International Trade Commission (ITC) is an independent, nonpartisan, quasi-judicial federal agency. Congress established the ITC in 1916 as the U.S. Tariff Commission and renamed it as the U.S. International Trade Commission by the Trade Act of 1974. The ITC has broad investigative powers on trade matters and makes policy recommendations to the President and Congress. The Commission is responsible for:

- Investigation and determination of injury caused by subsidized or dumped foreign goods (sections 701 and 731)[11] and of import relief for domestic industries (section 201)
- Independent analysis and information available for legislative and executive branches and support on matters of tariffs and international trade competitiveness of U.S. firms
- Maintenance of the Harmonized Tariff Schedule of the United States
- Generalized Scheme of Preferences (GSP)
- East-West trade; investigations of injury caused by subsidized or dumped goods
- Import interference with agricultural programs
- Unfair practices in import trade (section 337 of the Smoot-Hawley Tariff Act of 1930).

Virtually all of the major U.S. trade acts, past and present, have bestowed these responsibilities on the ITC (or Tariff Commission in the past). However, the President often directs the USTR to request that the ITC carries out or expedites an investigation of a particular case involving the above provisions, to initiate multilateral/bilateral discussions aimed at eliminating trade-distorting practices in a specific industrial sector, or to monitor imports subject to these provisions.

There are six commissioners, each appointed by the President for a nine-year term. Of the six, not more than three may be of the same political party. The President designates the Chairman for a two-year term, and successive Chairmen may not be of the same political party.

Among the nine ITC offices, the Office of Operations carries out its main function. There are six offices under the Director of the Office of Operations: Office of Investigations, Office of Industries, Office of Economics, Office of Tariff Affairs and Trade Agreements, Office of Unfair Import Investigations, and Trade Remedy Assistance Office. The Office of Investigations deals with cases of the countervailing duty and antidumping duty. It also reviews cases of escape clause and market-disruption investigations to determine both whether or not imports have injured or threatened to injure a U.S. industry and whether imports interfere with agricultural programs. The Office of Industries conducts studies of U.S. industry performance, factors influencing U.S. competitiveness, and the impact of international trade on U.S. industry. The Office of Economics provides advice to Congress and the President on international trade issues and conducts general trade research. The Office of Tariff Affairs and Trade Agreements produces the Harmonized Tariff Schedule of the United States and the database for bilateral and multilateral trade negotiations such as the Uruguay Round, U.S.-Canada Free Trade Agreement, and NAFTA. It reviews the GSP program and carries out rule-of-origin studies. The Office of Unfair Import Investigations investigates claims of unfair import competition, especially allegations of patent or trademark infringement. Finally, the Trade Remedy Assistance Office provides technical assistance to small businesses seeking benefits or relief.

6.4 PRIVATE SECTOR ADVISORY COMMITTEES

As discussed in chapter 1, the private sector plays an important role in the legislative process for trade laws. Likewise, the USTR seeks advice on trade policy formation from the private-sector advisory committees. The committees provide the President with information on the priorities and direction of U.S. trade policy. Three-tier advisory committees assisted by the relevant executive departments are: (1) the advisory committee for trade policy and negotiations; (2) the policy advisory committee for the overall economy; and (3) the sector advisory committee. The first tier consists of a group of presidential appointees. It is the most senior level representing government, labor, industry, agriculture, small business, service industries, retailers, consumer interests, and the public. The second tier represents whole sectors of the economy such as manufacturing industry, agriculture, labor, and services. The third tier consists of experts from various fields. The USTR and the relevant departments appoint members for the latter two tiers.

6.5 POLICY IMPLICATIONS

Often, some foreign countries attempt to contrive a political solution for trade disputes with the United States. This effort stems from their misunderstanding of U.S. trade laws and policy institutions. A political solution is virtually impossible for two reasons. First, there are highly complex legal and institutional aspects of trade policy and detailed inter-agency processes of policy implementation. Section 8 of Article 1 of the U.S. Constitution mandates that Congress be responsible for levying taxes and duties and thus for managing trade policy. This responsibility implies that trade policy is within the congressional domain and is dictated by trade laws. Among the six major trade remedy provisions discussed in chapter 4, for example, three provisions (Section 301, Super 301, and Special 301), are, in principle, implemented by the USTR, one (Section 201) by the USTR and ITC, and the remaining two (Sections 701 and 731) by the ITA and ITC through quasi-judicial processes. Second, the origin of protectionism lies often within self-interest of rent-seeking groups. They put pressure on legislators representing their districts for the development of protective policies and the passage of protective laws through various promotional activities. These pressures become a Congressional concern that is ultimately directed at the White House.

U.S. trade policy in reality approximates the following scenario: an industry association hires a lobbyist in order to secure market shares in home and foreign countries. The lobbyist advises the association to continue a rally for trade barriers domestic and against foreign trade barriers country, while he politicizes the case through his tactical skills such as a seminar or his own or contracted research detailing foreign trade barriers. At election time, he wages the electoral campaign. He orchestrates the media through the editorial board or columnist for endorsements. At the time of international trade negotiations, the lobbyist often threatens to oppose the trade pact in Congress unless a phrase is reversed for better protection of domestic firms. Congressional representatives on behalf of their constituents take the issue to the White House. The USTR and/or the ITA, depending on the statutes for a particular case, announce an investigation into charges. The inquiry starts a quasi-judicial process in accordance with the statutory timetables that could eventually lead to U.S. retaliation.[12]

In order to resolve trade disputes with the United States, it would be more effective for foreign countries to have a long-term and comprehensive solution derived from market principles that are also pursued by the WTO and OECD, rather than seeking a short-term, partial, and political solution through individual channels.

6.6 SUMMARY AND CONCLUSIONS

The USTR, ITA, and ITC are the three entities primarily responsible for actual implementation of U.S. trade policy. The USTR, as the principal advisor to the President and Congress, plays the central role in developing, coordinating, and implementing U.S. trade policy. The USTR focuses on unfair foreign trade practices, identification of trade liberalization countries, identification of intellectual property rights priorities, and the escape clause. The ITA in the Department of Commerce also plays a key role in trade policy and implementation. The ITA's primary responsibilities are the investigation of countervailing duty and antidumping duty cases. The ITC, an independent agency, plays a quasi-judicial function in making either affirmative or negative determinations in countervailing, antidumping duty and safeguard cases. It also investigates such cases and determines the extent of industrial injury. The ITC therefore parallels the role judge, while the ITA is comparable to a prosecutor.

Three-tier private sector committees under the USTR are involved in formulation of U.S. trade policy. They provide information and advice to the President on the priorities and direction of trade policy.

Although Congress has increasingly delegated policy authority to the Administration, trade policy and its implementation are actually generated through interbranch politics between the legislative and executive branches. Congress has moved the responsibility for implementing policies from the President to the USTR and requires him/her, as the chair of the Trade Policy Committee, to keep five advisors from the Committee on Ways and Means and five advisors from the Committee of Finance informed of U.S. trade policy agendas and issues. Within the executive branch, the USTR reports directly to the President as a cabinet member as well as a member of the National Economic Council. The U.S. trade policy institution itself is impeccable. However, it is an intricate system.

In conclusion, U.S. trade policy is a collective action taken by complex trade policy institutions. Given the complexity, it is erroneous to believe that U.S. trade policy decisions are readily reversible by a specific individual such as the President or a powerful legislator. In the event of trade disputes with the United States, it is appropriate for foreign countries to take a long-term, comprehensive approach based on market principles rather than seeking a short-term, partial, and political solution from the systemic operation of policy through individual channels.

NOTES

1. The formal rules of individual and organizational interactions include a legal system, government regulation, and policy measures. See Douglas North, *Institutions, Institutional Change, and Economic Performance* (New York, NY: Cambridge University Press, 1990) for the definition of institutions in detail.

2. The Reagan administration established the Economic Policy Council (EPC) and Domestic Policy Council (DPC) in 1985 to replace the seven existing Cabinet Councils and the Senior Interagency Group. The EPC advised the President, who chairs the

Council, on all areas of national and international economic policy and oversees the coordination and implementation of the administration's economic policies. The EPC is composed of the Secretaries of State, Treasury (Chairman Pro Tempore), Agriculture, Commerce, Labor, the Director of the Office of Management and Budget, the USTR, and the Chairman of the Council of Economic Advisers. The heads of the national security departments and agencies participate, as needed, in Council meetings. Note that all members of the Trade Policy Committee (TPC), including the USTR, automatically become members of the EPC. The EPC was superseded by the NEC.

3. USTRs in the past (not the STRs) and present are Rubin Askew (1979–1981), William E. Brock (1981–1985), Clayton K. Yeutter (1985–1989), Carla Hills (1989–1993), Micky Cantor (1993–1996), Charlene Barshefsky (1997–2000), Robert B. Zoellick (2001–2005), and Rob Portman (2005–present).

4. See U.S. House of Representatives, Committee on Ways and Means, *Trade Legislation Enacted into Public Law*, 1981 through 1988 (Washington, D.C.: U.S. GPO, January 1989), 374–75.

5. See the relevant sections in chapter 4 for details.

6. See Section 242 of the Trade Expansion Act of 1962.

7. See Section 1621 of the OTCA of 1988.

8. P.L. 480 is the Agricultural Trade Development and Assistance Act of 1954, as amended.

9. The efficiency loss from political power games played between the legislative branch and the executive branch is a primary concern of public choice economists.

10. See Chapter 4 for ITA's roles.

11. See Chapter 4 for ITC's roles.

12. This scenario is a version adapted from an article published in *Newsweek* (July 1995): 42, as modified by the author.

Chapter 7

Trade Policy in Action

U.S. trade policy under GATT$_{1947}$ was basically oriented toward free trade. Its primary purpose was to reduce tariff and nontariff barriers across countries through seven rounds of the GATT. However, global recessions in the 1970s and early 1980s caused by oil crises and a strong American anti-inflationary policy, forced all countries to choose protective trade policy courses.[1] The United States began to be concerned about its declining world market shares of manufactured goods in comparison with those of foreign countries, especially Japan and high performance Asian economies. Table 7.1 shows U.S. exports and imports of goods in 1985 and 2001. Exports and imports of manufacturing goods have been predominantly larger than those of agricultural goods. They accounted for 88 percent (86 percent in 1985) and 84 percent (figure unavailable in 1985) with respect to total exports and imports in 2001 (1985), respectively. Exports and imports of agriculture goods accounted only for 8 percent and 4 percent in 2001 (14 percent and 6 percent in 1985). Given the massive trade deficits, especially under the adverse trends in manufacturing exports and imports, and fiscal deficits that started to accumulate in the early 1980s, the United States determined to open foreign markets aggressively by legislating the OTCA of 1988. This act has provided the United States with the legal basis for a drastic change in trade policy from singly focused to multifaceted, that is, trade policy coordinated with multilateral agreements, regional negotiations, and bilateral initiatives. Such a policy has naturally entailed the strict enforcement of trade laws, monitoring the implementation of commitments by foreign countries, and frequent disputes with foreign countries on transparent and accessible institutions at all levels.

The U.S. economy (of 10 trillion dollars of its GDP as of 2002) is massive. Its foreign sector is now large enough to affect significantly not only the

Table 7.1. U.S. Merchandise Exports and Imports (Billions of dollars)

	1985[1]		2001[2]	
	Exports	Imports	Exports	Imports
Total	215.9	338.1	718.8	1145.9
Food, feeds, and beverages		49.4	46.6	
Industrial supplies and materials	54.8	62.6	160.1	273.9
Capital goods, except autos	79.3	61.3	321.7	298.0
Autos and parts	24.9	64.9	75.4	189.8
Consumer goods	NA	NA	88.3	284.3
Others	27.2	97.9	—	—
Addendum:				
Agriculture	29.6	20.0	55.2	39.5
Manufacturing	186.3[a]	NA	640.2	950.7
High technology	NA	NA	199.6	195.2

NA = Not available.
[a] Nonagricultural products

Sources:
1. Council of Economic Advisers, *Economic Report of the President* (Washington, D.C.: February 2003), 393 and 396.
2. USTR, *2003 Trade Policy Agenda and 2002 Annual Report,* (Washington, D.C.: U.S. GPO, 2003), Annex I, 4, and 8; Balance of Payments Basis.

domestic economy but also many foreign economies. The United States accounts for roughly 20 percent of world goods trade and 16 percent of world service trade. The impact of U.S. trade policy on the domestic economy and the world economy is considerable. The Council of Economic Advisors states that "Fully one-third of the strong economic growth America has enjoyed in the 1990s has come from exports,"[2] and that "our economic strategy has focused on opening markets around the world. Today, with more than 300 new trade agreements in place, including the North American Free Trade Agreement and the Uruguay Round agreements, American workers and firms are competing in more markets than even before, and our economy is stronger for it."[3] These statements imply how serious the United States has pursued trade expansion premised on opening foreign markets by means of various trade agreements at all levels.

This chapter examines actual trade policy in the United States during recent years. Sections 1 through 3 outline policies under multilateral, regional, and bilateral agreements. In the event of violation of any of these agreements by a foreign country, the foreign country is subject to trade remedy measures discussed in chapter 4. Section 4 discusses U.S. enforcement activities involving actual trade remedy cases. Such a policy requires not only enforcement but also monitoring activities and thus often results in trade disputes with foreign countries. The number of trade disputes and settlements is quite extensive. Chapter 8 will separately discuss the cases. Section 5 presents the priorities of future American trade policy agendas. Section 6 summarizes the chapter and states concluding remarks.

7.1 TRADE POLICY UNDER MULTILATERAL AGREEMENTS[4]

Among the seven rounds of the GATT prior to the Uruguay Round, the Kennedy Round (sixth round) and the Tokyo Round (seventh round) are the most notable ones. Trade laws enacted in the 1960s and 1970s mandated that both of these rounds pursue and complete multilateral trade negotiations. The Kennedy Round (1962–1972) reduced the average tariff rate by about 35 percent, making it the most striking success since the GATT went into effect. When the GATT was established in 1947, the tariff rate was almost 40 percent. In 1962, it dropped to a level slightly above 15 percent. The rate fell to below 10 percent in 1972 after the Kennedy Round. In the United States, tariffs on manufactured goods decreased by roughly one-third, although they were left intact on the agricultural goods.

The Tokyo Round (1973–1979) was held in Geneva to reduce NTBs in addition to furthering tariff cuts. One hundred and two (102) participating countries began negotiations in 1973 and completed the round in 1979. They agreed to reduce tariff rates on manufactured goods in developed countries by about one-third of the existing rates, phased in over eight years. The average tariff rate was brought down to 4.7 percent in 1987. However, the negotiating countries failed to reach any agreement on barriers to agricultural trade. Despite its limited achievement, the Tokyo Round is significant because it provided an important forum for negotiations in NTB areas such as subsidies and countervailing measures, technical barriers to trade (or the Standard Code), import licensing procedures, customs valuations, antidumping and the replacement of antidumping code in the Kennedy Round, and government procurement.

The GATT's contribution to trade liberalization is incontestable. Despite the successive reductions of tariffs imposed on manufacturing goods, however, the scope of $GATT_{1947}$ was narrow. The Uruguay Round extended it to cover the service sector, though only partially the agricultural sector. The United States believes that this new multilateral agreement boosts not only the U.S. economy but also the global economy, as lower trade barriers covering a broader area create new export opportunities and the new rules give business greater confidence on open export markets and that competition in foreign markets will be fair.[5] The UR is the basis of U.S. multilateral trade policy at present. The principal American trade remedy provisions are subject to compliance with the UR. Section 4 will discuss some of the specific cases.

7.2 TRADE POLICY UNDER REGIONAL AGREEMENTS

This section focuses on U.S. trade policy in connection with the NAFTA, the most active regional agreement at present. The primary objective of U.S. policy has always been trade expansion with Canada and Mexico through lower trade barriers.

In 1993, U.S. goods faced an average tariff barrier of 10 percent, two and a half times greater than the 4 percent rate the U.S. imposed on Mexican goods. Mexico's average tariff on U.S. exports today has decreased to about 2 percent. The NAFTA has brought tariff barriers to the near-parity. It requires gradual reductions in tariff barriers over fifteen years. By 2008, tariffs will no longer pose a barrier to trade. In addition, NTBs in the areas of import licensing, local content, and trade balancing were eliminated or resolved.

Contrary to initial concerns about the NAFTA, especially in the United States, it has performed superbly not only for the United States but also for other member countries. The NAFTA has considerably expanded trade among the three countries since it took into effect on January 1, 1994. Canada is now the United States's foremost export market and single largest trading and investment partner while Mexico is the United States's fourth (was second) largest export market.[6] What are effects of the NAFTA on the U.S. economy? Table 7.2 presents data on the U.S. economy under the NAFTA during the period of 1993–1998 (the first five year period, excluding 1993). The data shows that NAFTA's contribution to the U.S. economy is significant. U.S. exports of goods to Canada and Mexico increased by 55 percent and 90 percent, respectively. The success of the NAFTA is particularly evident when compared with U.S. trade to the rest of the world. American exports to NAFTA countries were up 17 percent in 1997, outpacing total U.S. export growth to the world of 10 percent, and they were up 5 percent in 1998 ($12 billion) when U.S. exports to the world dropped slightly (by –0.9 percent). U.S. exports to Mexico alone rose almost 11 percent in 1998.

The NAFTA has also fostered higher wage jobs. U.S. exports of goods to Mexico in 1998 supported almost 1 million jobs with a net increase of about 350,000 jobs since 1993. American exports to Canada supported about 1.7 million jobs, about 300,000 more than since 1993. The total U.S. exports of goods due to the NAFTA resulted in 2.7 million jobs carrying higher wages.

More importantly, the United States provided training and skills to augment the quality of American workers.

Table 7.2 shows also U.S. exports and imports of goods to the NAFTA member countries for the latest period (1999–2000). U.S. exports of goods to Canada (the largest U.S. export market accounting for 23 percent of U.S. exports) are up by nearly 40 percent since 1994. Since the same year, U.S. exports to Mexico (U.S. export market accounting for 14 percent of U.S. exports) have increased 91 percent. U.S. imports from Canada (the largest single country supplier of goods to the United States accounting for 18 percent of U.S.

Table 7.2. NAFTA and U.S. Economy (1993–1998)

1993–1998[1]
Increase in U.S. Exports of Goods
   and Services to the World   45%
   U.S. Exports of Goods   47%
   U.S. Exports of Goods to NAFTA Members
     Canada   55% ($56 billion); total exports of $156 billion
     Mexico[2]   90% ($37 billion); total exports of $79 billion
Number of Higher Wage Jobs Supported by U.S. Exports to NAFTA Members in 1998
     Canada   1.7 million jobs with net increase of 300,000
     Mexico   1.0 million jobs with net increase of 350,000

U.S. Exports and Imports of Goods by NAFTA Member Country
(1999-2002; Billions of Dollars)

	Canada		Mexico	
	Exports	Imports	Exports	Imports
1999	166.6	198.7	86.9	109.7
2000	178.9	230.8	111.3	135.9
2001	163.4	216.3	101.3	131.3
2002[3]	159.7	208.5	97.2	134.1
Average Percentage Change (1994–2002)	39.6%	62.4%	91.1%	171.0%

1. The NAFTA entered into effect in 1994.
2. U.S. trade performance with NAFTA partners has exceeded the performance of trade with the rest of the world. This growth occurred steadily every year despite the decline in exports to Mexico in 1995 due to the peso crisis and related severe recession, and more recently, despite the negative impact of the Asian financial crisis.
3. Annualized based on January–November 2002 data.

Sources:
(1) Period: 1993–1998 (the first five year period of the NAFTA beginning from 1994). U.S. Administration, *NAFTA Works for America: Administration Update on the North American Free Trade Agreement 1993–1998* (Washington, D.C.: U.S. GPO), 4–8.
(2) Period: 1999–2002 (the latest data available for this purpose) USTR, *2003 Trade Policy Agenda and 2002 Annual Report* (Washington, D.C.: U.S. GPO), Appendix I, 5, and 9.

imports) have grown by 62 percent since 1994. U.S. imports from Mexico (the second largest country supplier of goods to the United States accounting for 12 percent of U.S. imports) have increased 171 percent since 1994.

There are, of course, critics suggesting the failure of the NAFTA or its insignificant effects on the U.S. economy. They point out the U.S. trade deficit with Mexico. However, counterarguments suggest the trade deficit that is partly due to the devaluation of Mexican peso, low trade barrier of the United States that was already substantially reduced through multilateral trade negotiations, or relatively small Mexican economy in comparison with the U.S. economy.[7]

Environmental repercussions as a result of increased regional trade were another serious concern at the time of NAFTA negotiations. However, the NAFTA countries cooperate closely with each other to control pollution through action plans under the environmental supplemental agreement to NAFTA drafted by the North American Agreement on Environmental Cooperation (NAAEC) and the Commission for Environmental Cooperation (CEC). The CEC has protected U.S. wildlife habitats and coastal waters.

There are also few areas that have become increasingly controversial. The rules of origin, a problem that emerges from any free trade agreement, mandates strict adherence to an elaborate set of the rules. Another problem is concerned with the trade diversion effects stemming from economic integration. A free trade area increases intraregional trade among the member countries, but it can divert trade by agreement from a more efficient, lower-cost country outside the free trade area to a less efficient, higher-cost country within the free trade area.

Any unfair trade practices against the United States pursued by Canada and Mexico are resolved by the dispute settlement mechanism of the NAFTA.

Overall, the assessment of the NAFTA is positive to date without any serious disputes among the member countries.

7.3 BILATERAL INITIATIVES

As of 2002, the United States made 246 bilateral agreements with seventy-one countries in the Americas (including Canada, Mexico, Brazil, and the Southern Cone, the Andean Community, Central America, and the Caribbean), Europe (Western and Central Europe and the newly independent states of Eastern Europe), Asia and the Pacific (Australia and New Zealand, ASEAN, Korea, India, China, Japan, Taiwan, Hong Kong), the Middle East, and Africa. The Administration continues to seek bilateral deals with other current trading partners at present including: countries in the Central America and South

America, Asia, and Africa. Table 7.3 shows the number of bilateral agreements made with major trading partners. Like other types of agreements, the primary objective of bilateral agreements is mostly concerned with market-opening processes. The numbers of agreements with Canada, EU, Japan, Korea, and China are notably high. As shown in table 7.4, these countries trade heavily with the United States. U.S. merchandise exports and imports and trade deficits in 2002 by country indicate that the EU is the market of the United States's second largest merchandise exports, largest merchandise imports, largest two-way trade and investment, and third largest merchandise trade deficit; Japan is the country of the United States's sixth largest merchandise exports, dropped from the third in 1996, and second largest merchandise trade deficit; Korea is the United States's fifth largest export market in 1996; and China is United States's seventh largest market ascended from the fourteenth market in 1996 and the largest trade deficit country (fourth largest in terms of merchandise trade deficit).[8] Canada is the United States's first market and Mexico is the United States's fourth export market. U.S. bilateral policies to each of these countries are explained below. Note that they are subject to change in each year.

Table 7.3. Number of Bilateral Agreements since 1984: Selected Countries*

Country	Number of Agreements
Argentina	2
Australia	2
Brazil	1
Canada	10
China	10
EU	23
India	5
Indonesia	1
Israel	3
Japan	44
Korea	30
Mexico	2
Russia	6
Singapore	1
Taiwan	13
Thailand	3
55 other countries	90
71 countries	246

*Agreements that have entered into force since 1984. Excluded are agreements that have been negotiated but have not yet entered into force. Also excluded are other trade-related agreements and declarations.

Source: USTR, *2003 Trade Policy Agenda and 2002 Annual Report* (Washington, D.C., U.S. GPO, March 2003), Annex III, 1–16.

**Table 7.4.   U.S. Merchandise Exports and Imports in 2002
by Country and Region (Billions of dollars)**

Country	Exports	Imports	Trade Surplus (+) or Deficits (–)
Canada	163.4 (1st)	216.3 (2nd)	–52.9 (4th)
EU	158.8 (2nd)	220.1 (1st)	–61.3 (3rd)
Japan	57.5 (6th)	126.5 (5th)	–69.0 (2nd)
Korea[1]	25.1	23.2	1.9
China	19.2 (7th)	102.3 (6th)	–83.1 (1st)
Mexico	101.3 (4th)	131.3 (4th)	–30.0 (6th)
Pacific Rim[2]	104.8 (3rd)	147.3 (3rd)	–42.5 (5th)
Latin America[3]	58.2 (5th)	67.4 (7th)	–9.2 (7th)

1. Figures in 1997.
2. Except Japan.
3. Except Mexico.

Source: USTR, *2003 Trade Policy Agenda and 2002 Annual Report* (Washington, D.C.: U.S. GPO, 2003), Annex I, 5, and 9.

1. European Union

The Agenda for the New Transatlantic Partnership addressed at the U.S.-EU Summit in Madrid in 1995 sought U.S.-EU joint actions for expansion of multilateral as well as bilateral trade between the United States and the EU. Specific actions include joint efforts to reduce barriers to U.S.-EU trade and investment, to resolve trade disputes, to reduce regulatory burdens, to enhance customs cooperation, and to spur the transatlantic business dialogue. Areas currently under negotiation or consultation are standards, testing, labeling, and certification; intellectual property rights; government procurement; telecommunications; customs classification of information technology products; implementation of tariff commitments; the banana trade regime; humane trapping standards; approval of biotechnology products; a ban on growth promoting hormones in meat production; a large aircraft monitoring agreement; a voluntary eco-labeling scheme; canned fruit; veterinary equivalence; an SRM ban; and wine.

2. Japan

The United States has negotiated bilateral agreements with Japan in many areas. The United States took a comprehensive bilateral approach on the basis of the U.S.-Japan Framework for a New Economic Partnership signed in 1993. It focuses on two different aspects: negotiating new agreements and monitoring and enforcing a mechanism. Nine new agreements were concluded in 1997. Among them, the Enhanced Initiative on Deregulation and

Competition Policy is the most comprehensive one. It aims at promoting deregulation by strengthening competition enforcement, liberalizing the Japanese distribution system, and obtaining tangible deregulatory measures in four key sectors: telecommunications, housing, medical devices and pharmaceutical products, and financial services. Other agreements deal with the areas of wood products, sound recordings, tomatoes, telecommunications, government procurement, maritime and port practices, and Nippon Telegraph and Telephone procurement. Existing bilateral agreements signed mostly in the 1990s cover sectors such as autos and auto parts, insurance, flat glass, investment, construction, medical technology, satellites, computers and supercomputers, semiconductors, paper, rice, and civil aviation. Sound recordings and intellectual property rights, distilled spirits, consumer photographic film and paper, and testing of fruits are the sectors that involve multilateral disputes and WTO settlements, which also draw bilateral attention.

At present, bilateral trade activities between the two countries are more systematic than before. The U.S.-Japan Economic Partnership for Growth, signed in 2001, governs the bilateral trade. It includes regulatory reform, both sectoral and structural. The former includes the telecommunications, information technologies, medical devices and pharmaceuticals, financial services, and housing. The latter includes competition law and policy, transparency and other government practices, legal system and infrastructure, commercial law, and distribution.

The results of U.S. trade policy under the bilateral agreements are significant. Official estimates suggest that U.S. exports to Japan increased by 20 percent, with exports in those sectors covered by bilateral agreements. In addition, U.S. exports of private services accounted for 12.5 percent of total services exports in 1998.[9]

3. Korea

Agreements or commitments to liberalize trade include ones on auto market access, intellectual property rights, telecommunications, steel, cosmetics, financial services, distilled spirits, import clearance procedures, pharmaceuticals, screen quotas, agricultural products, government support for semiconductor production and exports, and food standards and labeling. It is also notable that an IMF macroeconomic stabilization package negotiated with the Korean government at the time of the financial crisis in November 1997 includes conditions aimed at eliminating trade- and competition-distorting policies through structural reforms. At that time, the United States stated that Korea should address systemic problems such as policy-driven lending, auto, steel, semiconductor and shipbuilding industries, export subsidies and financial market access, and import licensing and certification procedures. When the Trade Committee of the OECD reviewed the terms of Korea's admission to the OECD in May 1977, the United States was concerned about market access and distribution restrictions on autos, telecommunications, cosmetics, pharmaceuticals, and import clearances in Korea.

4. China

The United States normalized relations with China in an effort to open China's vast markets to American products, ranging from agricultural and manufacturing goods to services. Trade between the United States and China has primarily been based on the bilateral agreement reached in 1980 along with Most-Favored-Nation (MFN) treatment, which was subject to renewal at three-year intervals. The latest renewal was made in 1998.[10] The Intellectual Property Rights Enforcement Agreement, Memorandum of Understanding on Market Access, Agreement on International Trade in Commercial Space Launch Services, and an agreement on agriculture have all helped to resolve disputed trade issues between the United States and China.

The two countries also concluded a historic U.S.-China bilateral market access agreement in November 1999 and in October 2000. The United States passed legislation permitting a grant of permanent normal trade. All of these bilateral key agreements facilitated China's admission to the WTO in December 2001 (Taiwan became a member of the WTO on January 1, 2002). As China achieved resounding success, U.S. labor (the AFL-CIO) and industry groups filed increasingly more petitions calling for trade sanctions against China in less than three years (April 2004) since its accession to the WTO but the government rejected the request for stiff tariffs on imports from China.

5. Canada

Even with the U.S.-Canada Free Trade Pact and the NAFTA, there are still many other bilateral agreements made between the two countries, including agreements on softwood lumber, agricultures, and intellectual property rights.

6. Mexico

Since the NAFTA entered into force in 1994, bilateral trade between the United States and Mexico has substantially increased. The United States continues to broaden the range of negotiations with Mexico. Agreements include intellectual property rights, agricultural products, and telecommunications.

7.4 ENFORCEMENT ACTIVITIES
BY TRADE REMEDY MEASURES

The United States conducts trade policies on the basis of multilateral, regional, and bilateral agreements. Violations of these agreements by a foreign country are subject to U.S. trade remedy laws. Prior to the Uruguay Round, the trade remedy policy tools employed by the U.S. policy authorities were primarily the countervailing duty (CVD) and the antidumping duty (AD). The numbers of CVD and AD cases compiled in tables 7.10 and 7.11 are predominantly large in comparison with those for cases of Section 301, Super 301, Special 301, and section 201 in tables 7.5–7.9. Countries subjected to CVD and AD investigations were mostly developed or newly industrialized countries. In the past, most cases were concentrated in chemicals, food, iron/steel, and metal manufactures.[11]

The actual cases under the six primary trade remedy provisions are the central part of trade policy that characterizes the latest American trade policy. It is important to keep in mind that many cases are in the process of settlement or remain unresolved, appealed to the WTO's Appellate Body, or recurred after settlements.

1. Policy Actions under Section 301

Since the statute was first enacted in 1974, the number of investigation initiations by the USTR has steadily increased over time without revealing any particular pattern, while the number of active investigation has remained modest. Table 7.5 presents the number of initiations of investigation and the number of active investigations since 1989. There were ninety investigation initiations in 1992, 91 cases in 1993, 98 cases in 1994, 101 cases in 1995, 110 cases in 1996, 116 cases in 1997, 118 cases in 1998, 119 cases in 1999, 120 cases in 2000, 121 cases in 2001 and 2002. The numbers of cases in years prior to 1992 are not available. On the other hand, there were 20 active investigations in 1989, 16 cases in 1990, 15 cases in 1991, 7 cases in 1992, 5 cases in 1993, 7 cases in 1994, 6 cases in 1995, 9 cases in 1996, 12 cases in 1997, 13 cases 1998, 9 cases in 1999, 8 cases in 2000, 5 cases in 2001, and 3 cases in 2002. Table 7.6 outlines notable cases of active investigation by country since 1995. Each year, the countries listed in this table remain the same with few exceptions. The countries are the EU, Japan, China, Korea, Canada, Mexico, and several Latin American nations including Argentina and Brazil.

Table 7.5. Number of Initiations for Investigations and Number of Active Investigations by Section 301

Year	Number of Initiation for Investigations[1]	Number of Active Investigations
1989	NA	20
1990	NA	16
1991	NA	15
1992	90	7
1993	91	5
1994	98	7
1995	101	6
1996	110	9
1997	116	12
1998	118	13
1999	119	9
2000	120	8
2001	121	5
2002	121	3

1. Numbers since the statute was first enacted in 1974.
NA = Not available.

Source: Constructed by the author from data in USTR, *2003 Trade Policy Agenda and 2002 Annual Report* (Washington, D.C.: U.S. GPO), 233–36 and various other issues.

Table 7.6. Cases of Active Investigation under Section 301

Year	Country	Areas
1995	China	Intellectual property protection
	Japan	Auto parts replacement market; market access to consumer photographic film and paper
	Korea	Agricultural market access; steel pipe and tube
	EU	Banana import regime; union enlargement
	Columbia	Banana export regimes
	Canada	Communications practices
1996	Canada	Discriminatory treatment of foreign periodicals
	Portugal	Term of patent protection
	India	Patent Protection for pharmaceuticals and chemicals
	Pakistan	same as above
	Turkey	Discriminatory tax on box office revenue
	Australia	Subsidies affecting leather
	Argentine	Specific duties and NTBs affecting apparel textiles and footwear
	Indonesia	Practices benefiting domestic auto sectors
	Brazil	same as above
1997	Honduras	Protection of intellectual property rights
	Korea	Barriers to auto imports
	EU	Circumvention of export subsidy commitments on dairy products and market access for modified starch
	Canada	Export subsidies and market access for dairy products, practices affecting periodicals
	Japan	Market access barriers to agricultural products

Table 7.6. *(continued)*

Year	Country	Areas
	Pakistan	Patent protection for pharmaceuticals and agricultural chemicals
	Turkey	Discriminatory tax on box office revenues
	India	same as Pakistan above
	Australia	Subsidies on leather
	Argentina	Specific duties on textiles, etc.
	Indonesia	Promotion of motor vehicle sector
	Brazil	Practices regarding trade and investment in auto sector
1998	Mexico	Practices affecting high fructose corn syrup
	Paraguay	Intellectual property laws and practices
	Honduras	Protection of intellectual property rights
	Korea	Barriers to motor vehicles
	Canada	Export subsidies and market access for dairy products; practices affecting periodicals
	Japan	Market access barriers to agricultural products
	India	Patent protection for pharmaceuticals and agricultural chemicals
	Australia	Subsidies on leather
	Argentina	Specific duties
	Indonesia	Promotion of the motor vehicle sector
	Brazil	Practices regarding trade and investment in the auto sector
	EC	Importation, sale, and distribution of bananas
1999	Mexico	Practices affecting high fructose corn syrup
	Canada	Measures affecting tourism and sport fishing practices
	EC	(1) Importation, sale, and distribution of bananas
		(2) Measures concerning meat and meat products (hormones)

Other investigations involving WTO dispute settlement

Year	Country	Areas
	Canada	Practices affecting periodicals
	India	Patent protection for pharmaceuticals and agricultural goods
	Australia	Subsidies on leather
	Indonesia	Promotion of the motor vehicle sector
	Japan	Market access barriers to agricultural products
	Canada	Export subsidies and market access for dairy products
2000	Canada	Wheat trading practices
	EC	(1) Importation, sale, and distribution of bananas
		(2) Measures concerning meat and meat products (hormones)
2001	Ukraine	Practices regarding intellectual property laws
	Canada	Wheat trading practices
	EU	(1) Importation, sales, and distortion of bananas
		(2) Measures concerning meat and meat products
2002	Same as 2001	

Other investigations involving WTO dispute settlement

Year	Country	Areas
	India	Patent protection for pharmaceuticals and agricultural goods
	Australia	Subsidies on leather
	Indonesia	Promotion of the motor vehicle sector
	Japan	Market access barriers to agricultural products
	Canada	Export subsidies and market access for dairy products

Source: Constructed by the author from data in USTR, *2003 Trade Policy Agenda and 2002 Annual Report* (Washington, D.C.: U.S. GPO), 233–36 and various other issues.

2. Policy Actions under Super 301

Super 301 came into force in 1989 and expired in 1990. Executive Order 12901 reinstated it in 1994 and again in 1995. It was amended before extension to 1996–1997 and was embodied in Executive Order 13116.[12] Year 1999 marked the latest year of reinstatement.

Table 7.7 lists the highest priority cases with brief descriptions of each until 2002. In 1989, Super 301 was invoked to deal with ten priority cases against four priority countries: Korea, Japan, Brazil, and India in 1989. However, Korea agreed to liberalize foreign investment and import bans and to ease restrictions on agricultural products. Consequently, the three cases regarding Korea were removed from the list through bilateral negotiations. Taiwan (not listed in Table 7.5) avoided Super 301 by developing a trade action plan for opening markets by means of tariff reductions and import licensing.[13] The remaining six priority unfair practice cases with Japan, Brazil, and India were grouped into five broad categories as follows:[14]

- Quantitative restrictions and import licensing
  Restrictive licensing of agricultural and manufactured goods in Brazil
- Exclusionary government procurement
  Satellites in Japan
  Supercomputers in Japan
- Standards and technical barriers
  Forest products in Japan
- Trade-related investment measures
  Performance requirements in India
- Barriers to trade in services
  Insurance area in India.

Contrary to an expectation of aggressive investigations with the reinstitution of Super 301 in 1994, the USTR did not initiate new investigations since that year, presumably because Super 301 time limits were carefully drafted to work in conjunction with the GATT. The USTR thus decided to take cases directly to the WTO.[15, 16]

3. Policy Actions under Special 301[17]

Innovation is a primary source of economic progress in the United States.[18] U.S. exports and imports (volume of trade) of high technology goods with respect to total exports and imports accounted for 28 percent and 20 percent in 2001 and 2002, respectively. The role of Special 301 has become crucial. Bilateral and multilateral negotiations in the area of intellectual property rights

Table 7.7. Cases of Super 301

Year	Country	Reasons	Results
1989	Korea	Quantitative import restrictions	Agreed to eliminate bans on certain manufactured and agricultural goods
1989	Korea	Investment barriers	Agreed to revise or eliminate barriers to U.S. investment
1989	Korea	Unfair standards, testing and certification	Agreed to ease standards testing, labeling, and certification procedures
1989	Japan	Exclusionary government procurement practices for supercomputers	Pursuant to Section 310 (c) of Trade Act of 1974 in 1990, the USTR negotiated with Japan. Japan agreed to seek adequate funding for purchases of supercomputers, to use practical guidelines to select computers, and to provide a procedure for dealing with complaints. Investigation suspended.
1989	Japan	Exclusionary government procurement practices for satellites	Pursuant to Section 310 (c) of Trade Act of 1974 in 1990, the USTR and Japan negotiated. On 3 April 1990, Japan agreed to open government procurement of all satellites except R&D satellites. Investigation suspended.
1989	Japan	High tariffs and technical barriers, such as product standards, building codes, and testing and certification procedures	Pursuant to Section 310 (c) of Trade Act of 1974, the USTR and Japan negotiated. On 15 June 1989, Japan agreed to improve market access for U.S. companies and to address tariff miscalculation, certification standards, and tariffs. Investigation suspended.
1989	Brazil	Quantitative import restrictions, including import bans and restrictive licensing	Case was dismissed due to policy reforms by Brazil, which included import bans.
1989	India	Trade-related investment measures, i.e., requirements that investors must use local inputs and exports for a portion of production	Unresolved; listed as priority country in 1990.
1989	India	Barrier to entrance of U.S. insurance firms	Unresolved; listed as priority country in 1990.

(*continued*)

Table 7.7. **(continued)**

Year	Country	Reasons	Results
1990	India	Restrictions on potential U.S. investment, and unacceptable conditions on foreign firms already investing due to trade-related investment measures	On 14 June 1990, the USTR determined that the barriers are unreasonable and cause a burden to U.S. commerce, renewing its identification as a priority country; however, no action was taken because responsive action under Section 301 and Super 301 was not appropriate considering anticipation of India participating in the Uruguay Round.
1990	India	Barriers to trade in insurance	On June 14, USTR determined that barriers are unreasonable and cause a burden to U.S. commerce, renewing its identification as a priority country; however, no action was taken because responses under section 301 and Super 301 were not appropriate given the anticipation of India participating in the Uruguay Round.

1991 None

1992 None

1993 None

1994 None; but Super 301 was reinstated by Executive Order 12901 for 1994 and 1995, and amended to extend it to 1996 and 1997.

1995 None identified as a priority country; but the USTR noted that Japan and China may by identified as priority countries in the future.

Japan	Market access for wood and paper products
China	Market access for agricultural products

The USTR also noted that U.S. trade negotiating objectives should be addressed in connection with market access or measures on:

Korea	Market access to autos, medical devices, agricultural products, residue testing, and inspection requirements
EU	Utilities directive, eco-labeling directive, banana import regime, grain, and scallops
Germany	Power generation equipment
Japan	Distilled spirits
Canada	Dairy and poultry products
Mexico	Small package delivery services

1996 None identified. But the USTR initiated investigations of four new trade barriers:

Indonesia	National auto policy
Brazil	Auto program
Australia	Export subsidies on leather
Argentina	Import duties on textiles, apparel and footwear.

Except for the Brazilian case, WTO dispute settlement procedures were invoked for the remaining three.

Table 7.7. (continued)

Year	Country	Reasons	Results
	The USTR announced the adoption of a strategic enforcement strategy in an attempt to prevent future barriers through bilateral agreements with:		
	Japan	Automotive sector	
	Korea	Automotive sector	
	China	Automotive sector	
	India	Trade-related investment measures	
	Argentina	Trade-related investment measures	
	Malaysia	Trade-related investment measures	
1997	Korea	Barriers to auto imports	The USTR initiated Section 301 investigation with respect to policies such as cumulative tariff and tax disincentives, costly auto standards and certification procedures, auto financing restrictions, and bias against imported vehicles
	The USTR also announced enforcement of international trade agreements and U.S. trade Laws to be applied to:		
	Japan	Market access barriers to fruit	
	Canada	Export subsidies and import quotas on dairy products	
	EU	Circumvention of its export subsidy commitments on dairy products	
	Australia	Subsidies introduced to replace export subsidies on automotive leather	
1998	None issued due to expiration of Executive Order 12901. But the USTR terminated the one outstanding Super 301 investigation regarding Korean barriers to motor vehicles.		
1999	None identified as a priority country; but the USTR announced WTO dispute settlement cases:		
	EU	Avionics	
	India	Auto TRIMS	
	Korea	Barriers to import and distribution of foreign beef	
2000	None identified as priority country; But USTR announced WTO dispute settlement cases:		
	India and Philippines	Auto investment measures	
	Brazil and Romania	Customs valuation practices	
	Countries of significant concern are:		
	EU	Subsidies for Airbus	
	Japan	Market access barriers in flat glass sector	
	Mexico	Customs valuation practices	
2001	None identified as a priority country		
2002	None identified as a priority country		

Source: Constructed by the author from data in USTR, *1990 Trade Policy Agenda and 1989 Annual Report* (Washington, D.C.: U.S. GPO, 1989), 72 and all of later issues.

have significantly reduced the number of countries that deny adequate and effective protection of U.S. intellectual property or deny fair and equitable market access to the United States. The U.S.-Japan Memorandum of Understanding on certain patent issues and the U.S.-China ITP Enforcement Agreement exemplify those cases successfully resolved by bilateral negotiations. Nonetheless, many foreign practices in this area are still unsatisfactory to the United States. The most controversial area throughout the world at present is pharmaceutical products.

The USTR classified countries into a *Priority Watch List* and *Watch Lists* from 1989 and added *Out-Of-Cycle Reviews and Concerns* since 1995.

Table 7.8 shows the number of countries in each category during the period from 1995 to 2001, because, prior to 1995, the USTR reported only the total number of countries in each category without breakdown since 1989. The number of countries on the Watch List remained high throughout this period. The number on the Priority Watch List increased dramatically from the year 2000, implying significant increase in frequency of litigation by foreign countries and intensity of the policy. Overall, the total number of countries, including the number in Out-Of-Cycle Reviews has steadily increased.

4. Safeguard Actions

Table 7.9 presents the number of petitions and actions taken under Section 201 during the period from 1989 to 2001. During this period, three petitions were filed until 1995, all terminated with negative decisions, and ten petitions were filed for the remaining period, most of the petitions with affirmative decisions made by the USTR and/or the President but overturned by the WTO (as the WTO began actively to settle disputes). However, the cases recurred often for another round of settlement, *perpetuated disputes*.

Petitions filed since 1997 proceeded to resolutions as follows:

- Wheat gluten—The President imposed quantitative restrictions on wheat gluten imported from all countries except Canada, Mexico, Israel, and CBI and Andean, and Trade Preference Beneficiaries for three years and one day (June 1, 1998–June 1, 2000). On July 31, 2000, a WTO panel reported that the safeguard measures were inconsistent with the WTO Agreement on Safeguard. The United States appealed the panel's negative decision to the Appellate Body.
- Lamb meat—A tariff-rate quota was imposed on lamb meat imported from the same countries as above for three years and one day (July 22, 1999–July 22, 2002). The USTR initiated an appeal of the WTO panel's negative decision to the Appellate Body on December 21, 2000.
- Steel wire rod—A petition was filed on imported wire rod on January 12, 1999. The ITC made an affirmative injury determination. The President im-

Table 7.8. Cases of Special 301

Year	Number of Countries on the Priority Watch List	Number of Countries on the Watch List
1989	8	17
1990	4	19
1991	6	23
1992	5	23
1993	8	17
1994	8	19
March 1995	8	24

South Africa, Turkey, Japan, Indonesia, and Argentina were maintained on the Watch List.

April 1996	8	26

Greece was maintained on the Priority Watch List. Paraguay, Italy, Thailand, Russia, Saudi Arabia, Argentina, and the Philippines were maintained on the Watch List; and Bulgaria and Bolivia were added to the Watch List.

April 1997	10	36

The Priority Watch List includes Ecuador, Paraguay, Bulgaria, and Turkey, with two countries subject to Out-Of-Cycle Reviews, whereas the Watch List includes Thailand, Luxembourg, Italy, Brazil, and Hong Kong, with seven countries subject to Out-Of-Cycle Reviews. Brazil, Bulgaria, Canada, Ecuador, Hong Kong, Italy, Luxembourg, Panama, Paraguay, Thailand, and Turkey were named for Out-Of-Cycle Reviews.

January 1998	3	

The Priority Watch List includes Paraguay, Turkey, and Ecuador. The Watch List includes Brazil and Hong Kong. Bulgaria is considered for possible inclusion on the Priority Watch List.

April 1998	1	15

Paraguay remains on the Priority Watch List. Five of forty-seven countries were named for Out-Of-Cycle Reviews: Bulgaria, Hong Kong, Columbia, Jordan, and Vietnam. Brazil was removed for all 301 lists.

May 1998

New Zealand was named for Out-Of-Cycle Review.

September 1998

Bulgaria was placed on the Watch List.

December 1998

Hong Kong, Columbia, Jordan, and Vietnam were reviewed.

February 1999	1	2

The Priority Watch List includes Ecuador, whereas the Watch List includes Columbia and Vietnam. Hong Kong, Ecuador, Columbia, and Vietnam were subject to Out-Of-Cycle Reviews.

April 1999	16	37

Countries named for Out-Of-Cycle Reviews include Israel, Kuwait, South Africa, Columbia, Poland, the Czech Republic, Korea, Malaysia, Hong Kong, Paraguay, and China.

December 1999	2	

Columbia, the Czech Republic, Hong Kong, and Malaysia remained on Out-Of Cycle Reviews. The first two remained on the Watch List.

Table 7.8.   (*continued*)

Year	Number of Countries on the Priority Watch List	Number of Countries on the Watch List
2000	16	39

The Priority Watch List includes Argentina, the Dominican Republic, Egypt, EU, Greece, Guatemala, India, Israel, Italy, Korea, Malaysia, Peru, Poland, Russia, Turkey, and the Ukraine. The Watch List includes countries that were placed on this list the last year but not removed from it this year, plus Armenia, Azerbaijan, Kazakhstan, Latvia, Lithuania, Moldova, Tajikistan, Turkmenistan, and Uzbekistan.

2001	16	32

The Priority Watch List includes Argentina, Costa Rica, the Dominican Republic, Egypt, the EU, Hungary, India, Indonesia, Israel, Korea, Lebanon, Malaysia, the Philippines, Russia, Taiwan, and Uruguay. The Watch List includes countries placed on the list the previous year but not removed from it this year, plus New Zealand, the Slovak Republic, and the United Arab Emirates.

2002	15	33

The Priority Watch List includes Argentina, Brazil, Columbia, the Dominican Republic, Egypt, the European Union, Hungary, India, Indonesia, Israel, Lebanon, the Philippines, Russia, Taiwan, and Uruguay. Thirty-three trading partners were placed on the Watch List.

Source: Constructed by the author from data in USTR, *2003 Trade Policy Agenda and 2002 Annual Report* (Washington, D.C.: U.S. GPO), 238–39 and various other issues.

posed a tariff-rate quota on wire rod imported from all countries except Canada and Mexico for three years and one day (March 1, 2000–March 1, 2003).

- Circular welded carbon quality line pipe—A petition was filed on June 30, 1999. On December 22, 1999, the ITC made an affirmative injury determination. The President increased the import-relief tariff imposed on line pipe from all countries except Canada and Mexico by 19 percent for three years and one day (March 1, 2000–March 1, 2003). Korea, Japan, and EU requested WTO consultations on June 13, 2000. The WTO established a panel at the request of Korea on October 23, 2000. For the settlement of disputes on imported steel by the WTO, see section 8.4 of chapter 8.

5. Countervailing Duty Actions

The United States imposes CVD on foreign subsidies that can be broken down into three different kinds:

- Export subsidies (those contingent upon export performance)—direct grants and loans, currency retention schemes, internal transport and foreign charges on export shipments, delivery of goods and services by government

Table 7.9. Actions under Section 201

Year	Number of Petitions	Industrial Area	USITC's Determination	Presidential Decision
1989	0			
1990	1	Camera	Negative	
1991	0			
1992	1	Extruded rubber thread	3-3 even	Negative
1993	0			
1994	0			
1995	1	Tomatoes	Negative	
1996	2	Tomatoes and Peppers	4-1 negative	
		Broom corn brooms from Mexico	4-2 affirmative	Negative after negotiations ordered for 90 days
1997	1	Wheat gluten[1]	Affirmative after pending	Quantitative restrictions for 3 years and 1 day announced in 1998
1998	2	Lamb meat[2]	6-0 affirmative	A tariff-rate quota for 3 years and 1 day announced in 1999
		Wire rod		
1999	2	Wire rod[3]	3-3 even	A tariff-rate quota for 3 years and 1 day announced in 2000
		Line pipe[4]	5-1 affirmative	An increase in duty announced in
2000				
2000	2	Crab meat	Negative	
		Extruded rubber	Negative	
2001	1	Steel products	Affirmative	In deliberation

1. All countries excluding Canada, Mexico, Israel, CBI and Andean and Trade Preference Beneficiaries.
2. In 2001, the WTO Appellate Body finds the U.S. safeguard measure on lamb meat inconsistent with the Safeguard Agreement and $GATT_{1994}$.
3. All countries except Canada and Mexico. The WTO finds the U.S. measure on line pipe inconsistent with the Safeguard Agreement and $GATT_{1994}$. In November 2003, the WTO issued a final ruling that U.S. safeguard tariffs violated international trade agreements. See chapter 10 (10.2 and endnote 11).
Source: Constructed by the author from data in USTR, *2003 Trade Policy Agenda and 2002 Annual Report,* (Washington, D.C.: U.S. GPO), 245–46 and various other issues.

on behalf of exporters, full or partial exemption, remission, deduction or deferral of direct or indirect taxes or social welfare charges for exports, drawback of import charges, and the provision of export credit and insurance against exchange risk at preferential rates.[19]
- Domestic subsidies (those provided to a firm or industry, or a group of firms or industries)—provision of capital, loans or loan guarantees, goods and services at preferential rates, grants of funds or forgiveness of debt, and assumption of costs or expenses of production and distribution.
- Upstream subsidies (subsidies on inputs)—a subsidy paid to a producer of an intermediate input if a finished good is manufactured from subsidized input and exported even if the producer of the finished product did not receive a subsidy.

Table 7.10 presents the numbers of CVD cases during the period from fiscal year 1980 to 2001. The numbers vary in each year but exhibit a signifi-

Table 7.10.   CVD Cases (Fiscal year: 1980–2001)

Year	Terminated	Negative	Affirmative	Total
1980	9	55	2	66
1981	16	0	1	17
1982	42	53	18	113
1983	3	2	3	8
1984	6	8	8	22
1985	18	12	8	38
1986	9	7	10	26
1987	3	1	4	8
1988	4	3	3	10
1989	1	0	2	3
1990	1	2	1	4
1991	5	3	1	9
1992	1	25	18	44
1993	0	0	1	1
1994	3	6	2	11
1995	0	0	2	2
1996	1	0	0	1
1997	1	4	1	6
1998	3	1	7	11
1999	6	5	6	17
2000	0	0	1	1
2001	4	5	15	24
Total	136	192	114	442
	(31%)	(43%)	(26%)	(100%)

Source: U.S. ITC, *Antidumping and Countervailing Duty Handbook,* 10th ed prepared by Robert Carpenter, Office of Investigation (Washington, D.C.: U.S. GPO, December 2002), E-5.

cant level that is maintained throughout the period. During this period, about 400 cases were investigated. Only 26 percent of the cases were affirmative. The countries subject to CVD investigations are developed and newly industrialized countries. According to the ITC data, they include Brazil (10.9 percent), France (8.4 percent), Italy (8.4 percent), Canada (6.3 percent), Germany (6.1 percent), Korea (5.7 percent), Spain (5.2 percent), U.K. (5.0 percent), Belgium (4.8 percent), Venezuela (3.8 percent), and all others (35.5 percent). The number of ITC's affirmative final injury determinations is relatively small. Industries subject to Section 701 are textiles (1980–1984), nonmetalic mineral manufacturers (1980–1985), nonferrous metal manufacturers (various years), and electrical machinery (1985–1988). During actual determination of material injury, the ITC takes into account numerous (fourteen) economic factors, including:

• Volume of imports,
• Effects on U.S. prices of similar goods,
• Effects on U.S. producers such as lost sales, market share, profits, productivity, return on investment, and capacity utilization.

6. Antidumping Duty Actions

Table 7.11 shows the number of AD cases during the period of fiscal year from 1980 to 2001. The first year (1980) is the year when Congress transferred the authority to investigate AD cases from the Department of Treasury to the Department of Commerce. Almost one thousand cases were initiated for the last twenty years. Affirmative decisions reached 42 percent. Top ten countries cited in antidumping cases are Japan (10.4 percent), China (8.4 percent), Korea (6.4 percent), Germany (6.1 percent), Taiwan (6.0 percent), Canada (4.8 percent), Brazil (4.7 percent), Italy (4.7 percent), France (3.7 percent), U.K. (3.6 percent), and all others (41.3 percent). Industries subject to Section 731 are textiles (1982–1988), non-metalic mineral manufacturers (various years), motor vehicles (1987–1992), telecommunications and sound (various years), electrical machinery (1985–1992), and office machines (1985–1993).

Economists have begun to realize that U.S. policy based on the eighty-year-old antidumping law is beginning to boomerang. Countries are increasingly levying duties against one another through their antidumping laws. Developing countries filed only a limited number of cases in the 1980s, but they brought 700 cases overall in the second half of the 1990s. The countries and products/industrial areas subject to AD investigations are similar to those of CVD investigations. Numbers of AD investigations are generally larger than those of CVD cases throughout the period, implying that U.S. trade policy is

Table 7.11 AD Cases (Fiscal year: 1980-2001)

Year	Terminated	Negative	Affirmative	Total
1980	10	15	9	34
1981	6	5	4	15
1982	28	25	12	65
1983	8	14	12	34
1984	29	13	16	58
1985	36	20	26	82
1986	12	14	37	63
1987	4	15	17	36
1988	3	14	21	38
1989	3	9	17	29
1990	2	4	15	21
1991	6	40	19	65
1992	4	47	38	89
1993	16	9	11	36
1994	4	26	29	59
1995	3	6	9	18
1996	2	2	9	13
1997	2	7	14	23
1998	0	11	22	33
1999	6	24	20	50
2000	2	15	18	35
2001	9	43	40	92
Total	195	378	415	988
	(20%)	(38%)	(42%)	(100%)

Source: U.S. ITC, *Antidumping and Countervailing Duty Handbook,* 10th ed. prepared by Robert Carpenter, Office of Investigation, (Washington, D.C.: U.S. GPO, December 2002), E-4.

more dependent on AD policy and that dumping may be a major unfair trade method of foreign countries engaged in disputes with the United States. There is a theory suggesting that subsidy causes dumping. Figure 7.1 exhibits scattered points and the regression line for total numbers of CVD and AD cases available in tables 7.10 and 7.11. Although the estimated value for the coefficient of correlation between AD and CVD is low, the asymptotic t-value for the slope coefficient confirms the causality.

Despite strenuous enforcement of trade remedy measures with multilateral, regional, and bilateral initiatives, effectiveness of the policy on the balance of payments is questionable. Note that:

- U.S. merchandise trade deficits mounted with all countries and regions
- Deficit grew with the NAFTA member countries
- Dramatic increase in deficit with China since China joined the WTO in 2001
- Deficits with Japan remained high.

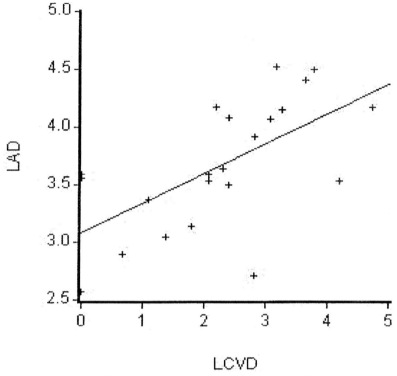

Figure 7.1. Scatter Points and Regression Line of AD and CVD in Natural Log
Regression equation:

$$LAD_t = 3.071 + 0.261\ LCVD_t + e_t$$
$$(15.796)\ (3.512)$$

$$R^2 = 0.382,\ SER = 0.454,\ DW = 0.797$$

where LAD = total number of cases of AD investigations (proxy for dumping) and LCVD = total number of cases of CVD investigations (proxy for subsidy) in natural log Asymptotic t-values in parentheses. Period of observation: 1980–2001. *Source:* Constructed by the author.

In his recent study, Prusa (2001) suggests that U.S. antidumping duties cause the value of imports to fall. Chapter 9 will discuss the effectiveness of the AD policy in detail with the CVD policy.

It is also important to note enormous social costs generated by the increased numbers of CVD and AD cases and their lengthy and complex quasi-judicial processes for final determination, as discussed in chapter 4, directly or peripherally to the United States and other countries. Chapter 10 will discuss this issue.

7.5 FUTURE COURSE OF U.S. TRADE POLICY

The United States believes that a strong multilateral trading system is necessary for the prosperity of not only the U.S. economy but also the entire global economy. In the future, the central thrust of trade policy will be again to open foreign markets and to expand trade. The administration will fully utilize the fast-track authority for trade promotion, renewed by the Trade Act of 2002.[20] Congress can accept or reject trade treaties but not amend them during the next five years, except for the antidumping laws.[21]

As of now, it is also highly likely that the trade policy agenda of the Administration would be to a large extent consistent with the future agenda of the WTO discussed in section 5.4 of chapter 5.[22] The United States will also continue to pursue regional and bilateral agreements with many countries. Unless the Omnibus Trade and Competitiveness Act of 1988 is significantly amended or a new trade law is enacted, the existing trade remedy previsions will continue to serve as the chief U.S. trade policy instruments.

Specific areas under the trade promotion authority include:

1. The Doha Negotiations

Two key built-in agenda for the Doha Round are the liberalization of trade in agriculture and services. The scope of trade negotiations for the United States ranges from the standing agenda, such as trade barriers and dispute settlement procedures, to priority areas, such as intellectual property rights in addition to the above Doha agenda. Recognizing the emerging importance of a strong high-tech sector, the United States is expected to protect the results of R&D such as biotechnology as the chief source of innovation in agriculture and medicine by means of Special 301 and the TRIPs agreement incorporated with various agreements including the 1991 U.S.-Japan Semiconductor Agreement, the Information Technology Agreement of 1997, the 1998 Agreement on Basic Telecommunications Services, and the 1999 Agreement on Financial Services.

2. Negotiations of Regional Trade Agreements

Extension of the NAFTA to the FTAA is the central agenda for the regional trade of the new administration. As part of the post-NAFTA agenda, issues negotiated at the meetings include market access, customs procedures and rules of origin, investment, standard and technical barriers, environment, government procurement, intellectual property rights, and dispute settlement.

3. Negotiations of Bilateral Agreements

The Administration will attempt to expand bilateral agreements to countries in Latin America, Southeast Asia, the Middle East, and Africa. The single most important bilateral concern of the United States is to build the ground for fair trade with China. With China, it is expected that the Administration will exert to ensure protection of U.S. intellectual property rights, nondiscriminatory taxation, market access in areas such as agriculture and financial services, transparency in trade regime, and distribution system.

4. Working Condition and Environment

The United States will continue to view adherence to international labor and environmental standards and to the protection and safety of consumers as fundamental human values. In detail, (i) internationally-agreed labor standards prohibit forced labor, exploitative child labor, discrimination in the workplace, and restrictions on collective bargain. The trading system is required to collaborate more effectively with the International Labor Organization (ILO), the relevant committees of the WTO, business, and citizen activists. The United States enforces the provisions of existing U.S. law that provide for withdrawal of U.S. trade preferences in cases of clear violation of worker rights; (ii) The trade and environmental issue addresses the need for environmental protection during the process of trade expansion. This issue has been pursued through the North American Agreement on Environmental Cooperation in the NAFTA, the Border Environment Cooperative Commission established by the U.S.-Mexico agreement at the time of the NAFTA, and the Committee on Trade and Environment of the WTO. In the future, this will continue to be a salient issue to be resolved through regional and multilateral forums, including FTAA, APEC, TEP, and the Committee on Trade and Environment of the WTO; and (iii) The issue on trade and consumer benefits addresses the argument for the open-market policy resulting in consumer benefits in terms of better prices, quality, and choice.

5. Monitoring and Enforcement

The Administration is highly likely to extend aggressively U.S. rights under various international trade agreements and to enforce effectively trade remedy provisions in order to protect U.S. interests through the WTO, regional agreements, bilateral agreements, and U.S. trade laws. The relevant provisions in the U.S. trade laws are Section 301, Special 301, Super 301, Section 1377 of the Omnibus Trade and Competitiveness Act of 1988 for telecommunications issues, Title VII of the enforcement of procurement agreements, and technical assistance to trading partners in an effort to implement the Agreement on Basic Telecommunications and TRIPs

6. Trade Capacity Building with Developing Countries

The United States believes that trade is critical to the growth of both developed and developing countries and that trade capacity should expand through its commitment to helping developing countries participate fully in the global trading system, As the largest single-country donor of trade-related technical assistance, the United States will continue to assist the developing countries for this purpose.

In addition to trade promotion authority discussed above, the future U.S. trade policy agenda includes trade adjustment assistance and the Generalized Scheme of Preference (GSP).

7. *Trade Adjustment Assistance*

It includes extension of the training period for American workers who lose their jobs and receive payments; extension of workers' benefits when manufacturing plants move to countries that have free or preferential trade agreements with the United States; and extension of health insurance to dislocated workers who would be eligible for refundable tax credit.

8. *GSP*

This authorizes the President to give preferential duty treatment to goods from developing countries, including Columbia, Peru, Ecuador, and Bolivia under the Andean Trade Preference Act, through 2006.

7.6 SUMMARY AND CONCLUSIONS

The Omnibus Trade and Competitiveness Act of 1988 dictates U.S. trade policy. The principal trade remedy provisions specified in the OTCA are the primary U.S. policy instruments. Coordinated use of multilateral, regional, and bilateral agreements is a characterization of the multifaceted policy nature.

This chapter examines actual U.S. trade policies employed in the recent past under each of the trade agreements. It focuses on policies involving trade barriers and disputes, two key agenda throughout the history of multilateral agreements since $GATT_{1947}$, under the Kennedy Round, the Tokyo Round, and the Uruguay Round; policies under the NAFTA and their effects on the U.S. economy; and policies on the basis of bilateral agreements with principal trading partners, the EC, Japan, China, Korea, and two NAFTA member countries.

Violation of any of these agreements by a foreign country is subject to enforcement by the trade remedy laws. This chapter analyzes actual cases of Section 301, Super 301, Special 301, Section 201, Section 701, and Section 731.

The U.S. trade policy agenda of the future includes trade promotion achieved through trade agreements by fast-track authority, values relating to labor and environmental standards, lower trade barriers in the areas of agricultural products, service industries, intellectual property, electronic commerce, and textiles; trade adjustment assistance for workers; and Andean trade preference and GSP for LDCs.

In conclusion,

- The scope of U.S. trade policy is broad.
- The numerous policy instruments are implemented through long and complex quasi-judicial processes.
- Fair trade policy requires the United States to pay a considerable social cost.

Chapter 10 will discuss fair trade policy and social cost.

NOTES

1. For example, imported automobiles were subject to U.S. quotas until 1985 and to voluntary export restraints (VERs) since then. Shortly afterward, Japanese-manufactured luxury cars and auto parts barely avoided U.S. sanctions. The textiles and apparel industry was in a similar situation at that time.

2. See the Council of Economic Advisors, *Economic Report of the President* (Washington, D.C.: U.S. GPO, 1999), 4.

3. See the Council of Economic Advisors, *Economic Report of the President* (Washington, D.C.: U.S. GPO, 2001), 4. Also see USTR, *2000 Trade Policy Agenda and 1999 Annual Report* (Washington, D.C.: U.S. GPO, 1999), 1. The USTR reports that it completed nearly 300 separate trade agreements only during the 1990s in order to open foreign markets under the rule of law, the trade policy tradition that has been maintained since the era of Franklin Roosevelt.

4. Other multilateral activities include trade and environment, trade and labor, the OECD, semiconductor agreements, and steel policy.

5. See USTR, *2000 Trade Policy Agenda and 1999 Annual Report* (Washington, D.C.: U.S. GPO, 1999), 1.

6. See table 7.4.

7. For devaluation effects of the Mexican peso, see Russell Hillberry and Christine McDaniel, "A Decomposition of North American Trade Growth Since NAFTA," *International Economic Review* (May/June 2002): 1–5; for small size of Mexican economy, see Edward Leamer, "Wage Effects of U.S.-Mexico Free Trade Agreement," in *The Mexico-U.S. Free Trade Agreement*, ed. Peter Garber (Cambridge, MA: MIT Press, 1993).

8. Balanced trade with these countries and responses to their unfair trade practices not covered in multilateral and regional trade agreements are the main objective of the U.S. market opening policy as pursued through bilateral trade agreements. For their trade barriers against the United States, see chapter 8, section 1 of this book.

9. See USTR, *2000 Trade Policy Agenda and 1999 Annual Report* (Washington, D.C.: U.S. GPO, 1999), 8–9.

10. Meanwhile, negotiations with the United States for the WTO admission of China have been underway for two decades until the United States has recently endorsed China's admission.

11. The history of trade protection for the U.S. steel industry is long and complex. The period of protection for steel is customarily broken down into three phases: 1969–1974, protection principally by voluntary export restraint (VER); 1978–1982, protection by a trigger price mechanism; and 1982 to the recent past, protection by both VER and Sections 701 and 731. See Jae Wan Chung, "Effects of U.S. Trade Remedy Law Enforcement under Uncertainty: The Case of Steel," *Southern Economic Journal* 65, no. 3 (July 1988): 151. Countries under Section 701 involving the iron/steel industry were Belgium, Brazil, Canada, France, Germany, Italy, Korea, Mexico, Singapore, Spain, Sweden, Taiwan, and Venezuela. Countries involving Section 731 were all of the above plus China, Japan, the Netherlands, Peru, Romania, South Africa, Thailand, and the United Kingdom.

12. See USTR, *2001 Trade Policy Agenda and 2000 Annual Report* (Washington, D.C.: U.S. GPO, 2000), 209 and various other issues.

13. The USTR considers this as the most significant example of the leverage exerted by Super 301.

14. See U.S. House of Representatives, Subcommittee on Trade of Ways and Means, *Hearing: USTR Identification of Priority Practices and Countries under Super 301 and Special 301 Provisions of the Omnibus Trade and Competitiveness Act of 1988* (Washington, D.C.: U.S. GPIO, 1998), 11.

15. The second round began on March 31, 1990 when the USTR issued *Foreign Trade Barriers 1990*, which is a comprehensive listing of foreign trade barriers. Based on this issue, the USTR was supposed to designate priority foreign countries and priority practices on the watch list by April 30.

16. See Maxwell Baucus, Memorandum to the USTR (submitted on January 30, 1990), 5.

17. Special 301 today includes new initiatives such as health-related intellectual property rights, on-going initiatives to secure full and timely implementation of WTO TRIPS, and pirate production and distribution of optical media like CDs, Video CDs, digital videodiscs, and CD ROMs.

18. See Council of Economic Advisors, *Economic Report of the President*, Washington, D.C.: U.S. GPO, 2003, 4.

19. Export subsidies are defined with reference to the GATT Subsides Code. Its annex provides a list of countervailable subsidies.

20. This section is based on USTR, *2004 Trade Policy Agenda and 2003 Annual Report* (Washington, D.C.: U.S. GPO, 2003).

21. The House passed the fast-track authority bill 215 to 212 on July 24, 2002, the Senate passed it 64 to 34 on August 1, 2002, and the President signed the bill on August 6, 2002. This legislation reinstates a power of five former Presidents until it lapsed in 1994.

22. President Bush signed a six-year farm bill on July 25, 2002, that increases subsidies substantially. Amid criticism from U.S. trading partners, the President has also proposed a global cut in farm subsidies and tariffs.

Chapter 8

Trade Disputes and Settlements

Since enactment of the OTCA in 1988, the United States has aggressively implemented its trade remedy policy. This policy has been controversial not only in the United States but also among foreign countries. In foreign countries, these controversies involve the compatibility of the trade remedy provisions with multilateral agreements and the implementation processes of the trade remedy provisions. Furthermore, foreign nations argue that each country has its own pace of economic development, social structure, and historical and cultural background, while the United States has applied a uniform definition of "unfair trade" to all foreign countries. The United States retorts that its responses to foreign trade practices are not necessarily unfair to those countries that violate multilateral, regional, and/or bilateral trade agreements.[1]

Requests for consultation brought by both the United States and foreign countries to the WTO during the period from 1995 to 2002, the first eight years of WTO operation, are substantially high. It is important to have insights into the pattern and nature of trade disputes, requiring us to analyze disputes that the United States brought against foreign countries to the WTO and disputes that foreign countries brought against the United States to the WTO. The foreign countries under consideration here are the countries in frequent trade dispute with the United States. They are the EU, Japan, Korea, China, Canada, and Mexico. The proportions of their disputes with respect to the total number of disputes brought to the WTO increased until 2000 and remained high throughout the period. The countries listed above are the same as those selected on their volumes of trade and the number of bilateral trade agreements available in section 7.3 of the preceding chapter. The rationale here is that the number of trade disputes of a particular foreign country with the

United States is positively correlated with its volume of trade with the United States, and that, if a foreign country trades more with the United States, the country has more chances to make bilateral trade agreements and faces more disputes with the United States.

This chapter is concerned with trade disputes between the United States and foreign countries and settlements at the WTO. The first section outlines foreign trade barriers to the United States, the initial step toward disputes and likely retaliations. Arguments concerning disputes of the foreign countries against the United States are discussed in the second section. The third section examines whether the trade remedy statutes are in accord with the GATT/WTO. The fourth section investigates the pattern of trade disputes between the United States and foreign countries to analyze the status of dispute settlement at the WTO for the past seven years. The last section draws conclusions.

8.1 FOREIGN TRADE BARRIERS

Trade disputes stem from trade barriers between the United States and foreign countries. The USTR has systematically compiled foreign trade to the United States. Most of the barriers, alleged as market-distorting measures by the United States but often contested by foreign countries, are within the purview of the trade remedy policy. A particular barrier of a foreign country is subject to U.S. retaliation. In the event of its failure to remove the barrier through bilateral consultation, the United States takes the case to the WTO for settlement and both countries are supposed to comply with the WTO decision. In order to provide valid commentary on trade disputes in the face of controversies about U.S. trade policy, it is important to have prior knowledge on foreign trade barriers conceived against the United States before switching our attention to the central issues on trade disputes and settlements.

This chapter begins with foreign trade barriers classified by the USTR:[2]

1. Import policies
2. Standards, testing, labeling, and certification
3. Government procurement
4. Export subsidies
5. Lack of intellectual property protection
6. Services barriers
7. Investment barriers
8. Anticompetitive practices
9. Trade restrictions affecting electronic commerce
10. Other barriers.

As shown in table 8.1, almost all of the foreign countries under consideration have trade barriers against the United States that correspond to each of the categories. Actual barriers in each category for each country are numerous. They include a large number of specific commodity items or policies. The items and policies keep changing over time. There are new trade barriers each year and many of the previous barriers remain for, or return after, several years as active cases. However, most of them have been standing barriers at least for the past several years. It is not appropriate to present them in detail here but important to make two propositions obtained carefully from the latest data available in the source cited in endnote 2 of this chapter by country under consideration:

• Despite trade agreements at all levels and strenuous implementations of the trade remedy policy during a long testable period, there is no clear evidence indicating alleviation of trade barriers to the United States with or without barriers in connection with service trade. This observation raises a serious question on the effectiveness of U.S. trade policy and the world trade system.
• Despite the long history of the NAFTA, trade barriers of Canada and Mexico to the United States still remain high, implying a possible limit of a regional trade agreement.

Table 8.1. Types of Trade Barriers in Selected Countries

Types of Trade Barriers	*Country*
(1) Import Policies	EU, Japan, Korea, China, Canada, Mexico
(2) Standards, Testing, Labeling, and Certification	EU, Japan, Korea, China*, Canada*, Mexico
(3) Government Procurement	EU, Japan, Korea, China, Canada*, Mexico
(4) Export Subsidies	EU, Korea*, China*, Canada*
(5) Lack of Intellectual Property Protection	EU, Japan, Korea, China, Canada, Mexico*
(6) Services Barriers	EU, Japan, Korea, China, Canada, Mexico*
(7) Investment Barriers	EU, Japan, Korea, China, Canada, Mexico*
(8) Anticompetitive Practices	Japan, Korea, China
(9) Electronic Commerce[1]	EU, Japan, Korea, China, Canada
(10) Other Barriers	EU, Japan, Korea, China, Canada**

Note: 1. Earlier issues of *National Trade Estimate Report on Foreign Trade Barriers* (FTBs) did not have this category.

* Countries of trade barriers listed newly in FTBs.
**Countries of trade barriers listed in earlier issues of FTBs but deleted from the issue in 2003 FTBs.

Source: Constructed by the author from data in USTR, *Foreign Trade Barriers* (Washington, D.C.: U.S. GPO), 2003 and earlier issues.

8.2 COMPLAINTS ABOUT U.S. TRADE REMEDY POLICY

This section discusses complaints of foreign countries toward the U.S. trade remedy policy in the order of the most frequent and pervasive disputes. The disputes are heavily concentrated on the countervailing duty (CVD) and antidumping duty (AD).

1. CVD and AD

A subsidy provided by a foreign government to an exporter who exports goods to the United States increases the price in its domestic market and decreases it in the home market, a result similar to that of Pigou's third-degree price discrimination for profit maximization of the monopolist. The United States levies the CVD to a foreign country because the foreign subsidy inflicts the *material injury* to U.S. industries, that is, *harm which is not inconsequential, immaterial, or unimportant*, as defined in the U.S. trade remedy law and the GATT/WTO. Apart from this statutory reason, there is a theoretical validity for the CVD. The Brander-Spencer strategic trade policy theory suggests that a foreign subsidy has a deterrent effect on U.S. firms attempting to enter into world markets in case of imperfect competition (contrary to Krugman who suggests that this effect can be neutralized by U.S. superiority in technology). The adverse welfare effects of a foreign subsidy on the U.S. economy can be another justification for a CVD. In the event of international rent-seeking, the United States may not be independent of the foreign welfare loss from the subsidy. The United States is forced to use scarce resources inefficiently or simply to face necessarily "directly-unproductive profit-seeking (DUP)" activities, the term used by Bhagwati (1982). Public choice economists assert that a significant portion of the subsidy tied with rent-seeking is political domain in nature. Complaints about the U.S. CVD policy by foreign countries will be discussed further in section 8.4.

Again, the statutory reason for AD is the material injury inflicted by foreign dumping on U.S. firms or industries. The national welfare loss in the United States through international rent-seeking is the underlying rationale for regulating such a monopolistic behavior. Since the "new protectionism" arose in the United States in the 1980s, antidumping policy has evolved along a path of ever increasing protection for U.S firms where ADs (and CVDs) have displaced tariffs and other NTBs as primary objects of multilateral negotiation.[3]

Most controversies over U.S. trade remedy policies are concerned more with actual implementation of the policies rather than the statutory reasons for material injury. Specific complaints regarding implementation of the AD/CVD policies are as follows:

(A) Dumping Margin

The International Trade Administration (ITA) computes the dumping margin (DM) by the three different methods discussed in chapter 4: (i) home market sales (weighted average of prices in the home market of the exporting country for goods similar to those exported to the importing country); (ii) third country sales (weighted average of prices for goods similar to those exported to a third country); and (iii) constructed value (sum of cost of production, operating expenses, and profit). These have numerous sources of bias.

For the first and second methods, the ITA generally calculates the average foreign market values of sales for six months to compare with the actual U.S. price of each entry. The difference between the average foreign market value and the U.S. price is regarded as the DM if the former is smaller than the latter. In the real world, such a comparison results in a statistical error in the event of price fluctuations over the period of measurement.[4] Furthermore, there are several sources of miscalculation of the dumping margin. As exhibited by the U-shaped average cost curve discussed in principles of microeconomics texts, firms usually pay a high average cost due to small output and large R&D expenditures in the early stages of production, especially in high technology industries. Expecting the average cost to be reduced in the future, firms often sell their products at a price below the production cost. Foreign countries believe that such a pricing strategy facilitates the introduction of new products in international markets and thus improves efficiency in the world economy. They should therefore be allowed, for a reasonable period of time, to recover the average total cost. However, the ITC considers such a practice to be dumping that is unfair to the United States.[5] A bias can also occur when the ITA makes cost-based adjustments to the foreign price for different physical characteristics, market circumstances, and levels of commerce between different countries. Although the ITA needs statistical inferences obtained from econometric analyses, it often bases its preliminary determination on the best available information if foreign producers do not comply with ITA's request for information, or if their information is inadequate; this allows the ITA more discretion toward the highest margin, contrary to what the Act states.[6]

The third method is used when home market sales are less than five percent of third country sales and when third country sales are few or nonexistent. The ITA must calculate an average variable cost and an average fixed cost. A method taken by the ITA is the specification of a minimum "general selling and administrative cost" of at least 10 percent of operating expenses and a profit of 8 percent of operating expenses plus general selling and administrative costs. This method contains arbitrary components that may yield a bias. The WTO has suggested a method to compute the dumping margin.

The sale price in an exporting country is comparable to that in the United States if both are based on the factory price. However, the ITC adjusts the sale price by the indirect expenditure for sale in the United States. Consequently, the sale price in the exporting country exceeds that in the United States if the indirect expenses for sale in the exporting country are higher than those in the United States. The purpose of the constructed value method is to compute the normal value, but the value is normally overestimated.

Foreign exchange fluctuations should also significantly affect the value for the dumping calculated by any of the three methods. However, there is a view that the United States does not take into account foreign exchange fluctuations.

(B) Biased Investigations of the AD and the CVD

Bhagwati (1988) and others argue that AD laws were designed for strategic use to maximize U.S. gain. For instance, the ITA procedures permit the ITA to compute dumping margins that could lead to positive margins. In fact, the definition of a dumping margin changed from the difference between the price in the home market and the price in a foreign market to the difference between the price in the home market and the foreign production cost in 1974. Furthermore, Congress transferred the authority to investigate AD cases from the Department of Treasury to the Department of Commerce and encouraged use of the constructed value for the dumping margin. The ITA and the ITC take petitions filed by any interest group or individual in the United States. They may also self-initiate and investigate a case. In any case, a foreign defendant is required to submit a massive amount of data within a short period. However, there is suspicion that the ITC uses data submitted by the plaintiff in the United States and that the ITC makes a negative determination arbitrarily. The high cost to the defendant incurred during a lengthy judicial process in the absence of a fair chance for defense can place the defendant in a gray area leading to out-of-court settlement with the plaintiff. The subsequent chapter will discuss extensive research done on adjudicatory behavior of policy institutions.

(C) The Sunset Clause

According to the Sunset Clause in the Uruguay Round, the period for any AD or CVD case is supposed to expire automatically after five years. However, agencies continue to monitor the case even after it is settled. Such a practice enables the U.S. plaintiff to save the initiating cost for filing another petition for the same case and requires the foreign defendant to pay the cost.

(D) Definition of the Same Product

The range of products subject to the AD and CVD depends on the definition of the *same* product. The definition may be drawn in terms of either *use* or *factor-intensity*. The United States broadens the range of products subject to the AD and CVD.

2. Section 301

There have been many questions and arguments about Section 301 and its related provisions because they are supposedly contradictory to the GATT/WTO framework. Japan first brought questions on Sections 301 and 304 to the WTO in 1995, followed by the EU twice, in connection with Sections 306–310 in 1999 and with Section 306 in 2000. The WTO ruled that Sections 301–310 were not in violation of the WTO agreements but should be consistent in their application.

3. Super 301

Super 301 has drawn the most strenuous complaints from foreign countries. Despite opposition by the executive branch, the Senate Committee on Finance passed the Baucus bill that proposed to extend Super 301 every five years. The unanimous passage of this bill clearly indicated that protectionism prevailed strongly in the legislative branch.

Critics of Super 301 argue that:

• The United States draws its own "unilateral" legal definition of unfair trade practices.
• Irrespective of the WTO's panel decision, the United States predetermines target countries in order to apply retaliatory measures selectively. Some even argued that it was designed to deal with the trade surplus of Japan at the time of chronic U.S. trade disparity.

However, the United States believes that there is no good alternative to Super 301 for two reasons:

• Although critics suggest that the United States should rely exclusively upon the GATT to settle trade disputes, GATT dispute settlement is not effective because each country has the right to block a GATT decision.
• The GATT does not deal with many of the trade problems that the United States faces, such as the distribution system, toleration of a cartel, and many technical barriers.

Among six priority practices conducted by three priority countries identified by the USTR in 1989, three different areas were cited against Japan (supercomputers, satellites, and finished forest products), one against Brazil (quantitative restrictions and import licensing), and two against India (investment and insurance). These three countries refused to negotiate with the United States, asserting that Super 301 was unilateral and was contrary to $GATT_{1947}$ or that their trade practices were fully compatible with the GATT.

In the cases involving Japan, the USTR argued that the U.S. share of the supercomputer market in Japan was exceedingly small in comparison with its shares in Europe and its home market because of government procurement policies and practices in Japan. It was also argued that Japan shielded its own satellite market because satellites were not used for commercial purposes, another example of government procurement policies and practices, and that Japan maintained numerous impediments to imports of finished wood products, including high tariffs and technical barriers. A hard line approach toward Japan in defending Super 301 turned its refusal around. In March 1990, Japan and the United States reached a supercomputer procurement agreement.

Brazil prohibited import items by means of NTBs including import licenses. After the change in Brazilian government, the new government made significant market reforms, leading to a considerable reduction in tariffs.

The two cases involving India were more complex as India refused to respond to Super 301 and remained closed in these two markets. India continued to maintain a policy on foreign investment that required governmental approval (without criteria from the U.S. perspective), required investors to use locally produced inputs regardless of quality, and imposed equity restrictions and restrictions on repatriation of capital. With some exceptions, the government owned all insurance business. Consequently, India was renewed by the USTR as the only priority country.

4. Special 301

The United States believes that failure of foreign countries to protect U.S. intellectual property rights has increasingly been a serious issue. A well-known example is U.S. computer software duplicated illegally by China in the mid-1990s. Foreign manufacturers of intellectual properties believe that the processes of petition, investigation and determination are biased against them. They complained that the period of investigation, is insufficient for a proper chance to defend their position.

5. Section 201

Actual numbers of Section 201 cases are relatively smaller than those of other provisions. However, this provision generates notable trade disputes at times. A case in the recent past was concerned with U.S. import-relief tariff imposed on steel pipe. In response to the requests made by Korea, Japan, and the EU, the WTO established a panel on June 13, 2000 and gave them the right to impose retaliatory tariffs in its final ruling. The United States withdrew the tariff in December 2003 accordingly.

8.3 ARE THE U.S. TRADE REMEDY STATUTES IN ACCORD WITH MULTILATERAL AGREEMENTS?

As the United States intensifies its trade remedy policy, trade remedy measures have become increasingly controversial. An immediate question arises as to whether the principal trade remedy provisions are in accord with the GATT/UR agreements. This section examines their conformity. Part II in GATT$_{1947}$ and Annex 1A and Annex 1C in Annex 1 in the Uruguay Round Agreement (UR) include provisions related to part of U.S. trade remedy laws. These provisions justify Sections 701, 731, 201, and Special 301, as discussed briefly below 1 through 4 in this section.

1. Section 701: Countervailing Duty

Articles VI, XVI, and XXIII in Part II of the GATT$_{1947}$ and Articles 1 through 32 included in the Agreement on Subsidies and Countervailing Measures in Annex 1A: Multilateral Agreements on Trade in Goods of the UR are concerned with subsidy and countervailing duty. The subsidy/countervailing duty in the Uruguay Agreement is based on Articles VI, XVI, and XXIII of GATT$_{1947}$ as negotiated in the Tokyo Round, (i.e., the 1979 GATT Subsidies Code). These articles define subsidy, introduce the concept of a "specific" subsidy, and contain disciplines or measures on the use of subsidies and countervailing duties, including calculation of the amount of a subsidy and the basis for determination of injury. According to the UR, all countervailing duties must be terminated within five years. The agreement defines "subsidies" as "financial contribution" provided directly and indirectly by a government and applies to nonagricultural products. There are three categories of subsidies: (i) prohibited subsidies; (ii) permissible, actionable subsidies; and (iii) permissible, non-actionable subsidies.[7] Prohibited subsidies are contingent upon export performance or upon the use of domestic inputs instead of imports. Actionable subsidies are those that demonstrably have adverse effects on other countries; such as, injury to an industry in another country, nullification, or impairment of benefits under the GATT, especially the benefits of bound concessions, and serious prejudice to interests.[8] Both prohibited subsidies and actionable subsidies are subject to dispute settlement procedures and to countervailing measures of the complaining country, if found by the DSB and not withdrawn immediately. However, the least developed countries are exempted from disciplinary measures on prohibited export subsidies. The countries with 3.25 percent or less than world trade share maintaining during two consecutive years get an additional two years for exemption. Non-actionable subsidies are subsidies provided for industrial research if the assistance is limited to 75 percent of research costs and precompetitive development activity if it is limited to 50 percent of the cost; for development in regions that are determined to be disadvantaged and are not targeted to a specific firm, industry, or group in the region; and for meeting new environmental standards by existing plant and equipment up to a one-time measure equivalent to 20 percent of the cost. The non-actionable provisions are exempted from trade remedies but expire after five years. In order to claim a non-actionable subsidy, the country must notify the Subsidy-Countervailing Measure Committee and provide sufficient evidence that the subsidies are non-actionable. For developing countries, the export subsidy prohibition takes effect in 2003. Overall, section 701 is consistent with the Agreement on Subsidies and Countervailing Measures in $GATT_{1947}$/UR.

2. Section 731: Antidumping Duty

The Agreement on dumping and antidumping measures (Article VI of $GATT_{1994}$) in Annex 1A in the UR allows members to impose antidumping measures up to five years after the imposition date if a foreign country exports a product at a price below its *norm*al price and this dumping causes injury to a domestic industry.[9] If the dumping margin is less than 2 percent and imports of the good from the accused country constitute less than 3 percent of U.S. imports in the case of the United States (less than 7 percent in the case of all other countries), an investigation will not be initiated. This measure was initially negotiated during the Tokyo Round and was revised in the UR. The UR established more stringent, detailed criteria and procedures for the measurement of the dumping margin, the conduct of the antidumping investigation, assessment and collection of duties, and other aspects of antidumping practice. The agreement calls for the use of "constructed" value or export prices to third countries when home market sales are less than 5 percent of the sales to the importing country. The provisions on the antidumping duty (Section 731) imposed by the United States are compatible with those in the GATT/UR.

3. Section 201: Safeguard Measure

As was the case under Article XIX of $GATT_{1947}$, WTO members may restrict imports in order to protect a domestic industry, if it is threatened with serious injury from imports on the basis of Articles 1 through 12 in Agreement on Safeguards in Annex 1 of the UR. The Safeguards Committee of the WTO oversees the operation of the agreement. Articles XIX through XXI provide additional mechanisms for a country to protect domestic producers from injury resulting from increases in imports. The key agreement on safeguard actions requires members to observe comparable rules and transparent procedures including a clear definition of injury. It prohibits repeated applications of the measure to the same product and to products with an import-share less than 3 percent from a given developing country and 9 percent from all developing countries. The duration of a safeguard measure should not exceed four years, although this can be extended up to eight years. Any VERs, orderly marketing arrangements, or other similar measures are restricted and should have been phased out by the end of 1998. Safeguard measures taken prior to the UR agreement should be terminated within eight years or by the end of 1999, whichever comes later. Section 201 is conformable to the GATT/UR.

4. Special 301: Intellectual Property Rights Priorities

Uruguay Round Agreements contain Agreement on Trade-Related Aspects of Intellectual Property Rights (TRIPs) in Annex 1C. It includes copyright, trademarks or service marks, geographical indications, industrial designs, patents, and trade secrets and know-how. The first three parts of the agreement state provisions on the applicability of the most-favored-nation (MFN) clause (one of the fundamental principles of the GATT), standards concerning the availability, scope and use of TRIPs, and enforcement. The remaining parts address dispute settlement and transitional implementation arrangements. Special 301 is largely consistent with the GATT/UR.

5. Section 301 and Super 301

There have been serious controversies involving Section 301 and Super 301 in the absence of explicit provisions corresponding to them in GATT/UR. These provisions pertain to practices that are deemed unfair but are not within the purview of the $GATT_{1947}$.[10] Many critics suggest that policies on Section 301 and Super 301 are "unilateral" attempts to define what is fair or unfair. Although countercritics admit that both sections are unilateral, they argue that the critics assume that the United States should rely exclusively upon the ineffective GATT system to settle trade disputes, e.g., the distribution system in Japan under the GATT. They go on to argue that foreign trade practices defined as unfair by U.S. trade law were unfair on GATT's criteria and to suggest that the statutory time period for consultation, investigation, and determination by Section 301 and Super 301 was long enough to permit the GATT to settle disputes prior to U.S. retaliation.

A response to critics of U.S. trade policy is best described in the Baucus memo which reflects the Congressional position.[11] Senator Max Baucus (D-Montana), Chairman, International Trade Subcommittee in 1990, suggested

that Super 301 is not a sanction because the United States does not immediately retaliate but only gets results when it threatens to retaliate. He admits
that Super 301 is unilateral but rejects that the U.S. should rely exclusively
upon the GATT to settle trade disputes; GATT was not comprehensive
enough to address many of the international trade problems that the United
States faces and its dispute settlement was not binding.

The EU alleged that Section 301 is unilateral and Sections 304 to 306 do
not comply with the DSB. It is, however, notable that the panel, established
on March 2, 1999, concluded that U.S. trade law was not inconsistent with
U.S. obligations to the WTO, and it found no evidence against the United
States in determining every case subject to Section 301.[12]

Foreign countries in general have, however, strong antipathy toward Super
301 and feel that problems faced by the United States in connection with this
provision should be addressed within the purview of a new multilateral agreement.

8.4 TRADE DISPUTES AND SETTLEMENTS

This section analyzes trade disputes among countries and settlements by the
WTO. The new settlement mechanism available to all member countries of
the WTO has considerably increased the number of disputes filed with the
WTO in each year. Tables 8.2, 8.3, and 8.4 provide us with important insight
into the pattern and nature of trade disputes between the United States and
foreign countries. Table 8.2 shows the total number of requests for consultation brought to the WTO by all member countries in each year beginning
from 1995 to 2002. During its eight years in operation, member countries
filed a large number of distinct cases that totaled 297. Interestingly, the number of cases increased to a peak in the third year, decreased thereafter for a
few years, and then began to increase again. This pattern suggests that trade
disputes are not transitory. Table 8.3 presents the number of disputes brought
against foreign countries by the United States to the WTO and the number of
disputes brought against the United States by foreign countries to the WTO,
respectively, along with corresponding percentage figures.

Both numbers in this table are considerable over time. The United States
and a large number of foreign countries have exerted to take cases against
each other to the WTO. These cases imply mutual efforts of retaliations between the United States and foreign countries. Figure 8.1 exhibits the two different cases. The cases brought by the United States are larger than the cases
by foreign countries. The latter cases are likely the cases replicated against
the U.S. trade remedy policy by foreign countries. It is interesting to observe

**Table 8.2. Number of Requests for Consultation Brought
to the WTO by All Member Countries[1] (As of March 2002)**

Year	Number of Consultations
1995	25
1996	40
1997	50
1998	40
1999	30
2000	34
2001	40
2002	38
First 8 years in operation	297

1. Numbers brought by both the United States and foreign countries.

Source: Constructed by the author from data in USTR, *2003 Trade Policy Agenda and 2002 Annual Report,* (Washington, D.C.: U.S. GPO, March 2003), 47–62, and various other issues.

that the latter cases are smaller than the former cases until the year 1999 but larger after that year. This reversal implies a *boomerang effect* of U.S.-initiated retaliatory measures. Table 8.4 presents numbers of cases between the United States and the EU.

The EU has had more complaints lodged against the United States than the United States has had over the EU in recent years, implying EU's intensified retaliatory efforts over time.

Table 8.3. United States as Plaintiff and Defendant

	As Plaintiff Number of Disputes Brought Against Foreign Countries to the WTO by the U.S./Total Number of Disputes Brought to the WTO	As Defendant Number of Disputes Brought Against the U.S. to the WTO by Foreign Countries/Total Number of Disputes Brought to the WTO
1995	7/25 (28%)	3/25 (12%)
1996	20/40 (50%)	4/40 (10%)
1997	30/50 (60%)	15/50 (30%)
1998	27/40 (68%)	12/40 (30%)
1999	24/30 (80%)	16/30 (53%)
2000	23/34 (68%)	25/34 (74%)
2001	18/40 (45%)	22/40 (55%)
2002	12/38 (32%)	26/38 (68%)
1995–2002	161/297 (54%)	123/297 (41%)

Note: The number in a particular year is not necessarily independent of the number in the previous year.

Source: Constructed by the author from data in USTR, *2003 Trade Policy Agenda and 2002 Annual Report* (Washington, D.C.: U.S. GPO, 2002) and various other issues.

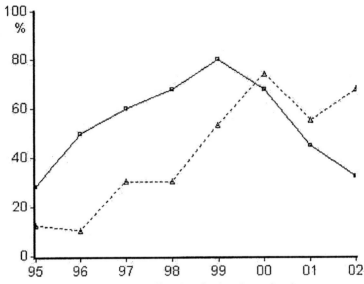

Figure 8.1.   United States as Plaintiff and Defendant in Trade Disputes.
Note: Percentage figures indicating the United States as the plaintiff in trade disputes (exhibited in the
solid line) = (number of disputes brought against foreign countries to the WTO by the U.S./total number of disputes brought to the WTO) × 100; percentage figures indicating the U.S. as the defendant
in trade disputes (exhibited in the dotted line) = (number of disputes brought against the United States
to the WTO by foreign countries/total number of disputes brought to the WTO) × 100. *Source:* Constructed by the author.

Appendices 8.1 and 8.2 list trade disputes filed with the WTO by the
United States and those by selected foreign countries in detail. Of the fifty-
two cases listed in appendix 8.1 for U.S. complaints to foreign countries,
three cases were settled immediately, nine cases were upheld at both panels
on the DSB and Appellate Bodies in favor of the United States, and one case
was not upheld at the Appellate Body. Among them, ten cases were concerned
with U.S. intellectual property rights, three with Section 701, and three with

Table 8.4.   Disputes between the United States and the EU

	U.S. Complaints to EU	EU Complaints to U.S.
1995	2	0
1996	4	1
1997	5	6
1998	5	6
1999	5	9
2000	4	15
2001	4	10
2002	3	11
1995-2002	32	58

Source: Constructed by the author from data in USTR, *2003 Trade Policy Agenda and 2002 Annual Report*
(Washington, D.C.: U.S. GPO, 2002) and various other issues.

Section 731. The lastest incident is the disputes over subsidies or tax break provided to the Airbus and Boeing. Most of the cases are disputes with EU, Japan, and Korea. Since the admission to the WTO in December 2001, China has not been on the list. However, the United States filed its complaints against China with the WTO for the first time in March 2004 in connection with unfair trade practices involving semiconductors.

Appendix 8.2 contains forty-six complaints of foreign countries toward the United States. Their complaints mostly involve Sections 701 and 731, indicating that the two provisions are dominant trade policy instruments of the United States. The cases of the EU are the largest; most of the Section 731 cases are concerned with Japan and Korea. There are two recent cases against the United States. One is the final ruling issued by the WTO in November 2003 that U.S. safeguard tariffs on steel, imposed up to 30 percent in March 2002 (for three years), violated international rules, which in turn gave the EU and several other countries the right to impose retaliatory tariffs up to 30 percent. As a result, the United States fully revoked the tariffs in December 2003. Another case ruled against the United States by the WTO is the case brought by Brazil in 2002. Brazil claimed that the United States illegally instituted a cotton subsidy in order to support the agricultural sector. The WTO ruled that U.S. cotton subsidies violated the WTO agreements in April 2004, forcing the United States to retract its subsidies much to the dismay of the cotton farmers, its lobbyists, and the members of Congress who hold these farmers as constituents.

Overall, the WTO system of dispute settlement demonstrates here the settlement process, which actually works and works fairly for all. However, many cases of trade disputes in appendices 8.1 and 8.2 have remained unsettled for several years.

Three distinct patterns emerge from tables 8.2 through 8.4 and appendices 8.1 and 8.2:

1. The number of trade disputes between the United States and foreign countries is considerable. A large number of disputes on the average imply that trade disputes have persisted and will persist over time.
2. The number of cases brought by the United States against foreign countries and the number of cases brought by foreign countries against the United States are almost the same, implying that mutual retaliations have prevailed. However, the former is greater than the latter for the earlier period of WTO operation and smaller for the latter period. The number of cases brought by foreign countries against the United States has notably increased in recent years, indicating that foreign countries have sharply escalated trade disputes with the United States in response to the trade remedy policy intensified by the United States.[13] This pattern confirms that U.S. trade policy tends to boomerang.

3. Although the WTO system of dispute settlement demonstrates an institutional power as a fair process, many cases remain unsettled for several years. The fair trade system is complex and its lengthy settlement processes are expensive.

There are numerous other measures and areas of disputes, often alleged to be inconsistent with GATT$_{1947}$, GATT$_{1994}$ or WTO rules (mostly brought by the EC, often joined by Japan and other countries). A policy measure becomes salient at times as trade issues change. Specific measures at present are:

- Section 110(5) of the Copyright Act
- Title VII of the Revenue Act of 1916 (entitled "Unfair Competition")
- Section 337 of the Tariff Act of 1930
- Section 306 of the Trade Act of 1974
- Dumping and Subsidy Offset Act of 2000 (Byrd Amendments)
- Rules of Origin

Consultations and negotiations between countries with or without involvement of the WTO are in progress for most of the cases. The above measures and issues are explained below:

1. Section 110(5) of the Copyright Act

This provision provides that certain retail establishments may play radio music without paying royalties to songwriters and music publishers. The EU, joined by Japan later, claimed that this provision is in violation of its TRIPS obligation. A panel found that this section is inconsistent with the United States's WTO obligation; the United States has agreed to respect this obligation. As of October 23, 2000, the EU requested the DSB's arbitration for a reasonable period for U.S. compliance with the panel's recommendation and ruling.

2. 1916 Revenue Act (often referred to as the Antidumping Act of 1916)

This Act allows for private claims against parties that import or assist in importing goods into the United States at a price substantially less than the actual market value or wholesale price. A panel found that the specific intent requirement of the Act does not satisfy the material injury test required by the Antidumping Agreement and that civil and criminal penalties in the 1916 Act go beyond the provisions of the Antidumping Agreement. The Appellate Body upheld the panel's finding that this provision is inconsistent with WTO rules. The EU and Japan requested the DSB's arbitration for the period of U.S. compliance with the pancl's determination. The arbitration proceeding was pending.

3. Section 337 of the Tariff Act of 1930

This provision is concerned with unfair import practices, mostly in connection with alleged infringement of intellectual property rights. It makes unlawful to engage in unfair acts or unfair methods of competition in the importation or sale of imported goods.

4. Section 306 of the Trade Act of 1974

This provision enables USTR to monitor foreign compliance with trade agreements with the United States. The Trade Representative focuses on the implementation of each measure undertaken or agreement entered into to provide satisfactory resolution of a matter subject to investigation or dispute settlement proceedings.

5. Continued Dumping and Subsidy Offset Act of 2000 (Byrd Amendment).

This act amended Title VII of the Tariff Act of 1930 to transfer import duties collected under U.S. antidumping and countervailing duty orders from the U.S. Treasury to the companies that filed relevant petitions. In the first annual distribution in January 2002, the United States dispensed $207 million mostly to steel producers. Many WTO members contested the compatibility with WTO rules. At the requests of the EU and ten other countries, along with six third party countries, the Appellate Body recommended to rescind the Byrd Amendment on September 16, 2002.

6. Rules of Origin

The rules of origin are not a provision included in the principal trade remedy law. The new rules of origin have been in effect since July 1996 as a measure primarily to restrict imports of textiles. The rules appear to be in conflict with WTO's Harmonized Rules of Origin. Prior to the new rules, the criterion for the definition of *origin* was the place where a textile good was designed and tailored. It is now the place where textile goods are actually manufactured or assembled. The new rules would discriminate against textiles designed in foreign countries in favor of textiles designed in the United States and manufactured in foreign countries.

8.5 SUMMARY AND CONCLUSIONS

Foreign countries argue that it is not fair to them to be subject to a trade remedy policy applied unilaterally by the United States on a uniform standard of *unfair trade*. The United States maintains that U.S. responses to foreign unfair trade practices are not necessarily unfair to foreign countries that violate multilateral, regional, and bilateral trade agreements and that trade remedy practices are applied on a case-by-case basis. Given these opposing views, trade disputes between the United States and foreign countries are inevitable.

Various trade issues disputes require us to understand foreign trade barriers alleged by the United States. These are the trade barriers broken down by the USTR into ten categories.

U.S. trade remedy policy has caused many serious controversies. A pertinent question is whether the principal trade remedy provisions are compatible with the Uruguay agreement. Sections 701, 731, and 201 conform to both the $GATT_{1947}$ and WTO. Regarding Section 301 and Special 301, though controversial, the WTO has confirmed that they do not contradict U.S. obligations to the WTO. Super 301 is the only provision that is not in accord with the GATT/WTO. There are numerous other controversial areas of disputes. Under the Doha Round, for instance, agriculture appears to remain as the area of most serious disputes.

Trade disputes between the United States and the EU are predominantly large in terms of number of cases of disputes. It is particularly important to focus on trade disputes between them as the EU has had more complaints initiated against the United States throughout the period. The EU, joined often by Japan and other countries, asserts that the inconsistencies in certain U.S. trade policy measures with the WTO rules necessitate further consultations or negotiations with the United States to establish a more functional system. Right or wrong, such an allegation complicates trade disputes further and the complexity involved with this allegation means more cost for settlement to both sides.

In conclusion, there are four notable outcomes obtained in this chapter.

- The total number of trade disputes has remained high, implying that, despite enforcement of the trade remedy laws, trade disputes will persist over time under the current fair trade system.
- Mutual retaliations between the United States and foreign countries are increasingly pervasive.
- Foreign countries replicate U.S. trade policy instruments and retaliations initiated by the United States against foreign countries began to boomerang.
- Many cases of trade disputes remain unsettled for several years or are recurrent. Settlements of such perpetuated disputes are costly to not only the United States but also the rest of the world.

APPENDIX 8.1 DISPUTES BROUGHT TO THE WTO
BY THE UNITED STATES AGAINST
FOREIGN COUNTRIES (SELECTED COUNTRIES)

Argentina	Year: 1966–1997–1998–1999 Reason: Duties and other measures affecting imports of footwear, textiles, and apparel Status: A panel upheld U.S. arguments; Argentina appealed the panel's decision to the Appellate Body; the Appellate Body upheld the panel's finding Year: 1999–2000–2001–2002 Reason: Patent and test data protection for pharmaceuticals and agricultural chemicals Status: Partial settlement and further consultation
Brazil	Year: 1996–1997–1998 Reason: Local content regime for automotive investment and discrimination against U.S. exports Status: After consultation, the two countries reached a settlement agreement in 1998 Year: 2000–2001–2002 Reason: Customs valuation Status: Consultation held; the United States continued to monitor the situation Year: 2000–2001 Reason: Patent protection on the grounds of possible violation of the TRIPs Status: The United States requested establishment of a panel. Both countries established the U.S.-Brazil Consultative Mechanism to accommodate their mutual desire.
Canada	Year: 1996–1997–1998–1999 Reason: Measures against split-run and other imported magazines Status: A panel upheld U.S. arguments to require Canada's compliance period of fifteen months; Canada appealed, and the United States cross-appealed; the Appellate Body rejected Canada's argument

Year: 1997–1998–1999–2000–2001–2002

Reason: Export subsidies and tariff-rate quotas on dairy products

Status: A panel upheld U.S. arguments, and the Appellate Body upheld the panel's finding. Canada implemented measures accordingly.

Year: 1999–2000–2001

Reasons: Patent protection term based on inconsistency with the TRIPs

Status: A panel upheld U.S. arguments, and the Appellate Body upheld the panel's finding. Canada amended its Patent Act to bring it into conformity with its obligations under the TRIPs agreement.

Year: 2000

Reason: Measures relating to Exports of Wheat and Treatment of Imported Grain

Status: In consultation

EU   Year: 1995–1996, 1998

Reason: Duties on imports of grains

Status: Settled

Year: 1995–1996–1997–1998–1999–2000–2001–2002

Reason: Regime for the importation, sale, and distribution of bananas

Status: Consultation; a panel and the Appellate Body upheld U.S. arguments; the United States suspended its increased duties.

Year: 1996–1997–1998–1999–2000

Reason: Beef hormone ban

Status: A panel and the Appellate Body upheld the claims of the United States

Year: 1996–1997–1998*

Reason: Reclassification of LAN adapter cards and multimedia PCs

Status: A panel upheld the claims of the United States, but the Appellate Body upheld the panel's decision on one issue. *Cases of Ireland and the U.K.

Year: 1997
Reason: Circumvention of export subsidy commitments on dairy products
Status: In consultation

Year: 1998*
Reason: Income tax subsidies to a company
Status: In consultation. *Case of France

Year: 1999*
Reason: Measures relating to the development of a flight management system
Status: In consultation. *Case of France

Year: 1999–2000–2001–2002
Reason: Protection of trademarks and geographical indicators for agricultural products and foodstuffs
Status: In consultation

Year: 1998–1999–2000*
Reason: Measures affecting the grant of copyright and neighboring rights
Status: After consultation, Ireland committed to implement comprehensive copyright reform legislation. *Case of Ireland

Year: 2001
Reason: Import surcharge on corn gluten feed
Status: No longer in dispute after the U.S. safeguard measure expired on June 1, 2001.

Year: 2002
Reason: Provisional safeguard measure on imports of certain steel products
Status: Consultation; a panel was established.

Japan   Year: 1995–1996–1997
Reason: Taxes on distilled spirits
Status: A panel upheld U.S. arguments, and the Appellate Body upheld the panel's finding

Year: 1996–1997
Reason: Sound recordings
Status: Settled

Year: 1996–1997[1]–1998
Reason: Measures on imported consumer photographic film
    and paper
Status: A panel established; the final panel report, in which
    Japan prevailed, was upheld.

Year: 1996–1997–1998
Reason: Measures on distribution services
Status: After consultation, Japan announced the abolition of
    its Large Scale Retail Stores Law.

Year: 1997–1998–1999
Reason: Measures affecting imports of agricultural products
Status: A panel upheld U.S. arguments, and the Appellate
    Body upheld the panel's finding

Year: 2002
Reason: Measures affecting the importation of apples
Status: Consultation; a panel was established.

Korea

Year: 1995–1996
Reason: Measures concerning the testing and inspection of
    agricultural products
Status: Discussions continued

Year: 1995
Reason: Measures concerning the shelf-life of products
Status: Partial settlement

Year: 1997
Reason: Requirements for importation of perishable prod-
    ucts
Status: In consultation

Year: 1997–1998–1999–2000
Reason: Taxes on alcoholic beverages
Status: A panel and the Appellate Body upheld the U.S. ar-
    gument

Year: 1999, 2001
Reason: Measures affecting imports of fresh, chilled, and frozen beef
Status: Consultations; the Appellate body upheld the panel report against Korea.

Year: 1999
Reason: Measures affecting government procurement
Status: Consultations held and a panel established.

Year: 2000
Reason: Measure affecting government procurement against the United States involving construction of the new Inchon International Airport
Status: A panel found the Agreement on Government Procurement did not cover this project.

Year: 2000
Reason: Measures affecting imports of fresh, chilled, and frozen beef
Status: A panel upheld U.S. arguments, and the Appellate Body upheld the panel's finding.

Mexico   Year: 1997–1998–1999, 2001
Reason: Antidumping investigation of high fructose corn syrup from the United States
Status: A panel upheld U.S. arguments; the Appellate Body agreed with the panel's findings.

Year: 2000–2001–2002
Reason: Measures affecting trade in live swine
Status: Resolved through consultations; the U.S. continues to monitor the case.

Year: 2000–2001–2002
Reason: Measures affecting telecommunications services
Status: A panel established at the request of the United States

Notes: Other countries in disputes with the United States include Australia, Belgium, Chile, Denmark, Greece, Hungary, Ireland, India, Indonesia, Pakistan, Philippines, Romania, Sweden, Turkey, and the U.K.

1. In the film market, Kodak has alleged that Fuji and the Japanese government have systematically conspired for years to keep Kodak from gaining a significant share of the Japanese market. Japan has asserted that the United States has threatened Japan by imposing tariffs unilaterally as a means to resolve the trade dispute and will ask the WTO to investigate how Kodak came to dominate the U.S. market.

Source: Constructed by the author from data in USTR, *2003 Trade Policy Agenda and 2002 Annual Report* (Washington, D.C.: U.S. GPO, March 2003), 47–62, and various other issues.

APPENDIX 8.2 DISPUTES BROUGHT TO THE WTO BY FOREIGN COUNTRIES AGAINST THE UNITED STATES (SELECTED COUNTRIES)

Argentina	Year: 1997 Reason: Tariff rate quota for peanuts and peanut butter Status: In consultation
	Year: 2002 Reason: Sunset reviews of antidumping measures on oil country tubular goods Status: In consultation
Brazil	Year: 1995* Reasons: Standards for reformulated and conventional gasoline Status:U.S. appealed the panel report. *Case with Venezuela
	Year: 2000–2001–2002 Reasons: Countervailing duties on certain carbon steel products Status: In consultation
	Year: 2001–2002 Reason: Calculation of dumping margin Status: In consultation
	Year: 2002 Reason: Equalizing excise tax imposed by Florida on processed orange and grapefruit products Status: Consultation; a panel was established.

Year: 2002
Reason: Subsidies on upland cotton
Status: In consultation

Canada   Year: 1998
Reason: Measures affecting imports of cattle, swine, and grain from Canada
Status: Consultation upheld

Year: 1999
Reason: Countervailing duty investigation with respect to live cattle
Status: Consultation; U.S. Department of Commerce made a final determination, terminating the case.

Year: 1999
Reason: Tariff reclassification of sugar syrups
Status: Consultation held

Year: 2000–2001
Reason: Measures treating export restraints as subsidies
Status: A panel was established.

Year: 2001–2002
Reason: Section 129(c)(1), Uruguay Round Act
Status: The panel refused Canada's request.

Year: 2002
Reason: Preliminary determinations with respect to certain softwood lumber from Canada
Status: Consultations; a panel released its report for and against the United States; the DSB adopted the panel's report.

Year: 2002
Reason: Final countervailing duty determination with respect to certain softwood lumber
Status: Consultation; a panel was established.

Year: 2002
Reason: Final dumping determination on softwood lumber
Status: Consultation; a panel was established.

Year: 2002
Reason: Investigation of the ITC in softwood lumber
Status: In consultation

EU   Year: 1997
Reason: Antidumping measures on imports of solid urea
    from the former West Germany
Status: Revoked by the United States

Year: 1997–1998
Reason: Rules of origin for textiles and apparel
Status: Resolved through consultations in 1997; the EU
    again requested consultation in 1998.

Year: 1997
Reason: Massachusetts Acts regulating State contracts with
    companies doing business with or in Burma
Status: In consultation

Year: 1997
Reason: Import suspension of EU poultry products
Status: In consultation

Year: 1998
Reason: Harbor maintenance fee
Status: In consultation

Year: 1999
Reason: Section 110(5) of the Copyright Act
Status: A panel established.

Year: 1999
Reason: Import measures on certain products from EU
    member countries
Status: A panel established.

Year: 1999
Reason: Section 211 of the 1998 Omnibus Appropriations
    Act complained by EU[3]
Status: The Appellate Body reported mixed results.

Year: 1999
Reason: Rule of origin for textiles and apparel
Status: Settled through consultations.

Year: 1997–1998–1999–2000–2001–2002
Reason: Foreign Sales Corporation (FSC) tax provisions
Status: A panel upheld EU's arguments, and the Appellate
  Body upheld the panel's finding; on November 15, 2000,
  Extra Territorial Income Exclusion Act of 2000 repealed
  and replaced the FSC. In response to the negative report
  with respect to the Act by the Appellate Body on January
  14, 2002, Congress held hearings.

Year: 1998–1999–2000–2001–2002
Reason: 1916 Revenue Act (often referred to as the Antidumping Act of 1916)
Status: Consultation held; a panel established, a panel upheld EU's arguments, and the Appellate Body affirmed
  panel's reports; Legislation to repeal the Act was introduced in 2001–2002 in Congress, but legislation was not
  completed.

Year: 2000–2001–2002
Reason: Section 110(5) of the Copyright Act
Status: A panel upheld EU's arguments; The United States
  and the EU requested arbitration.

Year: 2000
Reason: Import measures on certain products from EU
  member countries
Status: A panel rejected EU's arguments, and the Appellate
  Body affirmed the panel reports.

Year: 2000
Reason: Measures affecting textiles and apparel
Status: Resolved through consultations.

Year: 1998–1999–2000
Reason: Sections 301–310 of the Trade Act of 1974
Status: A panel found that the law was not inconsistent with
  the United States's WTO obligations.

Year: 1999–2000–2001
Reason: Definitive safeguard measures on imports of wheat
    gluten from the EU
Status: A panel upheld EU's arguments, but the Appellate
    Body reversed the panel's conclusion. However, the Ap-
    pellate Body ruled against the United States.

Year: 2000–2001–2002
Reason: Section 211 of the 1998 Omnibus Appropriations Act
Status: A panel was established. The Appellate Body re-
    versed part of the panel's findings and upheld another. On
    December 20, 2002, the two parties agreed to extend the
    time for the United States to implement the DSB recom-
    mendation.

Year: 1998–1999–2000
Reason: Imposition of countervailing duties on certain hot-
    rolled lead and bismuth carbon steel products originating
    in the United States
Status: A panel upheld EU's arguments, and the Appellate
    Body upheld the panel's finding. However, the counter-
    vailing duty order in question was revoked under the De-
    partment of Commerce's sunset review procedures.

Year: 2000
Reason: Section 337 of the Tariff Act of 1930
Status: The section was amended and consultations contin-
    ued.

Year: 2000
Reason: Section 306 of the Trade Act of 1974 and amend-
    ments thereto
Status: Consultations held.

Year: 2000–2001–2002
Reason: Countervailing duty measures concerning certain
    products from the EU
Status: Consultations held in connection with fourteen separate
    U.S. countervailing duty proceedings covering imports of
    steel and certain other products. The Appellate body re-
    versed part of panel's findings and affirmed another.

Year: 2000–2001–2002*
Reason: Countervailing duties on certain corrosion-resistant carbon steel flat products from Germany
Status: Consultations held in connection with a sunset review declined to revoke by the United States. The panel and the Appellate Body found in favor of the United States on all accounts. *Case of Germany

Year: 2000–2001–2002
 Reason: Safeguard measures on imports of line pipe and wire rod from the EU
Status: Consultation; a panel was established.

Year: 2001–2002*
Reason: Continued Dumping and Subsidy Offset Act of 2000 (Byrd Amendment)
Status: Consultations; The DSB adopted the panel and Appellate Body reports on January 27, 2003. The United States accommodated the DSB Recommendation and ruling. *Consultations requested by Australia, Brazil, Chile, EU, India, Indonesia, Japan, Korea, and Thailand on December 21, 2000, followed by Canada and Mexico on May 21, 2001.

Year: 2001–2002*
Reason: Antidumping duties on seamless pipe
Status: In consultation. *Case of Italy, complaining about the final results of a sunset review of the antidumping order.

Year: 2002*
Reason: Definitive safeguard measures on imports of certain steel products
Status: Consultation; panels were established; the United States abolished the safeguard measures. *Case with EU, Japan, Korea, China, Switzerland, and Norway; Canada, Mexico, New Zealand, and Venezuela as third parties

Year: 2002*
Reason: Sunset reviews of antidumping duty and countervailing duty on certain steel products
Status: In consultation. *Case with France and Germany

Japan   Year: 1995
Reason: Imposition of import duties on automobiles from
     Japan under Sections 301 and 304
Status: Withdrawn

Year: 1999–2000–2001–2002
Reason: Antidumping measures on certain hot-rolled steel
     products
Status: A panel was established. In response to Appellate
     Body's report, the two parties agreed to extend the period
     in this dispute until December 31, 2003.

Year: 2002
Reason: Sunset review of antidumping duty on corrosion-
     resistant carbon steel flat products
Status: Consultations; a panel was established.

Korea   Year: 1997–1998
Reason: Antidumping measures on color televisions
Status: After consultations and a panel requested by Korea,
     the United States terminated. Its inquiry and Korea with-
     drew its panel request pending final determination by the
     United States in 1998.

Year: 1997–1998–1999–2000
Reason: Antidumping measures on DRAMs
Status: Consultations held and a panel established at the re-
     quest of Korea; The panel rejected the arguments of Ko-
     rea and indicated that the U.S. standard was obscure; re-
     solved through consultations.

Year: 1999–2000–2001
Reason: Antidumping measures on stainless steel from Korea
Status: A panel accepted some of Korea's arguments.

Year: 2000–2001–2002
Reason: Definitive safeguard measures on imports of circu-
     lar welded carbon quality line pipe
Status: A panel was established. In response to Appellate
     Body's report, the two parties agreed to extend the period
     until December 21, 2003.

Venezuela[1]	Year: 1997
	Reason: EPA's regulations on reformulated and conventional gasoline
	Status: A panel and the Appellate Body upheld the case for Venezuela.
Group of Countries[2]	Year: 2000
	Reason: Continued Dumping and Subsidy Offset Act of 2000 (Byrd Amendments)
	Status: In consultations

Note: Other foreign countries include Australia, Chile, Columbia, Costa Rica, India, New Zealand, Malaysia, Pakistan, and Thailand.

1. The United States required foreign oil companies to reformulate gasoline they export to the United States immediately for environmental reasons while allowing domestic producers more time to do so. Venezuela, the largest exporter of gasoline to the United States, filed a petition with the WTO on the grounds that the United States violated the UR's fair trade agreement by discriminating against Venezuela. In its first determination since the UR agreement went into effect, a panel ruled against the United States on January 17, 1996. The Appellate Body upheld the panel's findings in May 1996.
2. Included are Australia, Brazil, Chile, the EU, India, Indonesia, Japan, Korea, and Thailand.
3. The fundamental issue in this case was whether the United States is permitted under TRIPs to deny trade mark ownership rights to certain foreign owners.

Source: Constructed by the author from data in USTR, *2003 Trade Policy Agenda and 2002 Annual Report*, (Washington, D.C.: U.S. GPO, March 2003), 52–62, and various other issues.

NOTES

1. See Maxwell Baucus, Memorandum to the USTR (submitted on January 30, 1990), 5.
2. USTR, *2003 National Trade Estimate Report on Foreign Trade Barriers* (Washington, D.C.: U.S. GPO, 2004), v–vi, 31–38, 47–75, 107–35, 194–228, 239–63, 271–78. Earlier issues had nine barriers. A new barrier listed in recent issues is electronic commerce.

3. See Bernard M. Hoeckman and Michel M. Kostecki, *The Political Economy of the World Trading System: From GATT to WTO* (Oxford: Oxford University Press, 1996), 177–80; Pietro Nivola, *Regulating Unfair Trade* (Washington, D.C.: The Brookings Institution, 1993), 31; and I. M. Destler, *American Trade Politics* (Washington, D.C.: Institute of International Economics, 1995), 154–55.

4. See Tracy Murray, "The Administration of the Antidumping Duty Law by the Department of Commerce," in *Down in the Dumps: Administration of the Unfair Trade Laws*, ed. Richard Boltuck and Robert E. Litan (Washington, D.C.: The Brookings Institution, 1991), 23–56 and N. David Palmeter, "The Antidumping Law: A Legal and Administrative Nontariff Barrier," in *Down in the Dumps: Administration of the Unfair Trade Laws*, ed. Richard Boltuck and Robert E. Litan (Washington, D.C.: The Brookings Institution, 1991), 64–94.

5. See Robert A. Cass and Richard D. Boltuck, "Antidumping and Countervailing Duty Laws: The Mirage of Equitable International Competition," in *Fair Trade and Harmonization: Prerequisites for Free Trade 2*, ed. Jagdish Bhagwati and Robert E. Hudec (Cambridge, MA: MIT Press, 1996), 366–67.

6. See Murray, "Antidumping Duty Law," 23–56 and Richard Boltuck and Robert E. Litan, "America's 'Unfair' Trade Laws," in *Down in the Dumps: Administration of the Unfair Trade Laws,* ed. Richard Boltuck and Robert E. Litan (Washington, D.C.: Brookings Institution, 1991), 15.

7. The term "actionable" implies actionable multilaterally and countervailable unilaterally.

8. An adverse effect of subsidies by one country on another country through price or volume/market share effects is called "serious prejudice."

9. Sales-below-cost formula is no longer used in determining fair prices. The level at which below-cost sales are regarded as substantial is 20 percent. The agreement calls for profits to be based on sales at above the cost of the product of the same producer.

10. See note 1.

11. See note 1.

12. See USTR, *2001 Trade Policy Agenda and 2000 Annual Report* (Washington, D.C.: U.S. GPO), 30–31.

13. See Boltuck and Litan, "America's 'Unfair' Trade," 5–6.

Chapter 9

Adjudicatory Behavior of Trade Policy Institutions and Effectiveness of Trade Remedy Policy

For the last two decades, economists have extensively carried out research on three major empirical questions in connection with implementation of the trade remedy laws:

- First, what are the determinants of petitions filed by U.S. firms/industries for safeguard (SG), countervailing duty (CVD), and antidumping duty (AD) actions? This is an important question because the decision-making process of the ITC (involving also the ITA for the latter two) begins chiefly with petitions and causes of petitions, which, if identified, are helpful in preventing trade disputes at the early stage.
- Second, how do the ITC and the ITA conduct its adjudicatory proceedings for CVD and AD cases? It has been widely speculated that the ITC does not conduct its adjudicatory proceedings for CVD and AD cases by rules (economic criteria for injury determination) but by discretion (political pressure). If political influence on ITC's decision-making process is empirically confirmed, it implies that politicians elevate the protection level to the maximum of their support on behalf of interested groups, thus creating a significant adverse welfare effect from major trade disputes especially when the filing involves many countries. If there is no interaction between special interest groups and politicians, however, rent-seeking behavior is insignificant.
- Third, how effective is trade remedy policy? This is a critical question because it is concerned with validity of trade remedy policy for the United States. As trade disputes among countries become increasingly complicated and settlements of disputes through complex, quasi-judicial process in accordance with the statutory time tables are costly not only to the United States but also the WTO; that is, the world as a whole.

This chapter examines each of these subjects in Sections 1, 2, and 3 in the above order. Since there are numerous studies done on each area, only the recent ones will be brought into perspective. Section 4 analyzes the trend of the U.S. trade balance during the period of active implementation of the trade remedy policy to provide its macroeconomic policy implications. The last section summarizes the chapter and draws conclusions.

9.1 DETERMINANTS OF PETITION

Economists have conducted research to identify the determinants of petitions (the pressure for protection) relating to the SG policy in the 1980s and AD and CVD policies in the 1990s. Table 9.1 presents their empirical results. The first three studies are concerned with determinants of petition for SG and the last two are concerned with determinants of petition for AD and CVD.

This section begins with Takacs (1981), who analyzed ITC's decisions in SG cases for the period between 1949 and 1979. Her hypothesis is that the petition for protection is caused by both macroeconomic conditions (GNP, unemployment, and unused capacity) and trade-related variables (trade deficits, imports and import penetration). The author carries out a *multiple regression analysis* on the relationships. Takacs confirms that both domestic and trade-related causal factors affect the decision to file cases under Section 201. She

Table 9.1. Determinants of Petitions

Author	Focus	Determinants
Takacs (1981)	SG	Macroeconomic conditions (GNP, Unemployment, unused capacity) and trade-related variables (trade deficits, imports and import penetration)
Salvatore (1987)	SG	GNP, import penetration, ratio of successful petitions and changes in trade laws
Coughlin, et al. (1989)	SG	Domestic factors (capacity utilization, profits, and inflation) and international factor (merchandise trade balance)
Krupp (1994)	AD	Import penetration, number of employees, dumping margin, and price-cost margins, production index
Chung (1999)	AD and CVD, and both combined together	Economic variables (import penetration and unemployment) and political economy variables (rent from trade protection and election dummy)

Source: Author's compilation. A similar table is available in Chung (1999), 377.

also takes into account in the model a legislative variable (lagged success rate of petitions) and two dummy variables. She reports their expected signs and statistical significance, confirming them as the principal determinants of the degree of protectionist pressure. Salvatore (1987) examines the causes and effects of protectionist pressure and SG petitions in the United States during the postwar period (1948–1985) of different exchange-rate regimes. He conducts a dynamic simulation with a system of simultaneous equations based on: (1) import penetration; (2) the number of SG petitions filed; and (3) the success ratio of petitions. Salvatore hypothesizes that import penetration is explained chiefly by the number of SG petitions filed, the ratio of successful petitions, and overvaluation of the dollar; the number of petitions by level of GNP, the ratio of successful petitions, and changes in trade laws; and the ratio of successful SG petitions by import penetration, positive trade balance, negative balance, and changes in the trade laws. The model is estimated by the *two-stage least squares method* (TSLS). Salvatore reports statistically significant results of the TSLS model with expected signs of estimated coefficients in general. It is notable that his *harassment thesis* postulates a negative correlation between import penetration and petitions, implying that the act of filing a trade complaint is effective in reducing import penetration. Coughlin, Terza, and Khalifa (1989) develop and estimate a *Poisson regression model* to explain macroeconomic determinants of the number of SG petitions.[1] The authors report that their model performs well under both *ordinary least squares* and *Box-Cox estimation*. Both domestic factors (capacity utilization rates, profits, inflation) and international factors (merchandise trade balance) affect the decision to file a petition under Section 201 (SG). Other explanatory variables under consideration include dummies for trade acts.

Krupp (1994) postulates a hypothesis that the probability of an antidumping (AD) filing is a positive function of an affirmative material injury and dumping margin identified by the ITA and a negative function of factors that reduce this likelihood. The author uses disaggregated panel data on the U.S. chemical industry for 1976–1988 to identify those factors. Import penetration (one of the important factors), number of employees, and the dumping margin are significant factors that explain the decision to file a petition. Price-cost margins and chemical production index are other important factors that influence the filing decision. In his *time-series analysis*, Chung (1999) uses petitions under Sections 701, 731, and both combined. The postulated hypothesis is that conventional economic variables (import penetration and unemployment) and political economy variables (rent accrued from trade protection and election dummy) are the primary explanatory variables for petitions for CVD and AD. The period of observation is the 1980s and early 1990 of active implementation of Sections 701 and 731. The maximum likelihood estimates of all explanatory variables confirm the statistical robustness. Significance of rent implies self-interested groups generate social welfare loss.

9.2 ITC'S DECISION-MAKING BEHAVIOR

There are numerous empirical studies done on ITC's decision-making behavior. Table 9.2 lists selected empirical studies done on ITC's decision-making behavior, mostly conducted in the 1980s and 1990s.[2] The objective of these studies is generally to ascertain whether the ITC observes *rules* or uses *discretion* when it makes the determination of SG, CVD, or AD in connection with Section 201, 701, or 731 cases, respectively.[3] Empirical results are almost equally divided into rules and discretion criteria regarding ITC decision-making. Some economists suggest that an industry-specific analysis of commissioners' behavior yields a more conclusive result.

Among three studies on the SG case, two report discretion whereas only one reports rules and discretion. On AD and CVD cases, the first five studies report rules and discretion, whereas the last three report discretion. Finger, Hall, and Nelson (1982) examine both the less-than-fair value (LFV); that is, AD and CVD cases and safeguard (SG) cases for the period (1975–1979) during which the Trade Act of 1974 was in force. They hypothesized the characteristics of the rules variables influence on the likelihood of an affirmative determination in the LFV cases and the characteristics of the political variables in the SG cases. Finger et al. employ the *logit method* to estimate the LFV models for both pricing determination and injury determination.[4] They find that variables in the rule set are influential for a pricing determination,

Table 9.2. Empirical Studies on ITC's Decision-Making Behavior

Author	Case	Rules or Discretion
Finger, et al (1982)	SG	Discretion
	AD and CVD	Rules and discretion
Baldwin (1985)	SG	Discretion
Moore (1992)	AD	Rules and discretion
Anderson (1993)	AD	Rules
Baldwin and	SG	Rules
Steagall (1994)	AD and CVD	Rules and discretion
Hansen (1990)	SG	Discretion
	AD and CVD	Discretion
Prusa (1991)	AD	Discretion
Hansen and Prusa (1997)	AD and CVD	Discretion

Source: Author's compilation. For a similar table, see Chung (1999), 377.

whereas variables in the political set are influential for an injury determination. No empirical results on SG cases are provided in the paper. Baldwin (1985) explores presidential actions on ITC import relief by the SG measure taken from 1975 to 1979. In his *logit model*, he takes into account the percentage of Commissioners favoring import relief and dummy variables. He reports that political factors influence presidential decisions. Moore (1992) investigates whether ITC's antidumping decisions are based on rules or politics. He analyzes individual commissioner votes in case of antidumping petitions for 1980–1986. The results estimated by the *probit method* suggest that ITC commissioners employ not only economic criteria in compliance with their legislative mandate but also the Congressional oversight process.[5] Anderson (1993) argues that earlier studies on ITC's decision-making in AD cases do not consider the extent to which agency decisions are based on the statutory requirements under which the agency operates. He tests four different models of ITC voting, two discretionary (the congressional reelection model and the interest group or congressional pressure model) and two statutory (the comparative static model and the trends model) for the last half of the 1980s and compares the discretionary model with the statutory model. The dependent variable in each model is a binary variable equal to one (1) in the case of affirmative decision. The discretionary model is not successful, but the statutory model is somewhat successful. The results imply that ITC decisions are not based on agency discretion, that is, political considerations or Congressional interests, but on statutory rules. Baldwin and Steagall (1994) attempt to ascertain how strictly the ITC follows statutory guidelines when it determines serious injury in SG cases and material injury in 701 and 731 cases. They use three different models specified for AD, CVD, and SG cases. Using AD and CVD cases for 1980–1990 and SG cases for 1974–1988, the authors obtain *probit regression* results suggesting that the ITC's determination is consistent with the law but is not strictly implemented as directed by the law.

Hansen (1990) analyzes the ITC's regulatory decision under Sections 731, 701, and 201 combined for the mid-1970s and the mid-1980s. She simultaneously accounts for explanatory variables on the supply side of trade protection (the ITC's decision to protect an industry—protection as the dependent variable (1) and otherwise (0)) and explanatory variables on the demand side of trade protection (industry decisions to seek trade protection as the dependent variable—application (1) and otherwise (0)). The explanatory variables of ITC decision (supply-side) include the location of the industry in a district of committee members and chairs by party (Ways and Means Committee and Trade Subcommittee), the elasticity of demand, capacity utilization, U.S. trade deficits, industry concentration ratios, percentage change in industry employment, percentage change in market share, and tariff rates. The explanatory variables of industry decisions (demand-side) are the last four determinants of ITC decision and an inclusive value that accounts for industries' anticipation of how the ITC will respond to their applications for protection and an information value for self-selecting application. Hansen employs a *nested logit technique* of McFadden (1978). The author concludes that trade protection is subject to domestic political forces. Prusa (1991) views AD cases of the steel industry as a two-stage decision problem. The industry makes the withdrawal decision of petition at the first stage or, if not, the ITC takes the case for the final decision at the second stage. He proposes two hypotheses on the factors influencing whether a case is withdrawn: self-selection by the domestic industry for settlement to avoid ITC final determination and political pressure for a negotiated settlement in U.S. interests. *Nested logit estimates* for the period of 1980–1988 generate various empirical results with or without economic variables, such as employment in the first-stage model, and employment and capacity utilization in the second-stage model. Prusa asserts that both the withdrawal decision and the injury decision are not influenced by economic criteria but by political pressure. In their best article of the year award, conferred by *Economic Inquiry* in October 1997, Hansen and Prusa suggest that accumulation of imports by the ITC, mandated by Congress in 1984 amendments of the AD and CVD laws, increases the probability of an affirmative injury determination and increases the number of unfair trading countries.

Overall, the ITC attempts to abide by rules, but discretion is overwhelmingly recognized. If the latter is the case, the ITC is likely to support self-interested groups.

9.3 EFFECTIVENESS OF TRADE REMEDY POLICY

Only a limited number of empirical researches are available. They are done with regard to sections 731 and 701. Table 9.3 contains only two of them. Both report that the trade remedy policy is partially and marginally effective. Herander and Schwartz (1984) carried out an interesting study. They suggest that import-competing American firms will increasingly rely on trade remedy measures, and thus foreign exporting firms will respond to the threat of retaliatory actions by adjusting their behavior. The authors investigate the effects of the threat of imposing AD by the United States on the pricing behavior; that is, the dumping margins, of foreign firms exporting to the United States from 1976 to 1986. They estimate three equations: domestic firm's complaint about dumping by foreign firms in the United States, ITC's material injury

Table 9.3.   Effectiveness of Trade Remedy Policies

Author	Case	Effectiveness
Herander and Schwartz (1984)	AD	Partially effective
Chung (1998)	AD and CVD	Effective but weak

Source: Author's compilation

determination, and the dumping margin. The first two are estimated to generate their predicted values for use as instrumental variables in the third equation. Although these equations are successfully estimated in terms of statistical significance, the third equation, which is the most important among the three, does not generate a satisfactory result.

In his relatively recent study, Chung (1998) investigates the impact of U.S. trade remedy law enforcement on import penetration of foreign-manufactured steel into the U.S. steel market between 1983–1992. To determine the relevant trade policy instruments and observation period, he begins his research with insights into the long and complex history of trade protection for the U.S. steel industry. The period of protection for steel is customarily broken down into three phases: 1969–1974, protection principally by voluntary export restraint (VER); 1978–1982, protection by a trigger price mechanism; and 1982 to the recent past, protection by both VER and trade remedy policies.[6] Among the various trade remedy provisions, the CVD and AD provisions are the ones most frequently invoked in connection with steel imports.[7] Unlike trade policies in the past, which were implemented fairly systematically (through tariffs and VERs) in response to changes in the trade balance, he focuses on the quasi-judicial process for CVD and AD cases, which begins with petitions filed randomly by firms, industries, and unions. American trade policy in the third phase therefore consists of both a systematic and an unsystematic component. This requires a researcher to incorporate uncertainty into any analytical model related to CVD and AD policies. Given the period of active implementation of the two provisions, it is necessary to separate the effect that is explained mainly by unsystematic policies from the total effect of systematic (tariffs and VERs) and unsystematic (CVD and AD) policies on the steel industry. Considering the history of trade policy and actual implementation of current trade remedy measures, Chung derives a probability-augmented model that incorporates explicitly with uncertainty into the theoretical model. He reports that the results obtained through a *time-series analysis*, the only such econometric technique recently employed in this area, indicate that the trade remedy policy is effective. However, the author notes that the degree of effectiveness in terms of elasticity is marginal.

Imported steel has been intensely subject to Sections 701 and 731 in the 1980s and the early 1990s. However, it was confirmed that CVD and AD policies, the two most prominent and frequently used policy instruments of the new protectionism, were not powerful enough to generate any significant effects on steel imports reduced over time.[8] Recently, a major interest group has turned to another policy measure. In March 2002, the President invoked Section 201 that increased the duty on imported steel products from 7 percent to 30 percent. This action was taken in response to pressure from the American steel industry (twenty-five steel manufacturing companies including U.S. Steel), which had been in trouble for the past five years. However, it only raised a strong opposition to U.S. trade policy by major steel exporting foreign countries, such as the EU, Russia, Japan, Korea, and China. The EU filed a suit against the United States with the Dispute Settlement Body (DSB) for settlement at the WTO in addition to other retaliatory actions. Korea followed soon thereafter, and the WTO upheld petitions filed by the EU and other countries.

9.4 TRADE REMEDY POLICY AND TRADE DISPARITY

The USTR reports that trade has significantly contributed to the U.S. economy. As shown in table 9.4, the USTR asserts that trade resulted in 28.6 percent of American economic growth, increased the number of jobs by 21 million, reduced the rate of unemployment by 4 percent, increased hourly wages by 6.5 percent, and enhanced industrial growth by 40.5 percent during the period from 1992 to 1999; trade increased nonresidential business investment by 10.4 percent from mid-1990 to 1999; and trade reduced the poverty level

Table 9.4. Contribution of International Trade to U.S. Economy

1992–1999		
	Growth	up by $2.1 trillion (28.6%)
	Employment	up by 21 million jobs; unemployment down by 4.0% (the lowest since January 1970)
	Living Standards	hourly wages for nonsupervisory workers up by 6.5%
	Industrial Growth	up by 40.5%
Mid-1990s–1999		
	Investment	nonresidential business investment up by 10.4%
1979–1999		
	Unemployment	record low of African-American and Hispanic unemployment

Source: Constructed by the author from USTR, *2000 Trade Policy Agenda and 1999 Annual Report* (Washington, D.C.: U.S. GPO: March 2000), 2–3.

and unemployment of African-Americans and Hispanics between 1979–1999.[9] The assessment implies an economy-wide positive effect of trade remedy policy, including its reflected effect on the trade balance.

Table 9.5 exhibits amounts of U.S. exports and imports of goods and the trade balance on merchandise account for the past twenty-two years (1980–2001). Note that the current account balance is not appropriate here because trade in services was not an active agenda prior to the Uruguay Round. Since the enactment of the Omnibus Trade and Competitiveness Act of 1988 (OTCA), U.S. exports steadily increased throughout the period, presumably because of active enforcement of the trade remedy policy. However, imports increased faster than exports, yielding merchandise trade deficits that

Table 9.5. Trends of U.S. Trade Balance and Fiscal Deficits (Billions of Dollars)

Year	Exports of Goods	Imports of Goods	Balance on Goods	Fiscal Surplus or Deficits[1]
1980	224.3	249.8	−25.5	−73.8
1981	237.0	265.7	−28.0	−79.0
1982	211.2	247.6	−36.5	−128.0
1983	201.8	268.9	−67.1	−207.8
1984	219.9	332.4	−112.5	−185.4
1985	215.9	338.1	−122.2	−212.3
1986	223.3	368.4	−145.1	−221.2
1987	250.2	409.8	−159.6	−149.8
1988	320.2	447.2	−127.0	−155.2
1989	359.9	477.7	−117.8	−152.5
1990	387.4	498.4	−111.0	−221.2
1991	414.1	491.0	−77.0	−269.3
1992	439.6	536.5	−96.9	−290.4
1993	456.9	589.4	−132.5	−255.1
1994	502.9	668.7	−165.8	−203.3
1995	575.2	749.4	−174.2	−164.0
1996	612.1	803.1	−191.0	−107.5
1997	678.4	876.5	−198.1	−22.0
1998	670.4	917.1	−246.7	69.2
1999	684.0	1030.0	−346.0	125.5
2000	772.0	1224.4	−452.4	236.4
2001	718.8	1145.9	−427.2	127.1
2002	NA	NA	−482.9	−157.8
2003p	NA	NA	NA	−304.2
2004p	NA	NA	NA	−307.4

1. On-budget and off-budget, fiscal years (October 1–September 20), p = projected.

NA = Not available.

Source: Council of Economic Advisors, *Economic Report of the President,* (Washington, D.C.: U.S. GPO, February 2004), 379 and 402.

have mounted over time except for deficits reduced in the two consecutive years of 1991 and 1992. The balance on merchandise account maintained a surplus for 1946–1970 (not shown in table 9.5), followed by deficits between 1971–2001 except for the two years of surplus in 1973 and 1975. Furthermore, deficit figures in billions of dollars rose from two-digit from 1977 to three-digit 1984–2001. Deficits began to decrease from 1989 down to two-digit numbers in 1991 and 1992. This result may be regarded as a favorable effect of the OTCA on the trade balance. However, such an impact lasted only for a few years. Trade gap steadily expanded thereafter back to the highest three-digit level ever reached (450 billion dollars) in 2000, and they have remained at a similar three-digit level. According to the latest trade statistics released by the Department of Commerce in May 2004, trade deficits swelled to a record level. As noted in chapter 7, U.S. merchandise trade balance by country and region are in deficit with respect to virtually all of them. Also designed to open foreign markets, the primary objective of U.S. trade remedy policy is not restricted solely to the trade balance. However, the trend of the trade balance defies prediction that the OTCA will abate the disparity problem. This is what motivated economists to investigate the effectiveness of trade remedy policy, as discussed in the preceding section. As long as the current policy stance is maintained, trade disparity is likely to remain unresolved in the end.

9.5 SUMMARY AND CONCLUSIONS

Economists have focused on three pertinent questions in connection with the implementation of trade remedy laws: determinants of petition filing, ITC's decision-making behavior, and the effectiveness of trade remedy policy. Each of these questions contains important policy implications. There have been numerous econometric analyses conducted relatively recently to try to answer these questions. This chapter has reviewed selected ones by each category.

To identify reasons for filing petitions, the authors estimate variously specified single equation models or a system of simultaneous equations. Most of the results estimated by ordinary least-squares, two-stage least-squares, logit, probit, or Poisson regression method confirm the statistical significance of macroeconomic variables and political variables, as hypothesized. A research confirms the statistical significance of rent. This result implies that self-interest groups generate social welfare loss.

The ITC's decision-making behavior is somewhat related to the determinants of petitions. However, the central question here is concerned with whether the ITC's adjudicatory proceedings in connection with AD and CVD cases are based on statutory rules or political discretion. The relevant empirical results are divided. Researchers suggest that the ITC makes the final injury determination based on statutory rules; but the significance of discretion is overwhelmingly recognized, implying that the ITC is likely to support self-interested groups.

Effectiveness of trade remedy policy is a crucial subject. Yet there are only a couple of studies done in the recent past. The latest study done by the time-series analysis suggests that trade remedy policy is effective but the degree of deterrent effects is small. U.S. trade policy is implemented very systematically and consistently. A macroeconomic overview does not exhibit a decidedly strong impact of current trade policy, and serious concerns remain on this question.

In conclusion,

• Significance of discretion implies that the ITC is likely to support self-interest groups.
• Given the marginal degree of deterrent effects of trade remedy policies, trade disparity is likely to remain unresolved in the long run.

NOTES

1. The Poisson specification postulates a hypothesis that the regression (SG or AD petitions) is a non-negative integer (a random variable) of skewed probability, distributed randomly, and independently over time.

2. Other notable studies that deal specifically with the actual decision-making of the ITC but are not discussed here are Judith Goldstein, "Political Economy of Trade: Institutions of Protection," *American Political Science Review* 80 (1986): 161–84; Judith Goldstein and Stefanie Lenway, "Interests or Institutions: An Inquiry into Congressional-ITC Relations," *International Studies Quarterly* (September 1989): 303–27, and Seth Kaplan, "Injury and Causation in USITC Antidumping Determinations: Five Recent Approaches," in *Political Implications of Antidumping Measures*, ed. P. K. Matthew Tharakan (Amsterdam: Elsevier, 1991).

3. The guidelines set forth in the statutes (or rules) are industry shipments, production, employment, cost of goods sold, net profits, productivity, investment, price, and wages.

4. The logit specification provides a model of probabilities (between 0 and 1 as dummies) that reflect the choice between two alternatives as depending on a linear combination of the observed explanatory variables with weights, given the coefficients to be estimated. The logit is based on the cumulative distribution function for a logistic random variable. The algorithms use an iterative method for convergence. For details, see any standard textbook for econometrics.

5. The probit specification is similar to the logit model. It also provides a model of probabilities (between 0 and 1 as dummies). The probit model is based on the standard cumulative normal distribution.

6. See Jae Wan Chung, "Effects of U.S. Trade Remedy Law Enforcement under Uncertainty," *Southern Economic Journal* 65 (July 1998): 151–59.

7. Observe that the number of AD investigations in the same period is significantly larger than the number of CVD investigations, that the number of ITC affirmative final determinations is relatively small, that other industries which were subject to Section 701 are textiles (1980–1984), non-metalic mineral (1980–1985), nonferrous metal (sporadic), and electrical machinery (1985–1988), and that other industries which are subject to Section 731 include textiles (1982–1985), non-metalic mineral (sporadic), motor vehicles (1987–1992), telecommunications and sound (sporadic), electrical machinery (1985–1992), and office machines (1985–1993).

8. See Chung, "Trade Remedy Law Enforcement," 151.

9. See USTR, *2000 Trade Policy Agenda and 1999 Annual Report* (Washington, D.C.: U.S. GPO, March 2000), 2–3.

Chapter 10

Fair Trade Policy, Social Cost, and Trade Policy Reform

Inter-industry trade is the pattern of trade compatible with the conventional theory that presupposes perfect competition. It includes classical theory (often referred to as the Ricardian law of comparative advantage), neoclassical theory (reciprocal demand analysis), and modern theory (the Heckscher-Ohlin proposition). As the dominant part of international economics for free trade, the conventional theory has governed the $GATT_{1947}$-WTO system of world trade for over half a century since 1947. The United States has long promoted free trade and played the leading role within the multilateral trade framework for free trade. However, this logically compelling theory does not explain a significant part of trade in the real world.

Modern trade revolves around the intrinsic market behavior of monopolistically competitive/oligopolistic industries (hereafter often referred to as imperfectly competitive industries). The core features associated with this type of industry structure are economies of scale, product differentiation, and thus intra-industry trade as the overriding pattern. These specific industries are highly significant within the U.S. economy and economies of other industrialized countries.

In theory, economies of scale provide imperfectly competitive industry with an incentive for specialization and thus for international trade. Trade increases the size of the market. A number of large firms in the expanded market can produce slightly differentiated products at a lower average cost. Product differentiation generated on a large scale in home and foreign countries results in *intra-industry trade* as a necessary consequence of imperfect competition.[1] Dumping is a kind of price discrimination. It is theoretically valid as the profit-maximizing behavior of the monopolist and imperfectly competitive producers that have considerable degrees of monopoly power in the market. Subsidy is justified as a policy device for expansion of the global market. However, the $GATT_{1947}$-WTO has prohibited both dumping and subsidy for over half a century. Although the United States began to regulate them long before the $GATT_{1947}$-WTO (chapter 2), dumping and subsidy have become the primary targets of trade policy in the United States in accord with the framework of free trade agreements, especially since the Omnibus Trade and Competitiveness Act (OTCA) of 1988 was enacted. Aiming at open, fair, and equitable access to foreign markets on the one hand and protection of domestic firms and industries from foreign competition on the other hand, the United States made a significant departure from free trade policy to a *free but fair trade* policy since the passage of OTCA.

There are industrial laws in almost all countries. In the United States, the common objective of numerous industrial laws is to prohibit price discrimination primarily in case of explicit collusion, monopolization, and anticompetitive mergers to promote competition in the domestic market rather than inhibiting directly or indirectly the profit-maximizing behavior of the monopolistic firms. However, part of U.S. trade remedy laws for fair trade prohibits the corresponding behavior of foreign monopolistic firms/industries in the United States to protect domestic firms/industries from foreign competition, resulting in foreign retaliations that, in turn, affect adversely U.S. firms/industries. It is paradoxical to allow imperfectly competitive firms/industries to exist lawfully in both countries and yet to declare the fundamental objective of daily business operations predatory to each other. In other words, fair trade policy based on criteria associated with free trade framework is illogical. Moreover, both U.S. trade laws and the $GATT_{1947}$-WTO agreement overlook economic reality. Given the widespread, global existence of monopolistic industries, the enforcement of trade remedy law by the United States is unable to transform market structure from imperfect to perfect competition in foreign countries. Failure to transform the fundamental nature of the markets explains the reason why disputes over the so-called unfair trade practices persist. Trade laws and international agreements are artificial rules governing trade conduct. If a law mandates that any particular business activity is illegal, it then becomes illegal regardless of economic rationale. Fair trade policy based on such a trade law or an agreement is the primary cause of trade disputes.

Each year, U.S. firms, corporations, and unions file a large number of petitions for protection from foreign dumping and subsidies. Trade law provisions require the policy authority (ITA and ITC) to conduct evidentiary hearings for each of these cases in accordance with lengthy and complex quasi-judicial processes. This statutory requirement entails enforcement by the trade policy authority to the maximum degree at any cost. Unlike in the past, however, trade disputes between the United States and foreign countries have become increasingly contentious, and the scope of dispute areas is expanding. Foreign countries now replicate U.S. trade remedy policy and step up their retaliation against U.S. actions. Consequently, the number of petitions filed with the WTO for settlement is growing. The social cost to the United States, especially from statutory processes for investigation and determination of antidumping duty and countervailing duty (AD-CVD) on a case by case basis each year at the local level (the United States) and the global level (the WTO), is enormous. It is compounded by implicit costs from ITC's discretionary proceedings in favor of domestic self-interested individuals (or groups) with or without Congressional involvement, the marginal effectiveness of AD and CVD policies, and the escalation of retaliation by foreign countries (chapters 8 and 9). Many economists have criticized U.S. fair trade policy. It was even described as one of the great intellectual frauds of the twentieth century.[2] Trade disputes are phenomena that occur when artificial trade rules attempt to reverse natural market processes in the real world economy. The high social cost for settlement of trade disputes suggests the need to optimize trade law enforcement and, ultimately, to reform the world trade framework in accordance with both economic rationale and market reality.

The primary objective of this chapter is to elicit the significance of social cost and the need to reform U.S. trade policy and world trade framework from chapters 1 through 9. Sections 1 and 2 present perspectives on U.S. trade remedy policy from law and economics, respectively. Section 3 discusses the social cost and the optimal trade intervention. An immediate need for minimization of the social cost arising from implementation of trade remedy policy and the ultimate reform of the global trade framework are the policy implications of this section. Section 4 summarizes and draws conclusions.

10.1 LEGAL PERSPECTIVE ON TRADE POLICY

There are several major industrial laws in the United States.[3] The Sherman Antitrust Act of 1890 is the first antitrust law enacted to prohibit the explicit collusive behavior of monopolistic firms. It has two substantive provisions. Section 1 makes illegal every contract, combination in the form of trust, or conspiracy in restraint of trade or commerce among the several States or with foreign nations. Section 2 prohibits monopolization of any part of the trade or commerce among the several States or with foreign nations.

The Clayton Act of 1914 is another antitrust law, which is actually a refinement of the Sherman Act. Section 2 outlaws price discrimination. Section 3 prohibits a producer from selling goods on the condition, agreement, or understanding that the purchaser shall not use or deal in the goods of a competitive seller. Section 7 states that no corporation shall acquire stock in another company for the objective of diminishing competition. This provision aims to prevent anticompetitive mergers.

The Federal Trade Commission Act of 1914 is also designed to foster competition in the U.S. economy. Section 5 in particular declares unfair methods of competition unlawful.

The primary objective of U.S. industrial laws is to promote competition by restricting monopolistic behavior of domestic firms/industries chiefly in the domestic market but not to inhibit the existence of those firms/industries. The underlying rationale for these industrial laws is that the concentration of economic power in large corporations and in combinations of business concerns reduces normal marketplace competition. There are antitrust cases filed with federal courts in the past, whether or not actually constituting violations of the Sherman Act. They include Standard Oil of New Jersey, U.S. Steel, Alcoa, United Shoe, and Microsoft. However, there is neither theory nor clear evidence suggesting that dumping, a case of price discrimination, by foreign monopolistic firms/industries in the United States necessarily leads to the collusive behavior, monopolization, or noncompetitive mergers that are subject to antitrust laws.[4]

Contrary to the objective of industrial laws, U.S. trade law today aims to protect domestic firms or industries from foreign competition. Although the Omnibus Trade and Competitiveness Act of 1988 explicitly states that its objective is to enhance also the competitiveness of American industry, this implies enhancement of competitiveness under a protective trade policy. The actual enforcement of principal trade remedy laws generally begins with petitions for protection from foreign competition, as exemplified by the AD-CVD policy that is heavily concentrated in terms of the number of petitions filed for investigation. Given the significance of intra-industry trade between monopolistic firms/industries in the United States and those in all developed foreign countries, the vicious circle between U.S. protection of U.S. monopolistic firms/industries at the expense of foreign monopolistic firms/industries and foreign retaliations against U.S. monopolistic firms/industries is a serious problem in the trade policy area. Mutual retaliations escalated by their policies inhibit direct competition between monopolistic firms/industries in the United States and those in foreign countries. Despite the intensive implementation of trade remedy policies, trade disputes between the U.S. and foreign countries persist and expand. The WTO is also responsible for this interactive behavior because the trade laws in both the United States and foreign countries are consistent with the multilateral trade agreements and penalizes dumping and subsidy activities on the same ground. This is an institutional problem created jointly by trade policies of all trading countries and the $GATT_{1947}$-WTO, necessitating them to reform their trade laws and international trade institution.

Trade remedy law prohibits price discrimination exercised by foreign firms in the U.S. markets, whereas the industrial laws prohibit price discrimination by domestic firms in domestic markets. One use of the same basic premise—price discrimination—inhibits open markets and competition while the other fosters it. There is clearly inconsistency between the trade law and industrial law.

10.2 ECONOMIC PERSPECTIVE ON TRADE POLICY

The concept of comparative advantage, the underlying rationale for classical, neoclassical, and modern trade theories, has long served as a theoretical basis for free trade. It presupposes perfect competition and generates a pattern of inter-industry trade. This theory has been the foundation for multilateral trade agreements made since $GATT_{1947}$. The overall direction of U.S. trade policy has generally been oriented toward free trade within the framework of multilateral agreements (chapter 6). However, the Omnibus Trade and Competitiveness Act of 1988 changed the direction of U.S. trade policy from free to *free but fair* trade maintained by means of trade remedy provisions (chapter 4) *within the free trade framework.*

This section is concerned with incompatibility between the fundamental objective of a firm (the profit-maximization) and the AD-CVD policy framework. Although AD and CVD policies are in accord with relevant provisions in the $GATT_{1947}$-WTO, they ignore economic rationale and industrial reality.

The industrial structure of the United States is characterized by imperfect competition. Industries in this category are critically important in light of their impact on the national economy. The size of firms in these industries is generally huge.[5] Large firms with increasing returns to scale produce slightly differentiated products at a lower average cost. Most other developed countries have a similar industrial structure. Product differentiation naturally results in intra-industry trade.

The trade pattern in industrialized countries is predominantly intra-industrial. The United Kingdom, France, Germany, United States, Canada, and Italy have high degrees of the Intra-industry Trade Index (IIT). Countries that trade heavily with the United States (Mexico, Korea, China, and Japan) also show relatively high values of the IIT.[6] Product categories with a relatively high index of intra-industry trade are inorganic chemicals, generators, industrial machinery, organic chemicals, toiletries and cosmetics, iron and steel, and household appliances.[7] It is important to stress that these industries are imperfectly competitive and that a number of imperfectly competitive industries overlap with the industries of intra-industry trade and with the industries involved in trade disputes with foreign countries (see appendices 8.1 and 8.2 in chapter 8).[8] The items subject to AD and CVD encompass a broad range of products. The industries involved in intra-industry trade of those items are concentrated among technology-embodied, capital-intensive, manufactured and import-competing goods that are also produced by other industrial countries.

The theory of price discrimination is a branch of the theory of monopoly in microeconomics. It suggests that, if the market is segmented by different price elasticities in the absence of commodity reshipment, monopolistic producers (monopolist and imperfectly competitive producers who have considerable degrees of monopoly in the markets) can maximize profit by exercising price discrimination between markets. Despite the net national welfare loss from monopoly and imperfect competition, dumping is the expected normal business behavior of an imperfectly competitive firm operating under economies of scale and enhances the degree of competition in the international market. There is no good economic justification for dumping as particularly harmful. However, this behavior is classified legally as an unfair trade practice that undermines world trade. The $GATT_{1947}$-WTO and almost all countries, including the United States, prohibit dumping. Even if a country would legally provide a monopolistic firm with unlimited opportunity for dumping, however, no firm would indefinitely exercise it in the face of possible bankruptcy.

Turning to the subsidy, there are two different perspectives. One views a subsidy negatively and the other views it positively. The negative view suggests that export subsidies result in a welfare loss, although the loss by a tariff-equivalent subsidy (the production distortion) is less than the loss by the corresponding tariff (the sum of the production distortion and the consumption distortion) if goods sell at world price. Wide-spread use of export subsidies by many countries could undermine the world trade order. What is worse is that certain industries in many countries survive only with such subsidies. The agricultural sector is an example.[9] On the contrary, the positive view suggests that subsidies raise national and global welfare by domestic and foreign firms unless trade practices by means of subsidies are extreme. In response to the Brander-Spencer theory of strategic trade policy suggesting that a subsidy to a domestic oligopolistic (imperfectly competitive) firm deters the entrance of foreign competitors into the market, Krugman (2003) believes that the superior technology of a foreign firm may override the deterrent effect.[10, 11] He suggests that dynamic increasing returns to scale (external economies at the industrial level) justify a subsidy because a country enables to produce the subsidized goods and the increased supply to the world market raises the volume of trade. The rationale here is similar to the infant industry argument. If a subsidy is regarded as unfair trade practice and hence penalized by a country's trade law and the $GATT_{1947}$-WTO, it is then contradictory to permit the escape clause (Section 201 in the United States) as a fair trade provision, especially if the provision is abused by subsidy-seeking interest groups (chapter 9).

The economy of a country consists of the domestic and foreign sectors. This dichotomy leads us to believe that the origin of most trade disparities lies in the foreign sector and that trade policy is primarily responsible for resolving trade disparities. However, the foreign sector is not independent of the domestic sector. Their intersection through various economic identities and functions suggests that the principal origin of a chronic trade disparity may also rest on the domestic sector. In the case of the United States, there are two primary causes of trade disparity from the domestic sector. One is the cause from the factor market. Facilities for the production of capital-intensive goods in a capital-abundant United States as a country of mature industries are relatively obsolete and deteriorated. Such a long-run problem of *plant-cycle dynamics* is coupled with high factor cost. Given the concentration of trade disputes in technology-capital-intensive industries, the United States needs, most of all, to increase *investment for replacement* in this specific industrial sector. The other is the cause from the product market. The theory of (Shephard) duality existing between the output function and the cost function is an important part of modern microeconomics. Even apart from the Shephard duality respect, the Heckscher-Ohlin model confirms that commodity and factor trade are substitutes for each other. It is then reasonable to believe that trade policy for productive factors is the mirror image of trade policy for commodities. In this sense, erosion of the once mighty reputation of products "Made in (the) USA" and relatively high prices in comparison with the *quality* become other serious problems reflected into the trade sector.

The cases of automobile and steel, two important industries in the U.S. economy, represent problems of plant-cycle dynamics and product quality. The automobile industry was protected by import quotas and voluntary export restraints (VER), mostly tied to Japan, after the oil crises in the 1970s. The auto industry has already made a significant concession to foreign manufacturers by giving up its market shares in the domestic and foreign markets. It continues to lose the market share. The latest news reported that overall sales of Japanese automobiles in the United States rose approximately 20 percent, whereas GM and Ford had their bond ratings reduced to junk status by Standard & Poor's. This report exemplifies a negative perception on the quality of American products of consumers in home and foreign markets. The steel industry has undergone three phases of protection: Primarily by VER in 1969–1978, by a trigger price mechanism in 1978–1982, and by VER and trade remedy policy from 1982–present.[12] Numerous studies have been done on U.S. trade protection for steel and automobiles during these periods. Included are Crandall (1987), who investigated the case of steel and automobiles, Tarr (1979) on steel, and Walter (1983) on steel. Unlike previous studies focusing on the welfare effect of trade protection, studies done by Eichengreen and van der Ven (1984) and recently by Chung (1998) are concerned with AD and AD and CVD combined, respectively. Despite a lengthy history of protective trade policies lasting for periods long enough to test their effectiveness and contrary to policy implications of most of the research, the two important industries are still experiencing frequent disputes with foreign countries and keep calling for protection.[13]

The history experienced by these two industries provides us with valuable insights into the underlying problems. The fundamental problem may not necessarily be foreign dumping and subsidy but comparative disadvantage incurring from the lack of investment for replacement of deteriorated and obsolete production facility and from the relatively poor quality of products. Then the routine enforcement of trade remedy laws under the OTCA could be a costly misjudgment by producing only a patchwork solution that leaves the long-term problem of trade disparity unresolved. A trade policy attempting to resolve domestic market failure is then a second-best argument.

Free trade is difficult to achieve, and fair trade is costly to maintain. In any event, it is necessary to alleviate trade disputes involved with the current trade policy. In order to resolve the chronic problem of trade disparity, U.S. trade policy needs to incorporate the economic rationale and the real world of business. Rather than strict enforcement of the AD/CVD-oriented policy, it is urgent for the United States to stimulate private investment for replacement embodied with new technology and to improve product quality.

10.3 SOCIAL COST OF TRADE POLICY, OPTIMAL TRADE INTERVENTION, AND TRADE POLICY REFORM

International trade may be compared to an ordinary game. Nothing is wrong with players expecting each other to conduct a fair game on the basis of an agreed set of rules. If the agreed rules are unrealistic and thus costly to observe, however, it is reasonable to optimize the intensity of rule observance or else modify the rules. The AD and CVD in the United States, two dominant trade policy instruments that are in accord with $GATT_{1947}$-WTO, are the serious arguments corresponding to this game pattern.

This section begins with the AD policy because dumping by any country is the behavior that is intrinsic to profit-maximizing, imperfectly competitive firms. This behavior will continue to occur as long as imperfect competition exists. No country, including the United States, prohibits the existence of imperfect competition *per se*, while almost every country restricts the behavior of foreign imperfectly competitive firms.

Implementation of the AD policy regulating foreign dumping is unreasonable and unrealistic for the following three reasons:

1. The regulatory power in one country is by no means capable of converting a foreign industrial structure of imperfect competition into one of perfect competition. In the absence of a strong economic rationale, this protective policy will be effective marginally and for the short run (chapter 9).
2. The long and complex quasi-judicial processes required for investigation and determination of AD cases (chapter 4) and the WTO's dispute settlement procedures (chapter 6) involve tracking down foreign dumping on a case-by-case basis each year. These processes are highly costly to the United States at the national as well as the global levels.
3. Such a social cost is compounded by both frequency and intensity of retaliations by foreign countries (chapter 8). Although it has eluded precise measurement, thus requiring further research, this cost is undoubtedly significant. There is no doubt that stricter enforcement of AD law by the United States results in a higher budgetary burden on U.S. trade policy agencies and the U.S. share of the WTO budget in addition to the trade-related cost to relevant private sectors and individuals. The net budget authority figures (actual) for the USTR and ITA are 38 million dollars and 417 million dollars, respectively, for FY 2003. Total spending by the ITC in FY 2002 was 52 million dollars. The annual budget for the WTO was approximately 123 million dollars.[14]

The social cost of protective policies has two different aspects. One aspect is the positive relationship of the social cost with respect to enforcement of AD policy. This part of the social cost accrues from the long and complex quasi-judicial processes for investigation and determination, as mandated by trade remedies laws. As stated in Chapter 4, the principal amendments were made in 1988 to strengthen the trade remedy provisions of the 1974 Trade Act. The amendments include: transferring authority from the President to the USTR; making provisions mandatory in the event of an obvious trade agreement violation or unjustifiable practice; and tightening time limits on all investigations and actions. Stringent enforcement means greater appropriations for more intensive enforcement activities by the policy authority and a higher probability of passing along more disputes to the WTO for settlement. As a result, the social cost increases as the trade authority intensifies policy enforcement.

The other aspect is the social cost—that is the negative function of the social cost with respect to AD enforcement. As the U.S. trade policy authority enforces AD policy to a greater degree, foreign countries reduce their dumping activities in the United States at least in the short-run. This effect reduces the social cost for the United States (chapter 9). Both the positive function and the negative function require the policy authority to reconcile the economic rationale and enforcement of trade remedy law for the optimal degree of enforcement at their intersection point. It is the level at which the social cost function, the sum of these two opposite functions, is minimized.[15] Any further degree of enforcement beyond the optimal level results in a higher social cost to the United States. The U.S. trade policy agency and the WTO should jointly undertake their leadership to optimize trade policy interventions for all countries.

On the CVD policy, export subsidy is not a profit-maximizing behavior of both competitive and imperfectly competitive firms/or industries. Subsidy paid to a competitive firm or industry, such as, the agricultural industry, undermines only the world trade order in the absence of justification of subsidy. However, subsidy to imperfectly competitive firms/industries (under increasing returns to scale) promotes international trade and the CVD policy reduces dumping by the subsidy-dumping causality (chapter 8) and the social cost from the AD policy. Validity of stringent subsidy justifies the CVD policy.

10.4 SUMMARY AND CONCLUSIONS

Imperfect competition characterizes the industrial structure of developed countries. Product differentiation, intra-industry trade, and dumping/subsidy are natural consequences of increasing returns to scale of large firms in monopolistically competitive and oligopolistic industries. From the perspective of economics, dumping is profit-maximization behaviors of typical business firms in this industrial category.

No country prohibits the existence of this dominant industrial structure by law. The United States allows monopolistic competition and oligopoly to exist lawfully in the markets. However, dumping by a foreign country is predatory in the United States. U.S. trade remedy law requires the ITA and ITC to implement AD policy. Unlike the industrial laws, which attempt to foster perfect competition in a domestic market, current trade law policy aims to enhance the competitiveness of domestic firms/industries by protection from foreign competition. Trade remedy law is in conflict with antitrust laws. It also contradicts economic theory and reality.

It is important to keep in mind the following real world phenomena:

- The volume of trade among developed countries within the total volume of world trade is huge,
- Imperfect competition is the dominant industry structure in industrial countries,
- Intra-industry trade among industrial countries is a significant pattern of trade in terms of both volume of trade and the range of products, and
- There is a significant overlap between the industrial areas of intra-industry trade and those of U.S. trade disputes with foreign countries.

Trade disputes persist because artificial trade rules override the natural operation of an economy. They occur more frequently and on a larger scale today. The social cost involved with trade disputes and settlements is enormous. It does not permit the United States to pursue a protective policy indefinitely, especially in light of the marginal effectiveness of trade remedy policy, the dynamic problem of domestic plant cycles, and the problem of product quality as the fundamental causes of trade disparity, and retaliations intensified by foreign countries.

Free/fair trade is neither wrong nor undesirable. However, free trade presupposes perfect competition, which exists only rarely in the real world. While the domestic market behavior of imperfect competition is lawfully permitted or is left intact, intrinsic market behavior of imperfect competition in foreign countries is illogically declared as predatory within the free trade framework. Free trade is virtually impossible to achieve, and fair trade is costly to maintain.

- It is necessary to optimize the degree of trade intervention for the minimum social cost and to reform the world trade framework by embracing the industrial reality of imperfect competition.
- This book proposes to abolish the AD policies and the CVD policies applied to imperfectly competitive industries in not only the United States but also all foreign countries in collaboration with the WTO, so that monopolistic firms/industries in all countries can freely compete to each other.

World trade system evolves along the path that embodies the *Economic Darwinism* with or without AD/CVD in the long-run anyway.[16] However, the system with the antidumping duty and countervailing duty is costly to maintain for all trading countries. In case of the United States, the problem of the trade sector will persist as long as disparities in the domestic factor market and product market remain unresolved, requiring trade policy to incorporate with domestic economic policies.

NOTES

1. For the proposition on "economies of scale, imperfect competition and intra-industry trade," see Paul R. Krugman, "Increasing Returns, Monopolistic Competition, and International Trade," *Journal of International Economics* 9, no. 4 (November 1979): 469–79; Elhanan Helpman, "Increasing Returns, Imperfect Markets, Trade Policy," in *Handbook of International Economics I*, ed. Ronald E. Jones and Peter B. Kenen (Amsterdam: Elsevier, 1984); Elhanan Helpman and Paul R. Krugman, *Market Structure and Foreign Trade* (Cambridge, MA: MIT Press, 1985); and Paul R. Krugman and Maurice Obstfeld, *International Economics* (Boston: Addison and Wesley, 2003). In this chapter, I define imperfect competition as broadly as possible. It includes not only monopolistic competition but also oligopoly. In the latest issue of *Economic Report of the President* (Washington, D.C.: U.S. GPO, 2004), 230–31, the Council of Economic Advisors indicates the importance of intra-industry trade.

2. See James Bovard, *Fair Trade Fraud* (New York: St. Martin Press, 1991).

3. The references for each industrial law for antitrust policy in the United States are not provided here because they are widely introduced in textbooks for introductory economics, intermediate microeconomics, and industrial economics.

4. While the Department of Justice is responsible for enforcement of the Sherman Act and the Clayton Act, the Federal Trade Commission (FTC) enforces both the Federal Trade Commission Act and the Clayton Act. For other industrial laws, see the Robinson-Patman Act of 1936 (the amended version of the Clayton Act of 1914) and the Wheeler-Lea Act of 1938 (the amended version of the Federal Trade Commission Act of 1914). The former prohibits price discrimination and expulsion of small competitors by large producers through selective, discriminatory price cuts (Section 2(a)). The latter empowers the Federal Trade Commission to investigate unfair or deceptive methods of competition in commerce (Section 5(a)(1)). The EU and Japan also have industrial laws similar to those of the United States. The Treaty of Rome of 1957 (especially Articles 85 and 86 in Title V), amended by treaties agreed to at Maastricht in 1993 and Amsterdam in 1999, and the Antimonopoly Law of 1947 (especially Sections 3, 15, 19, and 25) in Japan are the basis of competition policy. The Directorate General of the EU, the Japan Fair Trade Commission (JFTC), and the Ministry of International Trade and Industry (MITI) in Japan are responsible for these policies, respectively.

5. In the United States, monopolistically competitive industries include food products, household appliances, apparel, detergents, toothpaste, and most consumer services; oligopolistic industries include nonferrous metals (aluminum and copper), sugar, heavy machinery, steel, automobiles, potash, dynamite, oil, cigarettes, and anthracite coal. See George J. Stigler, "The Kinky Oligopoly Demand Curve and Rigid Prices," *Journal of Political Economy* 55 (October 1947): 432–46 and *The Concentration of Industry* (Homewood, IL: Richard D. Irwin, 1968); and Joe E. Bain, *Barriers to New Competition* (Cambridge, MA.: Harvard University Press, 1956). Stigler identified the last seven industries as oligopolistic. Their importance in the U.S. economy justifies the serious attention of economists to oligopoly. The U.S. Bureau of the Census periodically takes a Census of Manufactures classified into the North Ameri-

can Industry Classification System (NAICS), which has replaced the Standard Industrial Classification (SIC) for over sixty years. If the four largest firms in an industry combined together supply 40 percent or more of industry sales, it is believed that each must be aware of the others. Such industries are oligopolies. Economists also use the Herfindahl index for industrial concentration in order to identify oligopolistic industries.

6. Intra-industry Trade index (IIT) was developed by Herbert G. Grubel and Peter J. Lloyd, *Intra-industry Trade* (London: Macmillan, 1975). Studies conducted on intra-industry trade in relatively recent years include Don P. Clark, "Recent Evidence on Determinants of Intra-industry Trade," *Weltwirtschaftliches Archiv* (1993) and David Greenway, R. Hine, and Chris Milner, "Vertical and Horizontal Intraindustry Trade: A Cross Industry Analysis for the United Kingdom," *Economic Journal* (1995). See Steven Husted and Michael Melvin, *International Economics*, 6th ed. (Boston: Pearson Addison-Wesley, 2004) and Helmut Forstner and Robert Balance, *Competing in a Global Economy: An Empirical Study on Specialization and Trade in Manufactures* (London: Unwin Hyman, 1990).

7. See U.S. Bureau of the Census, *International Trade in Goods and Services*, FT 900 (Washington, D.C.: U.S. GPO, 2004).

8. The industries include chemicals, food, iron/steel, metal manufacturers, and automobiles.

9. Subsidies paid to the agricultural sector by many countries is controversial. However, this controversy is irrelevant here, because the agricultural industry is not imperfectly competitive.

10. See Krugman and Obstfeld, *International Economics* (2002), 140-155.

11. See James Brander, "Intraindustry Trade in Identical Commodities," *Journal of International Economics* 11 (1981): 1–14.

12. There are numerous studies done on U.S. trade protection for steel and automobiles during these periods. Included are Crandall (1987), who investigated the case of steel and automobiles, Tarr (1979) on steel, and Walter (1983) on steel. Unlike previous studies focusing on the welfare effect of trade protection, studies done by Eichengreen and van der Ven (1984) and recently by Chung (1998) are concerned with AD and AD and CVD combined, respectively.

13. See section 8.4 in chapter 8.

14. The sources for these figures are Office of Management and Budget (OMB), *Appendix: Budget of the United States Government*, Fiscal Year 2005 (Washington, D.C.: U.S. GPO, 2005); http://www.usitc.gov; and http://www.wto.org.

15. To illustrate, a positive function and a negative function can be represented, respectively, by simple equations:

$$y = ax^2 + bx + c \text{ and } y = g - hx,$$

where y = social cost, x = enforcement of the trade remedy law; $a > 0$, $b \leq 0$, $c \geq 0$, $g > 0$, $h > 0$, and $b^2 \leq 3ac$.

The total social cost function to minimize is:

$$2y = (ax^2 + bx + c) + (g - hx).$$

The first-order condition for the minimum is:

$$dy/dx = ax + (1/2)(b - h) = 0,$$

yielding the extreme value for minimum social cost: $x^* = (h - b)/2a > 0$.
The second-order condition for the minimum is:

$$d^2y/dx^2 = a > 0.$$

Social cost in connection with optimal choice was discussed as early as in the 1960s and is still a serious subject of interest today. See Gary S. Becker, "Crime and Punishment: An Economic Approach," *Journal of Political Economy* 76 (March 1968): 169–217, James M. Buchanan, *Cost and Choice: An Inquiry in Economic Theory* (Chicago: Markham Publishing, 1969), George J. Stigler, "The Optimum Enforcement of Laws," *Journal of Political Economy* 78 (May 1970): 526, Gary S. Becker and George J. Stigler, "Law Enforcement, Malfeasance and Compensation of Enforcers," *Journal of Legal Studies* 3 (1974): 1–8, Stephen Shavell, "Optimal Structure of Law Enforcement," Journal of Law and Economics 36, no. 1 (April 1993): 255–87, and Gary S. Becker and Casey B. Mulligan, "Deadweight Cost and the Size of Government," *Journal of Law and Economics* 46, no. 2 (October 2003): 293–340 for discussions on an approach similar to this in details. The optimal tariff rate is the traditional measure of the optimal trade intervention. Since the 1950s, Harry Johnson and others have discussed the optimal tariff rate at which the marginal gain from improved terms of trade equals the marginal welfare loss from a tariff.

16. *Economic Darwinism* is the term suggested by Caroline Chung.

Epilogue

American trade policy is a crucial subject to not only the United States but also foreign countries. It is a multifaceted policy that encompasses a broad spectrum of integral components. This book explores American trade policy in perspective from U.S. trade laws and international trade agreements.

The framework of international trade maintained by the United States for over half a century since 1947 is based on the rationale for free trade of the GATT/WTO. Free trade presupposes perfect competition. However, most markets are not competitive. Given the frequent trade disputes stemming from industrial sectors of imperfect competition and their tendencies perpetuated under fair trade policy, the social cost incurred from the quasi-judicial processes of dispute settlements is enormous to the United States and the rest of the world. Fair trade policy by means of trade remedy laws in the free trade framework is illogical. This book addresses the needs to optimize trade remedy law enforcement by the United States and to reform trade policy in each country, including the United States, and to reform the world trade framework in concert with the WTO by embracing economic principle and the real world of both competitive and imperfectly competitive markets, especially for trade among industrialized countries. Uniqueness of this book is to *elicit* the above arguments from each of the chapters that constitute the book.

The Omnibus Trade and Competitiveness Act of 1988 changed the direction of U.S. trade policy from *free* to *free but fair trade*. U.S. responses to alleged foreign unfair trade practices loom large in present-day trade disputes. American trade policy is sound overall but encounters a number of serious problems in the implementation of provisions for the policy. These problems are:

- *Trade disputes are not transitory.*
- *Mutual retaliations are increasingly common.*

- *U.S.-initiated retaliations tend to boomerang.*
- *Many trade disputes remain unsettled for several years or are recurrent.*

Furthermore, numerous studies on the ITC's decision-making behavior report evidence indicating:

- *Self-interested groups generate social cost.*
- *The ITC is based on rules, but discretion is not eliminated.*

These results imply a considerable waste of scarce resources. There is also empirical research that is concerned with the effectiveness of trade remedy policy. The results suggest that:

- *U.S. trade remedy policy is marginally effective.*

Despite the active implementation of trade remedy policy for a long period, U.S. trade balance does not show any sign for improvement. A significant portion of trade disparity in the United States rests on the distorted domestic factor markets and poor quality of products rather than insufficient enforcement of trade laws.

- *Trade disparities are likely to remain unresolved in the long run.*

The pattern of trade under the theory of comparative advantage (classical, neoclassical, and Heckscher-Ohlin theories) is inter-industry trade. This theory has governed the world framework of free trade for over half a century. An underlying assumption of the theory is perfect competition. However, most markets in the real world, both domestic and international, are not competitive. The industry structure of developed countries is predominantly characterized by imperfect competition. Intra-industry trade is the dominant pattern of trade under the theory of imperfect competition.

- *Intra-industry trade is pervasive and accounts for most of world trade.*

Although the overall direction of U.S. trade policy has changed from free to free but fair trade, it still rests on the free trade framework of multilateral agreements. It is contradictory to allow imperfectly competitive firms or industries to exist lawfully in the domestic market and yet to declare the profit-maximizing behavior of imperfectly competitive firms or industries of foreign countries unlawful in both the United States and foreign countries. Given foreign retaliations, this contradiction brings about a self-denial of a legitimate existence of imperfect competition in the domestic market.

- *Fair trade policy within the free trade framework is illogical, perpetuating trade disputes because of the ignorance of economic rationale.*

Among various trade remedy policies, antidumping duty (AD) is the policy instrument used most heavily by the United States. Dumping is the profit-maximizing behavior of imperfectly competitive firms or the monopolist. The long and complex quasi-judicial process required to investigate and determine antidumping duties on a case-by-case basis each year at the local level (the United States) and the global level (the WTO) are extremely costly to the United States and the world as a whole. Despite positive assessments of trade policy by the U.S. government, strict enforcement of the trade remedy laws can be a costly misjudgment, achieving only a patchwork solution in the short run.

- *Trade remedy policies should be enforced in an optimal manner.*

U.S. trade policy to date has focused on tracking down violations of agreements by foreign countries case by case rather than attempting to remove the causes of disputes. Such a policy should not be a long-term goal.

Drawing from inferences made throughout this book, the author concludes that the new system should be comprehensive to ensure mutual benefits for all trading countries by minimizing the social cost. Ineffectiveness and inefficiency of the trade policy thus set practical limits on U.S. trade policy. Competition between domestic and foreign imperfectly competitive firms is also a competition.

- *The AD policy should be abolished.*
- *Stringent use of CVD policy applied only to monopolistic firms/industries is reasonable.*

This book does not suggest that the United States has never been unfair to foreign countries and thus foreign countries should comply with U.S. trade policy, nor that the United States has always been unfair to foreign countries and thus should abandon its trade policy. It suggests that, given the current trade policies employed by all countries and the world trade system, reconciliation of dissonance from widespread trade disputes among countries is costly to all.

In conclusion,

- *The United States needs to reform U.S. trade policy/institutions and the world trade framework in concert with the WTO by embracing the real world of both competitive and imperfectly competitive firms/industries, especially for trade among industrialized countries, so that monopolistic firms/industries too can globally compete to each other.*
- *The problem of trade disparity is not resolved solely by trade policy. It needs to incorporate with the domestic factor market policies to stimulate private investment for replacement of deteriorated and obsolete facilities of production and to improve quality of products.*

April 2005

GATT$_{1947}$: Components

PART I

PART II

Article XX	General Exceptions
Article XXI	Security Exceptions
Article XXII	Consultation
Article XXIII	Nullification or Impairment

Part III

Article XXIV	Territorial Application-Frontier Tariffs—Customs Unions
Article XXV	Joint Action by the Contracting Parties
Article XXVI	Acceptance, Entry into Force and Registration
Article XXVII	Withholding or Withdrawal of Concessions
Article XXVIII	Modification of Schedules
Article XXIX	Relation of This Agreement to the Chapter for an International Trade Organization
Article XXX	Amendments
Article XXXI	Withdrawal
Article XXXII	Contracting Parties
Article XXXIII	Accession
Article XXXIV	Annexes

Note: This book (mostly in chapter 5) focuses on Articles I in Part I, VI, XVI, XIX, XXII, and XXIII in Part II.

Source: U.S. Department of State, *General Agreement on Tariffs and Trade* 1 (Washington, D.C.: U.S. GPO, 1949), 8–71.

Uruguay Round Agreements: Components

Agreement Establishing the World Trade Organization

Article I	Establishment of the Organization
Article II	Scope of the WTO
Article III	Functions of the WTO
Article IV	Structure of the WTO
Article V	Relations with Other Organizations
Article VI	The Secretariat
Article VII	Budget and Contributions
Article VIII	Status of the WTO
Article IX	Decision-Making
Article X	Amendments
Article XI	Original Membership
Article XII	Accession
Article XIII	Non-Application of Multilateral Agreements between Particular Members
Article XIV	Acceptance, Entry into Force, and Deposit
Article XV	Withdrawal
Article XVI	Miscellaneous Provisions

ANNEX 1

ANNEX 1A: Multilateral Agreements on Trade in Goods
General Agreement on Tariffs and Trade 1994
Agreement on Agriculture
Agreement on the Application of Sanitary and Phytosanitary Measures
Agreement on Textiles and Clothing

Agreement on Technical Barriers to Trade

Agreement on Trade-Related Investment Measures

Agreement on Implementation of Article VI of the General Agreement on Tariffs and Trade 1994

Agreement on Implementation of Article VII of the General Agreement on Tariffs and Trade 1994

Agreement on Preshipment Inspection

Agreement on Rules of Origin

Agreement on Import Licensing Procedures

Agreement on Subsidies and Countervailing Measures

Agreement on Safeguards

ANNEX 1B: General Agreement on Trade in Services

ANNEX 1C: Agreement on Trade-Related Aspects of Intellectual Property Rights

ANNEX 2: Understanding on Rules and Procedures Governing the Settlement of Disputes

ANNEX 3: Trade Policy Review Mechanism

ANNEX 4: Plurilateral Trade Agreement

Agreement on Trade in Civil Aircraft

Agreement on Government Procurement

International Dairy Agreement

International Bovine Meat Agreement

Note: This book (mostly in chapter 5) discusses Agreements I–IV, VI, and VII in Agreement establishing the WTO, agreements in Annexes 1A, 1B, and 1C, and part of Annex 4.

Source: 1. Office of the United States Trade Representative, *Uruguay Round: Final Texts of The GATT, Uruguay Round Agreements Including the Agreement Establishing The World Trade Organization As Signed on April 15, 1994,* Marrakech, Morocco, (Washinton, D.C.: U.S. GPO, 1994), 2. World Trade Organization, *WTO* (France: St. Juste-la-Pendue, 1995).

Appendix III

NAFTA: Outline

1. Elimination of Tariffs and Nontariff Barriers

Within 10 years of January 1, 1994, all tariffs will be eliminated on North American industrial products traded among Canada, Mexico, and the United States. A few tariffs on U.S. exports of agricultural products to Mexico will be phased out over fifteen years. As provided in the U.S.-Canada Free Trade Agreement (CFTA), the United States and Canada will eliminate all duties by 1998. On January 1, 1994, approximately 50 percent of U.S. industrial exports to Mexico (including machine tools, medical equipment, semiconductors and computer equipment, and telecommunications electronic equipment) will be immediately eligible for duty-free treatment in Mexico; 65 percent of products within five years, including light trucks, most auto parts, and paper products; all except for corn and beans in ten years. Mexico eliminates nontariff barriers and other trade-distorting restrictions, including most import licenses. NAFTA also eliminates other Mexican barriers, such as local content requirements.

2. Reduction of Tariffs on Motor Vehicles and Parts

The United States and Mexico, which has the fastest growing major auto market in the world, will eliminate tariffs on passenger cars, light trucks, and other vehicles and parts over a transition period. Mexico will immediately cut its tariffs on cars and light trucks in half and on U.S. parts exports by 75 percent within five years. U.S. exports of medium and heavy trucks can enter Mexico duty-free after five years. Local content requirements phased out over ten years. The NAFTA strengthens and harmonizes safety, emissions, and fuel efficiency standards of the United States.

3. Rules of Origin

In general, a good must contain substantial North American content and be eligible for benefits from tariff cuts under the NAFTA. In the case of autos, the NAFTA requires 62.5 percent North American content (50 percent in the case of the CFTA).

4. Safeguards

In case of serious injury threatened to or inflicted on an industry by a surge of imports, the country can suspend its tariff elimination once for up to three years or four years in the event of sensitive products bilaterally against the exporting country. The NAFTA retains global safeguards.

5. Telecommunications

The NAFTA ensures the availability of private leased lines on the public telephone network and telecommunication equipment such as phones, faxes, and computers. Access to Mexican public telephone networks to interconnect private networks should be nondiscriminatory to the United States. The NAFTA eliminates regulatory barriers such as licensing, permits, legislation, or notification procedures, etc. Investment restrictions in Mexico should be removed by July 1995.

6. Textiles and Apparel

All countries eliminate immediately over ten years tariffs on textiles and apparel that meet rules of origin of yarn produced in North America. Trade barriers on $250 million (over 20 percent) of U.S. exports to Mexico should be eliminated immediately, with another $700 million in six years. The U.S. textile quota from Mexico ends immediately.

7. Agriculture

The NAFTA immediately eliminates Mexico's duty for one-half of U.S. farm exports and will phase out remaining Mexican tariffs within ten to fifteen years. The NAFTA immediately eliminates all nontariff barriers, including Mexico's import licensing system, which has been the largest barrier to U.S. farm exports to Mexico.

8. Financial Services

The agreement expands trade in financial services, including banks and securities firms, insurance companies, leasing and factoring companies, and nonbank lenders. It recognizes the right to establish a commercial presence, the right to purchase services across borders, nondiscrimination, and transparency. By the year 2000, Mexico will open its closed financial markets in the absence of restrictions.

9. Services Other Than Financial Services

Following the CFTA, the NAFTA covers numerous services markets with the exception of aviation transport, maritime, and basic telecommunications: accounting, advertising, architecture, broadcasting, commercial education, construction, consulting, engineering, enhanced telecommunications, environmental services, health care management, land transport, legal services, publishing, tourism. The NAFTA allows countries to trade services without discrimination against foreign firms. Each country has excluded certain sensitive sectors from coverage. Mexico has excluded public notaries, Canada has retained its cultural exclusion from the CFTA, and the United States does not remove or weaken U.S. licensing and certification requirements.

10. Investment

The NAFTA expands investment opportunities by removing investment barriers, providing fairness for investors, such as the right to repatriate profits and capital, the right to fair compensation in the event of expropriation, the right to international arbitration in disputes between investors and governments, and the elimination of investment distortions. Except for a few closed domestic markets considered to be "Constitutional" activities retained by Mexico (energy and railroads), U.S. companies have the right to establish firms in Mexico and Canada or acquire existing firms. Mexico removes governmental approval for opening up new opportunities in certain areas (food processing, construction, mining, and selected petrochemicals), drops domestic content rules and export performance requirements. NAFTA investment provisions do not cover maritime, basic telecommunications, government-sponsored technology consortia and R&D programs, and existing state and local measures.

11. Intellectual Property Rights

The NAFTA clarifies and expands intellectual property rights for copyrights, patents, and trademarks and applies stronger enforcement internally and at the border. U.S. high technology producers are better protected under the NAFTA.

12. Government Procurement

Except for national security procurement, NAFTA member countries open government procurement of not only goods but also services such as construction contracts, environmental services, and computer hardware and software services by federal government departments, agencies and enterprises. Therefore, U.S. supplies have immediate access to the Mexican government procurement market, including PEMEX (national oil company) and CFE (national electric company). The NAFTA bans certain discriminatory practices.

13. Antidumping and Countervailing Duty Matters

A binational panel reviews determinations of such duties. The panel's decision is binding. The NAFTA will result in no change to U.S. antidumping and countervailing duty laws.

14. Dispute Settlement

The NAFTA encourages resolution of trade disputes through consultation between the countries in disputes. If consultation fails, the trilateral Free Trade Commission, which comprises each country's top trade official and private sector experts, will hear disputes involving interpretation or application of the NAFTA. If arbitration by the Trade Commission fails, a country can seek a bilateral or trilateral panel decision. The panel consists of private sector trade experts. Dispute resolution will normally be completed in less than one year. The panel's decision is binding.

Note: Given the relatively small volume of trade between Canada and Mexico, this section outlines highlights of the NAFTA only on the part agreed between the United States and Mexico. Appendix III to chapter 5 of this book summarizes the U.S.-Canada Trade Pact.

Sources: 1. U.S. Department of Commerce, "Key Provisions of the North American Free Trade Agreement," in *North American Free Trade Agreement* (Washington, D.C.: U.S. GPO), 3–11; Office of the Press Secretary, The White House, *The North American Free Trade Agreement*, Press Release (August 12, 1992), 1–6.

Bibliography

CHAPTER 1

Becker, Gary S. "A Theory of Competition among Pressure Groups for Political Influence." *Quarterly Journal of Economics* 98, no. 3 (August 1983): 371–400.

Bhagwati, Jagdish. "Directly-Unproductive Profit-Seeking (DUP) Activities." *Journal of Political Economy* 90, no. 5 (October 1982): 988–1002.

Buchanan, James M., and Gordon Tullock. *Calculus of Consent.* Ann Arbor, MI: University of Michigan Press, 1965.

Chung, Jae W. "Insights into Trade Protection under U.S. Trade Remedy Laws." *Journal of Policy Modeling* 21, no. 3 (1999): 375–87. © 1999 Society for Policy Modeling.

Coughlin, Cletus C., Joseph V. Terza, and Noor A. Khalifa. "Determinants of Escape Clause Petitions." *Review of Economics and Statistics* 71, no. 2 (May 1989): 341–47.

Council of Economic Advisers, *Economic Report of the President*, Washington, D.C.: U.S. GPO, 1996 various issues.

Krueger, Anne, O. "Political Economy of the Rent-seeking Society." *American Economic Review* 64, no. 3 (June 1974): 291–303.

Krupp, Corinne. "Antidumping Case in the US Chemical Industry: A Panel Data Approach." *Journal of Industrial Economics* 42, no. 3 (September 1994): 299–311.

Magee, Stephen P., William A. Brock, and Leslie Young. *Black Hole Tariffs and Endogenous Policy Theory.* Cambridge: Cambridge University Press, 1989.

Mueller, Dennis C. *Public Choice.* New York: Cambridge University Press, 1979.

Oleszek, Walter J. *Congressional Procedures and the Policy Process.* Washington, D.C.: Congressional Quarterly Press, 1978.

Olson, Mancur, *The Logic of Collective Action*, Cambridge, MA: Harvard University Press, 1965.

Pugel, T.A., and I. Walter "U.S. Corporate Interests and the Political Economy of Trade Policy." *Review of Economics and Statistics* 67, no. 3 (August 1985): 465–73.

Rowley, Charles K., Willem Thorbecke, and Richard E. Wagner, *Trade Protection in the United States*, Brookfield, VT: Edward Elgar Publishing, 1995.

Salvatore, Dominick. "Import Penetration, Exchange Rates, and Protectionism in the United States." *Journal of Policy Modeling* 9, no. 1 (Spring 1987):125–41. © Society for Policy Modeling, 1987.

Takacs, Wendy E. "Pressures for Protectionism: An Empirical Analysis." *Economic Inquiry 19*, no. 4 (1981): 687–93.

Tiefer, Charles. *Congressional Practice and Procedure.* New York: Greenwood Press, 1989.

Tollison, Robert D. "Rent Seeking: A Survey" *Kyklos* 35 (1982): 575–602.

Tullock, Gordon. "The Welfare Costs of Tariffs, Monopolies, and Theft." *Western Economic Journal* 5 (June 1967): 224–32.

U.S. House of Representatives., *How Our Laws are Made*, revised and updated by Edward F. Willett, Jr., Esq. Washington, D.C.: U.S. GPO, 1990.

——. *Overview and Compilation of U.S. Trade Statutes.* Washington, D.C.: U.S. GPO, 1995.

——. *The Constitution of the United States of America.* Washington, D.C.: U.S. GPO, 2003.

CHAPTER 2

Allen, Robert Loring, and Ingo Walter. "The Formation of United States Trade Policy: Retrospect and Prospect." *The Bulletin*, nos. 70–71, New York: New York University, February 1971.

Baldwin, Robert, E. *The Political Economy of U.S. Import Policy.* Cambridge, MA: MIT Press, 1985.

Bernanke, Ben S. "Nonmonetary Effects of the Financial Crisis in the Propagation of the Great Depression." *American Economic Review* 73, no. 3 (June 1983): 257–76.

Bhagwati, Jagdish. *Protectionism.* Cambridge, MA: MIT Press, 1988.

Bidwell, Percy W. *Tariff Policy in the United States.* New York: Putnam, 1933.

Callahan, Colleen, Judith A. McDonald, and Anthony Patrick O'Brian. "Who Voted for Smoot-Hawley?" *Journal of Economic History* 54, no. 3 (1994): 683–90.

Clubb, Bruce E. *U.S. Foreign Trade Law.* New York: Little, Brown, and Company, 1991.

Crucini, Mario J. "Sources of Variation in Real Tariff Rates: The United States, 1900–1940." *American Economic Review* 84, no. 3 (June 1994): 732–43.

——. and James Kahn. "Tariffs and Aggregate Economic Activity: Lessons from the Great Depression." *Journal of Monetary Economics* 38, no. 3 (1996): 427–67.

Cupitt, Richard T., and Euel Elliott. "Schattschneider Revisited: Senate Voting on the Smoot-Hawley Tariff Act of 1930." *Economics and Politics* 6, no. 3 (November 1994): 246–51.

Dobson, John M. *Two Centuries of Tariffs.* Washington, D.C.: U.S. GPO, 1976.

Eichengreen, Barry. *The Political Economy of the Smoot-Hawley Tariff.* Cambridge, MA: NBER, 1986.

Field, Alexander, J. "Asset Exchanges and the Transaction Demand for Money, 1919–29." *American Economic Review* 74, no. 1 (March 1984): 43–60.

Friedman, Milton, and Anna Jacobson Schwartz. *A Monetary History of the United States, 1896–1960.* Princeton, NJ: Princeton University Press, 1963.

Gordon, Robert A. *Economic Instability and Growth: The American Record.* New York: Harper and Row Publishers, 1974.

Irwin, Douglas. "The Smoot-Hawley Tariff: A Quantitative Assessment." *Review of Economics and Statistics* 80, no. 2 (1998): 326–34.

Irwin, Douglas, and Randall S. Kroszner. "Log-Rolling and Economic Interests in the Passage of the Smoot-Hawley Tariff Act." *Carnegie-Rochester Series on Public Policy* 45 (1996): 173–200.

Kindleberger, Charles. *The World in Depression, 1929–1933.* Berkeley and Los Angeles: University of California Press, 1973.

Krueger, Anne, O. *Economic Policies at Cross-Purpose.* Washington, D.C.: The Brookings Institution, 1993.

Lake, David A. *Power, Protection, and Free Trade.* Ithaca, NY: Cornell University Press, 1988.

Mankiew, N. Gregory. *Macroeconomics.* 2d edition, New York: Worth Publishers, 1994.

McDonald, Judith, Anthony Patrick O'Brien, and Colleen Callahan. "Trade Wars: Canada's Reaction to the Smoot-Hawley Tariff." *Journal of Economic History* 57, no. 4 (1997): 802–26.

McDonald, Judith, Anthony Patrick O'Brien, and Colleen Callahan. "Trade Wars: Canada's Reaction to the Smoot-Hawley Tariff." *Journal of Economic History* 57, no. 4 (1997): 802–26.

Nivola, Pietro S. *Regulating Unfair Trade.* Washington, D.C.: The Brookings Institution, 1993.

Romer, Christina D. "Spurious Volatility in Historical Unemployment Data." *Journal of Political Economy* 94, no. 1 (February 1986): 1–37.

———. "Is the Stabilization of the Postwar Economy a Figment of the Data?" *American Economic Review* 76, no. 3 (June 1986): 314–34.

Schattschneider, E. E. *Politics, Pressures and the Tariff.* Englewood Cliffs, NJ: Prentice Hall, 1935.

Smith, Carolyn C. "Fast-Track Negotiating Authority for Trade Agreements and Trade Promotion Authority: Chronology of Major Votes." *CRS Report for Congress* received through the CRS Web, December 2001.

Stowell, Alan M., ed. *U.S. International Trade Laws.* Washington, D.C.: Bureau of National Affairs, 1989.

Taussig, Frank W. *The Tariff History of the United States.* 8th ed. New York: G. P. Putnam's Sons, 1931.

U.S. Congress. *Tariff Act of 1930.* Washington, D.C.: U.S. GPO, 1930.

———. *The Statutes at Large of the United States of America from March 1933 to June 1934* XLVIII, Part I. Washington, D.C.: U.S. GPO, 1934, 943–45.

———. *Trade Act of 1974.* Washington, D.C.: U.S. GPO, 1974.

———. *Trade Agreements Act of 1979.* Washington, D.C.: U.S. GPO, 1979.

U.S. Department of Commerce, Bureau of the Census. *Historical Statistics of the United States, Colonial Times to 1970*, Washington, D.C.: U.S. GPO, 1972.

U.S. House of Representatives, Committee on Ways and Means, 71st Congress, 1st Session. *Tariff Act of 1929: Hearings before the Committee on Ways and Means on H.R. 2667.* Washington, D.C.: U.S. GPO, 1929.

U.S. Senate. Committee on Finance, 71st Congress, 1st Session, *Tariff Act of 1929: Hearings before the Committee on Finance on H.R. 2667 Volume 5, Schedule 5: Sugar, Molasses and Manufactures.* Washington, D.C.: U.S. GPO, 1929.

U.S. Senate. *Hawley-Smoot Tariff Bill of 1930: Yea-and Nay Votes in the United States Senate*, compiled by C. A. Loeffler. Washington, D.C.: U.S. GPO, 1930.

Web Search. *The Tariff Act of 1930.* < http://www.law.cornell.edu>.

CHAPTER 3

Council of Economic Advisors. *Economic Report of the President.* Washington, D.C.: U.S. GPO, 1998 and 2004.

Lawrence, Robert Z., and Robert Litan. *Saving Free Trade: A Pragmatic Approach.* Washington, D.C.: Brookings Institution, 1986.

Marks, Stephen V. "Economic Interests and Voting on the Omnibus Trade Bill of 1987." *Public Choice* 75, no. 1 (January 1993): 21–42.

Nivola, Pietro. *Regulating Unfair Trade.* Washington, D.C.: The Brookings Institution, 1993.

Smith, Carolyn C. "Fast-Track Negotiating Authority for Trade Agreements and Trade Promotion Authority: Chronology of Major Votes." *CRS Report for Congress.* (December 18, 2001).

U.S. House of Representatives. *Congressional Quarterly Almanac* and *CQ Weekly.* Washington, D.C.: U.S. GPO, 1988.

———. *Overview and Compilation of U.S. Trade Statutes.* 1993 Edition. Washington, D.C.: U.S.GPO, January 1993.

U.S. Trade Representative. *1998 Trade Policy Agenda and 1997 Annual Report.* Washington, D.C.: U.S. GPO, 1997.

CHAPTER 4

Bello, Judith Hippler, and Alan F. Holmer. "The Heart of the 1988 Trade Act: A Legislative History of the Amendments to Section 301." In *Aggressive Unilateralism: America's 301 Trade Policy and the World Trading System,* edited by Jagdish Bhagwati and Hugh T. Patrick. Ann Arbor, MI: University of Michigan Press, 1990.

Boltuck, Richard, and Robert E. Litan, eds. *Down in the Dumps: Administration of the Unfair Trade Laws.* Washington, D.C.: The Brookings Institution, 1991.

Coughlin, Cletus C. "U.S. Trade-Remedy Laws: Do They Facilitate or Hinder Free Trade." *Review* 73, no. 4, The Federal Reserve Bank of St. Louis (July/August 1991).

Marks, Stephen V. "Economic Interests and Voting on the Omnibus Trade Bill of 1987." *Public Choice* 75, no. 1 (January 1993): 21–42.

Office of Federal Register, National Archives and Records Administration. *Federal Register, Presidential Documents* 59, no. 45 (March 1994): 10727.

Office of the United States Trade Representative. *Trade Policy Agenda and Annual Report.* Washington, D.C.: U.S. GPO, various years.

——. *National Trade Estimate Report on Foreign Trade Barriers.* Washington, D.C.: U.S. GPO, various years.

Rossidies, E. T., and A. Maravel. *United States Import Trade Law.* Salem, NH: Butterworth Legal Publishers, 1992.

U.S. House of Representatives, Committee on Ways and Means. *Trade Legislations Enacted into Public Law, 1981 through 1988.* Washington, D.C.: U.S. GPO, January 27, 1989.

——. *Overview and Compilation of U.S. Trade Statutes.* Washington, D.C.: U.S. GPO, 1995.

U.S. Senate. *Hawley-Smoot Tariff Bill of 1930: Yea-and-Nay Votes in the United States Senate*, compiled by C. A. Loeffler. Washington, D.C.: U.S. GPO, 1930.

CHAPTER 5

Baucus, Maxwell. Memorandum to the USTR. January 30, 1990.

Bhagwati, Jagdish N. *Protectionism.* Cambridge, MA: MIT Press, 1989.

Bhagwati, Jagdish N., and Hugh T. Patrick, eds. *Aggressive Unilateralism: America's 301 Trade Policy and the World Trading System.* Ann Arbor, MI: University of Michigan Press, 1990.

Council of Economic Advisers. *Economic Report of the President.* Washington, D.C.: U.S. GPO, 2004.

Hoekman, Bernard M., and Michel M. Kostecki. *The Political Economy of the World Trading System from GATT to WTO.* Oxford: Oxford University Press, 1996.

Jackson, John H. "The World Trade Organization, Dispute Settlement, and Codes of Conduct." In *The New GATT,* edited by Susan M. Collins and Barry P. Bosworth. Washington, D.C.: The Brookings Institution, 1994, 63–75.

Krueger, Anne O. *American Trade Policy: A Tragedy in Making.* Washington, D.C.: AEI Press, 1995.

Lustig, Nora, Barry P, Bosworth, and Robert Z. Lawrence, eds. *North American Free Trade: Assessing the Impact.* Washington, D.C.: Brookings Institution, 1996.

Sek, Lenore, *North American Free Trade Agreement.* Congressional Research Service (1992): 1–16.

Stiglitz, Joseph H. *Globalization and Its Discontents.* New York: W.W. Norton and Company, 2002.

U.S. Department of Commerce, International Trade Administration. *North American Free Trade Agreement.* 1992.

——. *Uruguay Round Update.* January 1994.

———. *The Case for NAFTA*. 1995.

———. *NAFTA Facts*, Document no. 1020, 4003, 8101 and 8102, 1996.

U.S. Departament of State. *General Agreement on Tariffs and Trade I*. Washington, D.C.: U.S. GPO, 1949.

U.S. House of Representatives, Committee on Ways and Means. *World Trade Organization: Hearing before Committee on Ways and Means*. Washington, D.C.: U.S. GPO, 1994.

USTR. *2000 Trade Policy Agenda and 1999 Annual Report*. Washington, D.C.: U.S. GPO, 2000 various issues.

———. *Uruguay Round:Final Texts of the GATT Uruguay Round Agreements including The Agreements Establishing The World Trade Organization as Signed on April 15, 1994, Marrakech, Morocco*. Washington, D.C.: U.S. GPO, 1994.

Weintraub, Sidney. "NAFTA Benefits Flow Back and Forth Across the Rio Grande." *The Wall Street Journal*. May 10, 1996.

White House. *The North American Free Trade Agreement: Fact Sheet*. August 12, 1992, 1–6.

World Trade Organization. *WTO*. France: St. Juste-la-Pendue, 1995.

WTO/GATT. "Agreement on Subsidies and Countervailing Measures." <http://www.itl.com>. WTO Website <http://www.wto.org>.

CHAPTER 6

Finger, J. M., H. K. Hall, and D. R. Nelson. "The Political Economy of Administered Protection." *American Economic* Review 72, no. 3 (June 1982): 452–66.

Hansen, Wendy L. "The International Trade Commission and the Politics of Protection." *American Political Science Review* 84, no. 1 (March 1990): 21–46.

Levinson, Marc. "Introducing Mr. Protection." *Newsweek* (July 1995): 42.

North, Douglas. *Institutions, Institutional Change, and Economic Performance*. New York: Cambridge University Press, 1990.

Office of the Federal Register/National Archives and Records Administration. *The United States Government Manual*. Washington, D.C.: U.S. GPO, 2001–2002.

U.S. House of Representatives, Committee on Ways and Means. *Overview and Compilation of U.S. Trade Statutes*. Washington, D.C.: U.S. GPO, 1995.

———. *Trade Legislation Enacted into Public Law*. 1981 through 1988, Washington, D.C.: U.S. GPO, January 1989.

<www.ita.doc.gov/about.html>.
<www.whitehouse.gov/nec/>.
<www.usitc.gov/geninfo.htm>.
<www.ustr.gov/about-ustr/ustrrole.shtm/>.

CHAPTER 7

Baldwin, Robert E. *The Political Economy of U.S. Import Policy*. Cambridge, MA: MIT Press, 1985.

Baldwin, Robert E., and Jeffrey W. Steagall. "An Analysis of ITC Decisions in Antidumping, Countervailing Duty and Safeguard Cases." *Weltwirtschafliches Archiv* 130, Heft 2 (1994): 290–308.

Baucus, Maxwell. Memorandum to the USTR. 1990.

Bhagwati, Jagdish, and Hugh T. Patrick, eds. *Aggressive Unilateralism: America's 301 Trade Policy and the World Trading System.* Ann Arbor, MI: University of Michigan Press, 1990.

Bhagwati, Jagdish, and Robert Hudec, eds. *Fair Trade and Harmonization.* Cambridge, MA: MIT Press, 1995.

Boltuck, Richard, and Robert E. Litan, eds. *Down in the Dumps: Administration of the Unfair Trade Laws.* Washington, D.C.: Brookings Institution, 1991.

Chung, Jae Wan. "Effects of U.S. Trade Remedy Law Enforcement under Uncertainty: The Case of Steel." *Southern Economic Journal* 65, no. 1 (July 1998): 151–59.

Destler, I. M. *American Trade Politics.* Washington, D.C.: Institute for International Economics, 1995.

Feigenbaum, Susan, and Thomas D. Willett. "Domestic versus International Influences on Protectionist Pressure in the United States." In *Exchange Rates, Trade and U.S. Economy*, edited by Seven W. Arndt, Richard J. Sweeney, and Thomas D. Willett. Cambridge, MA: American Enterprise Institute and Ballinger Publishing Company, 1985, 181–90.

Goldstein, Judith. "Political Economy of Trade: Institutions of Protection." *American Political Science Review* 80, no.1 (1986): 161–84.

Hillberry, Russell, and Christine McDaniel. "A Decomposition of North American Trade Growth Since NAFTA." *International Economic Review.* Office of Economics, United States International Trade Commission (May/June 2002): 1–5.

Kaplan, Seth. "Injury and Causation in USITC Antidumping Determinations: Five Recent Approaches." In *Political Implications of Antidumping Measures,* edited by P. K. Matthew Tharakan, Amsterdam: North-Holland 1991, 143–73.

Krueger, Anne O. *American Trade Policy.* Washington, D.C.: AEI Press, 1995.

Leamer, Edward. "Wage Effects of U.S.-Mexico Free Trade Agreement." In *The Mexico-U.S. Free Trade Agreement*, edited by Peter Garber. Cambridge, MA: MIT Press, 1993, 57–125.

Messerlin, Patrick A. "Antidumping." In *Completing the Uruguay Round: A Results-Oriented Approach to the GATT Trade Negotiations*, edited by Jeffrey J. Schott. Washington, D.C.: Institute for International Economics, September 1990, 108–29.

Murphy, Louis J. "Successful Uruguay Round Launches Revitalized World Trading System." *Uruguay Round Update.* International Trade Administration, U.S. Department of Commerce (January 1994): 1–23.

Murray, Tracy. "The Administration of the Antidumping Duty Law by the Department of Commerce." In *Down in the Dumps: Administration of the Unfair Trade Laws*, edited by Richard Boltuck and Robert E. Litan. Washington, D.C.: The Brookings Institution, 1991, 23–56.

Nivola, Pietro. *Regulating Unfair Trade.* Washington, D.C.: The Brookings Institution, 1993.

Office of the Federal Register, National Archives and Records Administration. *Federal Register*. Washington, D.C.: U.S. GPO, 2002 various issues.

Prusa, Thomas J. "On the Spread and Impact of Antidumping." *Canadian Journal of Economics* 34, no. 3 (August 2001): 591–611.

U.S. Administration. *NAFTA Works for America: Administration Update on the North American Free Trade Agreement 1993–1998.* Washington, D.C.: U.S. GPO, July 1999.

U.S. Department of Commerce. *U.S. Global Trade Outlook, 1995–2000.* Washington, D.C.: U.S. GPO, March 1995.

U.S. House of Representatives, Subcommittee on Trade of Ways and Means. *Hearing: USTR Identification of Priority Practices and Countries under Super 301 and Special 301 Provisions of the Omnibus Trade and Competitiveness Act of 1988.* Washington, D.C.: U.S. GPO, 1998.

U.S. International Trade Commission. *Operation of the Trade Agreements Program.* Washington, D.C.: U.S. GPO, 1998.

———. *Annual Report.* Washington, D.C.: U.S. GPO, 1990–1999.

———. *The Year in Review.* Washington, D.C.: U.S. GPO, FY 2000–2003.

———. *The Year in Trade.* Washington, D.C.: U.S. GPO, FY 2000–2003.

USTR. *2004 Trade Policy Agenda and 2003 Annual Report.* Washington, D.C.: U.S. GPO, March 2003 and all of the earlier issues.

———. *Uruguay Round: Final Texts of the GATT Uruguay Round Agreements including the Agreements Establishing the World Trade Organization as Signed on April 15, 1994, Marrakech, Morocco.* Washington, D.C.: U.S. GPO, 1994.

———. *Foreign Trade Barriers.* Washington, D.C.: U.S. GPO, 2003 various issues.

CHAPTER 8

Baldwin, Robert E. *The Political Economy of U. S. Import Policy.* Cambridge, MA: MIT Press, 1985.

Baldwin, Robert E., and Jeffrey W. Steagall. "An Analysis of Factors Influencing ITC Decisions in Antidumping, Countervailing Duty and Safeguard Cases." *NBER Working Paper*, no. 4282 (1993): 1–47.

———. "An Analysis of ITC Decisions in Antidumping, Countervailing Duty and Safeguard Cases." *Weltwirtschafliches Archiv* Band 130, Heft 2 (1994): 290–308.

Baucus, Maxwell. Memorandum to the USTR. January 30, 1990.

Bhagwati, Jagdish. *Protectionism.* Cambridge, MA: MIT Press, 1988.

———. "Directly-Unproductive Profitseeking (DUP) Activities." *Journal of Political Economy* 90, no. 5 (October 1982): 988–1002.

Bhagwati, Jagdish, and Hugh T. Patrick, eds. *Aggressive Unilateralism: America's 301 Trade Policy and the World Trading System.* Ann Arbor, MI: University of Michigan Press, 1990.

Bhagwati, Jagdish, and Robert E. Hudec, eds. *Fair Trade and Harmonization* 1 and 2. Cambridge, MA: MIT Press, 1996.

Boltuck, Richard, and Robert E. Litan. "America's "Unfair" Trade Laws." In *Down in the Dumps: Administration of the Unfair Trade Laws*, edited by Richard Boltuck and Robert E. Litan. Washington, D.C.: Brookings Institution, 1991, 1–22.

Brander, James A. "Strategic Trade Policy." In *Handbook of International Economics III*, edited by G. Grossman and K. Rogoff. Amsterdam: Elsevier Science B.V., 1995, 1395–1455.

Brander, James A., and Barbara J. Spencer. "Export Subsidies and International Market Share Rivalry." *Journal of International Economics* 16, no. 1/2 (February 1985): 83–100.

———. "Tariff Protection and Imperfect Competition." In *Monopolistic Competition and International Trade,* edited by H. Kierzkowski. Oxford: Oxford University Press, 1984.

Cass Robert A., and Richard D. Boltuck. "Antidumping and Countervailing-Duty Law: The Mirage of Equitable International Competition." In *Fair Trade and Harmonization: Prerequisites for Free Trade 2*, edited by Jagdish Bhagwati and Robert E. Hudec. Cambridge, MA: MIT Press, 1996, 351–414.

Council of Economic Advisors. *Economic Report of the President.* Washington, D.C.: U.S. GPO, February, various years, including 1996 and 1999.

Destler, I. M. *American Trade Politics.* 2d ed. Washington, D.C.: Institute for International Economics, 1991.

Feigenbaum, Susan, and Thomas D. Willett. "Domestic versus International Influences on Protectionist Pressure in the United States." In *Exchange Rates, Trade and U.S. Economy*, Cambridge, edited by Seven W. Arndt, Richard J. Sweeney, and Thomas D. Willett. Cambridge, MA: American Enterprise Institute, 1985, 181–90.

Francois, Joseph F., N. David Palmeter, and Jeffrey C. Anspacher. "Conceptual and Procedural Biases in the Administration of the Countervailing Duty Law." In *Down in the Dumps: Administration of the Unfair Trade Laws*, edited by Richard Boltuck and Robert E. Litan Washington, D.C.: The Brookings Institution, 1991, 95–140.

Goldstein, Judith. "Political Economy of Trade: Institutions of Protection." *American Political Science Review* 80, no. 1 (1986): 161–84.

Helpman, Elhanan. "Increasing Returns, Imperfect markets, and Trade Policy." In *Handbook of International Economics 1*, edited by Ronald E. Jones and Peter B. Kenen. Amsterdam: North Holland, 1984, 325–65.

Helpman, Elhanan, and Paul Krugman. *Trade Policy and Market Structure.* Cambridge, MA: MIT Press, 1989.

Hoeckman, Bernard M., and Michel M. Kostecki. *The Political Economy of the World Trading System: From GATT to WTO.* Oxford: Oxford University Press, 1995.

International Trade Commission. *Annual Report.* Washington, D.C.: U.S. GPO, various years.

———. *Antidumping Duty Determinations.* Washington, D.C.: U.S. GPO, various years.

———. *Countervailing Duty Determinations.* Washington, D.C.: U.S. GPO, various years.

———. *Escape Clause Determinations.* Washington, D.C.: U.S. GPO, various years.

Kaplan, Seth. "Injury and Causation in USITC Antidumping Determinations: Five Recent Approaches." Pp. 143–73 in *Political Implications of Antidumping Measures, edited by* P.K. Matthew Tharakan. Amsterdam, North-Holland: 1991.

Krueger, Anne O. *American Trade Policy.* Washington, D.C.: AEI Press, 1995.

Krugman, Paul R. "Increasing Returns, Monopolistic Competition and International Trade." in *International Trade: Selected Readings*, 2d ed., edited by Jagdish Bhagwati. Cambridge, Mass.: MIT Press, 1996.

———. "Scale Economies, Product Differentiation, and the Pattern of Trade." *American Economic Review* 70 no. 3 (December 1980): 950–59.

Messerlin, Patrick A. "Antidumping." Pp. 108–29 in *Completing the Uruguay Round: A Results-Oriented Approach to the GATT Trade Negotiations,* edited by Jeffrey J. Schott. Washington, D.C.: Institute for International Economics, September 1990.

Murray, Tracy. "The Administration of the Antidumping Duty Law by the Department of Commerce." Pp. 23–63 in *Down in the Dumps: Administration of the Unfair Trade Laws*, edited by Richard Boltuck and Robert E. Litan. Washington, D.C.: The Brookings Institution, 1991,.

Nivola, Pietro. *Regulating Unfair Trade.* Washington, D.C.: The Brookings Institution, 1993.

Office of the Federal Register, National Archives and Records Administration. *Federal Register.* Washington, D.C.: U.S. GPO, 1993/1994.

Office of the United States Trade Representative. *2000 Trade Policy Agenda and 1999 Annual Report.* Washington, D.C.: U.S. GPO, various other issues.

———. *Uruguay Round: Final Texts of the GATT Uruguay Round Agreements including the Agreements Establishing the World Trade Organization as Signed on April 15, 1994, Marrakech, Morocco.* Washington, D.C.: U.S. GPO, 1994.

———. *1998 Trade Policy Agenda and 1997 Annual Report.* Washington, D.C.: U.S. GPO, March 1998.

———. *Foreign Trade Barriers.* Washington, D.C.: U.S. GPO, various issues.

Palmeter, N. David. "The Antidumping Law: A Legal and Administrative Nontariff Barrier." Pp. 64–94 in *Down in the Dumps: Administration of the Unfair Trade Laws*, edited by Richard Boltuck and Robert E. Litan, eds., Washington, D.C.: The Brookings Institution, 1991.

Rowley, Charles, Willem Thorbecke, and Richard Wagner. *Trade Protection in the United States.* Lock Institute. Brookfield, Vt.: Edward Elgar Publishing, 1995.

U.S. Department of Commerce. *U.S. Global Trade Outlook, 1995–2000.* Washington, D.C.: U.S. GPO, March 1995.

U.S. Government. *Administration Update on the North American Free Trade Agreement 1993–1998.* Washington, D.C.: U.S. GPO, July 1999.

WTO, website, <http//www.wto.org>.

CHAPTER 9

Anderson, Keith B. "Agency Discretion or Statutory Direction: Decision Making at the U.S. International Trade Commission." *Journal of Law and Economics* 36, no. 3 (October 1993): 915–35. © 1993 by The University of Chicago. All rights reserved.

Baldwin, Robert E. *The Political Economy of U.S. Import Policy.* Cambridge, MA: MIT Press, 1985.

Baldwin, Robert E., and Jeffrey W. Steagall. "An Analysis of Factors Influencing ITC Decisions in Antidumping, Countervailing Duty and Safeguard Cases." *NBER Working Paper*, no. 4282 (1993): 1–47.

———. "An Analysis of ITC Decisions in Antidumping, Countervailing Duty and Safeguard Cases." *Weltwirtschafliches Archiv* 130, Heft 2 (1994): 290–308.

Bhagwati, Jadish, and Hugh T. Patrick, eds. *Aggressive Unilateralism: America's 301 Trade Policy and the World Trading System.* Ann Arbor, MI: University of Michigan Press, 1990.

Bhagwati, Jagdish, and Robert Hudec, eds. *Fair Trade and Harmonization* 1 and 2, Cambridge, MA: MIT Press, 1996.

Boltuck, Richard, and Robert E. Litan, eds. *Down in the Dumps: Administration of the Unfair Trade Laws.* Washington, D.C.: Brookings Institution, 1991.

Chung, Jae Wan. "Effects of U.S. Trade Remedy Law Enforcement under Uncertainty." *Southern Economic Journal* 65, no. 1 (July 1998): 151–59.

———. "Insights into Trade Protection under U.S. Trade Remedy Laws." *Journal of Policy Modeling* 21, no. 3 (1999): 375–87.

Coughlin, Cletus C., Joseph V. Terza, and Noor A. Khalifa. "Determinants of Escape Clause Petitions." *Review of Economics and Statistics* 71, no. 2 (May 1989): 341–47. Copyright © 1989.

Council of Economic Advisors. *Economic Report of the President.* Washington, D.C.: U.S. GPO, February 1996 and 2004.

Department of Commerce. *U.S. Global Trade Outlook, 1995–2000.* Washington, D.C.: U.S. GPO, March 1995.

Feigenbaum, Susan, and Thomas D. Willett. "Domestic versus International Influences on Protectionist Pressure in the United States." In *Exchange Rates, Trade and U.S. Economy,* edited by Seven W. Arndt, Richard J. Sweeney, and Thomas D. Willett. Washington, D.C.: American Enterprise Institute, 1985, 181–90.

Finger, J. M., H. Keith Hall, Douglas R. Nelson. "The Political Economy of Administered Protection." *American Economic Review* 72, no. 3 (June 1982): 452–66.

Francois, Joseph F., N. David Palmeter, and Jeffrey C. Anspacher. "Conceptual and Procedural Biases in the Administration of the Countervailing Duty Law." In *Down in the Dumps: Administration of the Unfair Trade Laws*, edited by Richard Boltuck and Robert E. Litan. Washington, D.C.: The Brookings Institution, 1991, 95–140.

Goldstein, Judith. "Political Economy of Trade: Institutions of Protection." *American Political Science Review* 80, no. 1 (1986): 161–84.

Goldstein, Judith, and Stefanie Lenway. "Interests or Institutions: An Inquiry into Congressional-ITC Relations." *International Studies Quarterly 33*, no. 3 (September 1989): 303–27.

Hansen, Wendy L. "The International Trade Commission and the Politics of Protectionism." *American Political Science Review* 84, no.1 (March 1990): 21–46.

Hansen, Wendy L., and Thomas J. Prusa.. "Cumulation and ITC Decision-Making: The Sum of the Parts is Greater than the Whole." *Economic Inquiry* 34, no. 4 (October 1996): 746–69.

Herander, Mark G., and J. Brad Schwartz. "An Empirical Test of the Impact of the Threat of U.S. Trade Policy: The Case of Antidumping Duties." *Southern Economic Journal* 51, no. 1 (1984): 59–79.

International Trade Commission. *Annual Report.* Washington, D.C.: U.S. GPO, various years.

———. *Antidumping Duty Determination.* Washington, D.C.: U.S. GPO, various years.

———. *Countervailing Duty Determination.* Washington, D.C.: U.S. GPO, various years.

———. *Escape Clause Determinations.* Washington, D.C.: U.S. GPO, various years.

Kaplan, Seth. "Injury and Causation in USITC Antidumping Determinations: Five Recent Approaches." In *Political Implications of Antidumping Measures,* edited by P. K. Matthew Tharakan. Amsterdam: North-Holland, 1991, 143–73.

Krueger, Anne O. *American Trade Policy.* Washington, D.C.: AEI Press, 1995.

Krupp, Corinne. "Antidumping Cases in the US Chemical Industry: A Panel Data Approach." *Journal of Industrial Economics* 42, no. 3 (September 1994): 299–311. © Basil Blackwell Ltd. 1994.

Messerlin, Patrick A. "Antidumping." In *Completing the Uruguay Round: A Results-Oriented Approach to the GATT Trade Negotiations,* edited by Jeffrey J. Schott. Washington, D.C.: Institute for International Economics, September 1990, 108–29.

McFadden, Daniel. "Modeling the Choice of Residential Location." In *Spatial Interaction Theory and Planning Model,* edited by Anders Karlquist, Lars Lundqvist, Folke Snickars, and Jörgen W. Weibull. Amsterdam: North-Holland, 1978, 75–96.

Moore, Michael. "Rules or Politics?: An Empirical Analysis of Antidumping Decisions." *Economic Inquiry* 30, no. 3 (1992): 449–66. © Western Economic Association International, 1992.

Murray, Tracy. "The Administration of the Antidumping Duty Law by the Department of Commerce." In *Down in the Dumps: Administration of the Unfair Trade Laws,* edited by Richard Boltuck and Robert E. Litan. Washington, D.C.: The Brookings Institution, 1991, 23–56.

Nivola, Pietro. *Regulating Unfair Trade.* Washington, D.C.: The Brookings Institution, 1993.

Office of the United States Trade Representative. *2004 Trade Policy Agenda and 2003 Annual Report.* Washington, D.C.: U.S. GPO, and all earlier issues.

———. *Uruguay Round: Final Texts of the GATT Uruguay Round Agreements including the Agreements Establishing the World Trade Organization as Signed on April 15, 1994, Marrakech, Morocco.* Washington, D.C.: U.S. GPO, 1994.

Office of the Federal Register, National Archives and Records Administration. *Federal Register.* Washington, D.C.: U.S. GPO, 2001.

Prusa, Thomas J. "The Selection of Antidumping Cases for ITC Determination." In *Empirical Studies of Commercial Policy,* edited by Robert E. Baldwin. Chicago: University of Chicago Press, 1991, 47–71. © 1991 by The University of Chicago. All rights reserved.

Rowley, Charles, Willem Thorbecke, and Richard Wagner. *Trade Protection in the United States.* Locke Institute. Brookfield, VT: Edward Elgar Publishing, 1995.

Salvatore, Dominick. "Import Penetration, Exchange Rates, and Protectionism in the United States." *Journal of Policy Modeling* 9, no. 1 (Spring 1987): 125–41.

Takacs, Wendy E. "Pressures for Protectionism: An Empirical Analysis." *Economic Inquiry* 29. no. 4 (1981): 687–93. © Western Economic Association International, 1981.

U.S. House of Representatives, Committee on Ways and Means. *Overview and Compilation of U.S. Trade Statutes.* Washington, D.C.: U.S. GPO, August 1995.

CHAPTER 10

Bain, Joe E. *Barriers to New Competition.* Cambridge, MA: Harvard University Press, 1956.

Becker, Gary S. "Crime and Punishment: An Economic Approach." *Journal of Political Economy* 76, no. 2 (March 1968): 169–217.

Becker, Gary S., and George J. Stigler. "Law Enforcement, Malfeasance and Compensation of Enforcers." *Journal of Legal Studies* 3, no. 1 (January 1974): 1–8.

Becker, Gary S., and Casey B. Mulligan. "Deadweight Costs and the Size of Government." *Journal of Law and Economics* 46, no. 2 (October 2003): 293–340.

Bovard, James. *The Fair Trade Fraud.* New York: St. Martin Press, 1991.

Brander, James. "Intraindustry Trade in Identical Commodities." *Journal of International Economics* 11 (1981): 1–14.

Brander, James A., and Barbara J. Spencer. "Tariff Protection and Imperfect Competition." In *Monopolistic Competition and International Trade*, edited by H. Kierzkowski. Oxford: Oxford University Press, 1984.

Buchanan, James M. *Cost and Choice: An Inquiry in Economic Theory.* Chicago: Markham Publishing, 1969.

Chung, Jae Wan. "Effects of U.S. Trade Remedy Law Enforcement under Uncertainty: The Case of Steel." *Southern Economic Journal* 65, no. 1 (July 1998): 151–59.

Clark, Don P. "Recent Evidence on Determinants of Intra-industry Trade." *Weltwirtschatliches Archiv Band 129, Heft 2* (1993): 332–43.

Council of Economic Advisers. *Economic Report of the President.* Washington, D.C.: U.S. GPO, 2004.

Crandall, Robert W. "The Effects of U.S. Trade Protection for Auto and Steel." *The Brookings Papers on Economic Activity* I (1987): 271–88.

Eichengreen, Barry, and Hans van der Van. "U.S. Antidumping Policies: The Case of Steel." In *The Structure and Evolution of Recent U.S. Trade Policy*, edited by Robert E. Baldwin and Anne O. Krueger. Chicago: University of Chicago Press, 1984, 67–104.

Forstner, Helmut, and Robert Balance. *Competing in a Global Economy: An Empirical Study on Specialization and Trade in Manufactures.* London: Unwin Hyman, 1990.

Greenway, David, R. Hine, and Chris Milner. "Vertical and Horizontal Intraindustry Trade: A Cross Industry Analysis for the United Kingdom." *Economic Journal* 105, no. 433 (November 1995):1505–518.

Grubel, Herbert G., and Peter J. Lloyd. *Intra-Industry Trade.* London: Macmillan, 1975.

Helpman, Elhanan. "Increasing Returns, Imperfect Markets, and Trade Policy." In *Handbook of International Economics* 1, edited by Ronald E. Jones and Peter B. Kenen. Amsterdam: Elsevier, 1984, 325–65.

Helpman, Elhanan, and Paul Krugman. *Market Structure and Foreign Trade.* Cambridge MA: MIT Press, 1985.

Husted, Steven, and Michael Melvin. *International Economics.* Sixth ed. Boston: Pearson Addison-Wesley, 2004.

Kaufman, Patrick J., and Francine Lafontaine. "The Cost of Control." *Journal of Law and Economics* 37 1:2 (1994): 455–76.

Krugman, Paul R. "Increasing Returns, Monopolistic Competition, and International Trade." *Journal of International Economics* 9, no. 4 (November 1979): 469–79.

Krugman, Paul R., and Maurice Obstfeld. *International Economics.* Boston: Addison and Wesley, 2003.

Office of Management and Budget. *Appendix: Budget of the United States Government, Fiscal Year 2005,* Washington, D.C.: U.S. GPO, 2005.

Shavell, Stephen. "The Optimal Structure of Law Enforcement." *Journal of Law and Economics* 36 (1) (April 1993): 255–87.

Smith, Tom, and Robert E. Whaley. "Assessing the Cost of Regulation: The Case of Dual Trading." *Journal of Law and Economics* 37, 1:1 (1994): 215–46.

Stigler, George J. "The Kinky Oligopoly Demand Curve and Rigid Prices." *Journal of Political Economy* 55, no 5 (October 1947): 432–49.

———. *The Concentration of Industry.* Homewood, IL: Richard D. Irwin, 1968.

———. "The Optimum Enforcement of Laws." *Journal of Political Economy* 78, no. 3 (May 1970): 526–36.

Tarr, David G. "Cyclical Dumping: The Case of Steel Products." *Journal of International Economics* 9, no. 1 (1979): 57–63.

U.S. Bureau of the Census. *International Trade in Goods and Services.* FT 900. Washington, D.C.: U.S. GPO, 2004.

Walter, Ingo. "Structural Adjustment and Trade Policy in the International Steel Industry." In *Trade Policy in 1980,* edited by William E. Cline. Washington, D.C.: Institute of International Economics, 1983.

<www.usitc.gov/perfrmp/npdf>

<www.wto.org/english/thewto_e/whatis_e/whatis_e.htm>.

Index

230 *Index*

152; Duty, 7, 15, 26, 27, 37, 45, *46*, 47, 54, *55*, 62, 68, 80, 106,108, 111, 123, 137, 146–49, *171*, *172*, 175, *176*, *178*, 179–80, *181*, 182, 184–86, 189, 191–92, 194, 197, 199, 203

Antimonopoly Law of 1947, 198

antitrust: law, 189, 190, 196; policy, 198

APEC. *See* Asia-Pacific Economic Cooperation

Appellate Body (AB), 69, *74*, 75, *76*, 96, 130, 156, 158, *161–65*, 168, *169–73*

Appellate Review, 76

ASEAN. *See* Association of South East Asian Nations

ASEM. *See* Asia-Europe Meeting

Asia-Pacific Economic Cooperation (APEC), 77, 81, 84, 97, 139

Asia-Pacific region, 81

Askew, R. 112

assistance for: firms and industries, 61; workers, 61

Association of South East Asian Nations (ASEAN), 81, 84, 97

asymptotic t-value, 136, *137*

average: cost, 187, 191; cost curve, 147; fixed cost, 147; foreign market value, 147; total cost, 147; variable cost, 147

Bain, J., 198

balance of payments, *114*, 136

balance on current account, 33

balance on goods, 183

Baldwin, R. E., *14*, *178*, 179

barriers to trade in services, 126

Barshefsky, C., 112

Baucus, M., 142, 153, 173

Baucus bill, 149

Baucus Memo, 153

Becker, J. S., 11, 200

Bernanke, B., 20

Bhagwati, J., 11, 146, 152, 174

Bidwell, P. W., 28

bilateral: agreement, 22, 27, 34, 66, 82–83, 88, 118–22, 138–40; consultation, 68; initiatives, 65, 88, 113; trade, 82; trade agreement, 22, 141, 143, 144; (trade) negotiations, 103

Bilateral Commercial Agreement in 1980, 83

Bilateralism, 88

binary variables, 179

bipartisan coalition, 79

Bipartisan Trade Promotion Authority Act of 2001, 43

Black Tuesday, 19

Blair House Agreement, *70*

Blake Island, 91

Boltuck, R., 174

boomerang effect, 155

Border Environment Cooperative Commission, 139

bound tariff, 73

Bovard, J., 198

Box-Cox estimation, 177

Brander, J. A., 199,

Brander-Spencer strategic trade policy (STP), 146

Brock, W. E., 112

Brunei, 84

Buchanan, J. M., 11, 200

Bureau of: Economic Analysis (BEA), 106; Economic and Business Affairs, 106; International Labor Affairs, 107; the Census, *117*

Bush Administration, 137

Byrd Amendments, 158–59, *171*, *173*

Cabinet Council, 111

Callahan, C. J., 21

Cancún, *87*, 88

Cancún Ministerial Conference, 85, 87

Cantor, M., 112

CAP. *See* Common Agricultural Policy

capacity utilization, 135, *176*, 177, 179, 184

About the Author

Jae Wan Chung is Professor Emeritus of Economics at George Mason University in Fairfax, Virginia. He received his Bachelor of Commerce from Seoul National University in 1962, Ph.D. from New York University in 1972 and has subsequently taught both undergraduate and graduate level courses at George Mason University since 1972. Professor Chung served briefly at the World Bank as a consultant and the Inter-American Defense College as a seminar consultant. He also served as a visiting professor of Seoul National University, held positions at the Research Department of the Bank of Korea (1962–65), the University of Suwon in Korea as Professor of Economics and the Dean of the College of Economics and Business Administration (1997–2002). In addition, he served as a senior visiting research fellow of the International Economic Institute and a research advisor of International Economic Policy Institute in Korea during his leave periods.

Professor Chung is the author of *Utility and Production Functions: Theory and Applications* published by Blackwell Publishers (1994), as well as the author of numerous articles published widely in scholarly journals.